BLACK AND WHITE PHOTOGRAPHY IN PRACTICE

BLACK AND WHITE PHOTOGRAPHY IN PRACTICE

Jack Taylor

Element

DAVID & CHARLES
Newton Abbot London

An Element technical publication
Conceived. designed and edited by
Paul Petzold, Limited, London.

First published in 1984
Second impression 1985

British Library Cataloguing in Publication Data
Taylor, Jack
Black and White photography in practice.
1. Photography
I. Title
770' 28 TR146

ISBN 0-7153-8409-0

Designer Roger Kohn
Illustrator Janos Marffy

Typeset by ABM Typographics Limited, Hull
and printed in Great Britain
by Butler and Tanner Ltd, Frome
for David & Charles (Publishers) Limited
Brunel House Newton Abbot Devon

CONTENTS

1 QUALITIES OF THE BLACK-AND-WHITE PRINT

Photography is the art of converting a three-dimensional coloured scene into a two-dimensional reproduced image. For most colour photographers, this means obtaining a near-as-possible copy of the view in front of the camera, whether the final result is a slide or a colour print. More advanced colour photographers sometimes modify reality by using techniques to distort or change the contrast and/or colour.

However, because the conversion of the observed coloured scene is into shades of grey, black-and-white photographs *interpret* the scene rather than reproduce it. So, even in the 'straight' monochrome print, there is a translation of what we see into something quite different from reality. This inherent 'unreal' quality of black-and-white photographs, coupled with the many controls which can be used in monochromatic photography, has persuaded many serious photographers to adopt black-and-white rather than colour as the best medium for expressing their ideas.

The purpose of this book is to help increase visual awareness in black-and-white terms and to show how monochromatic images can be controlled from the visualisation stage through to the finished print. A thorough knowledge of the materials, processes and techniques involved must be acquired if the photographer is not to limit his vision.

As an introduction, it is worth examining the specific qualities of the black-and-white print, and considering why so many photographers prefer it.

Emphasis on content

Because the black-and-white print eliminates the variations provided by colour in the original scene, the viewer is forced to examine the content of a picture more carefully. He is not distracted by the behaviour or interplay of colours, so he must study the various component parts of the image and so make an effort to relate them to each other.

There are some subjects which seem to lend themselves naturally to black-and-white work rather than colour. Many photojournalists prefer to work in black-and-white: hard-hitting news photographs somehow gain extra strength from the use of monochrome. This is true even of war pictures, in which you might expect the gory nature of the subject to produce greater shock in the viewer when presented in full colour. The black-and-white photograph presents only stark facts; the viewer does not get the chance to find comfort in relaxing colours. Graphic content is more impactive than the reality of the colour image. On a more practical level cost constraints and speed of reproducing mean that most newspapers prefer black-and-white.

Black-and-white portraits often reveal more depth of character. The commercial portrait photographer may feel the need to dress-up his colour photographs to make them more appealing. He places them in fancy frames and offers a pseudo-canvas finish to resemble a painting, as if photography were a lesser form of painting rather than a medium in its own right.

The majority of memorable portraits, and those preferred by museums for their permanent collections, have nearly all been made in black-and-white. One has only to think of the fine portraits taken by Bill Brandt, Arnold Newman, Irving Penn and Brian Griffin to realise the truth of this. Colour portraits certainly offer a more accurate surface likeness of the subject but somehow colour gets in the way of searching more deeply into the human character.

Black-and-white photographs cannot always be superior to those in colour and some subject areas are invariably best recorded on colour film. Obvious examples are flowers and plants, which are usually rather dreary in monochrome—except where there is full and dramatic use of the grey scale, where the structure is the main aspect of the picture or the composition renders colour unnecessary. This is clearly demonstrated in the work of such masters of the camera as Imogen Cunningham and Edward Weston.

Certain subjects almost *demand* to be photographed in colour, for example, fairgrounds and circuses, or night scenes. But for every generalisation made about the use of colour or black-and-white, it is always possible to find the exception

1 The major characteristics of a black-and-white print are demonstrated here, ie. full tonal range from black through greys to white, good image definition (even though the picture is made from a 35mm negative), low graininess and greater emphasis on subject content because colour has been eliminated.

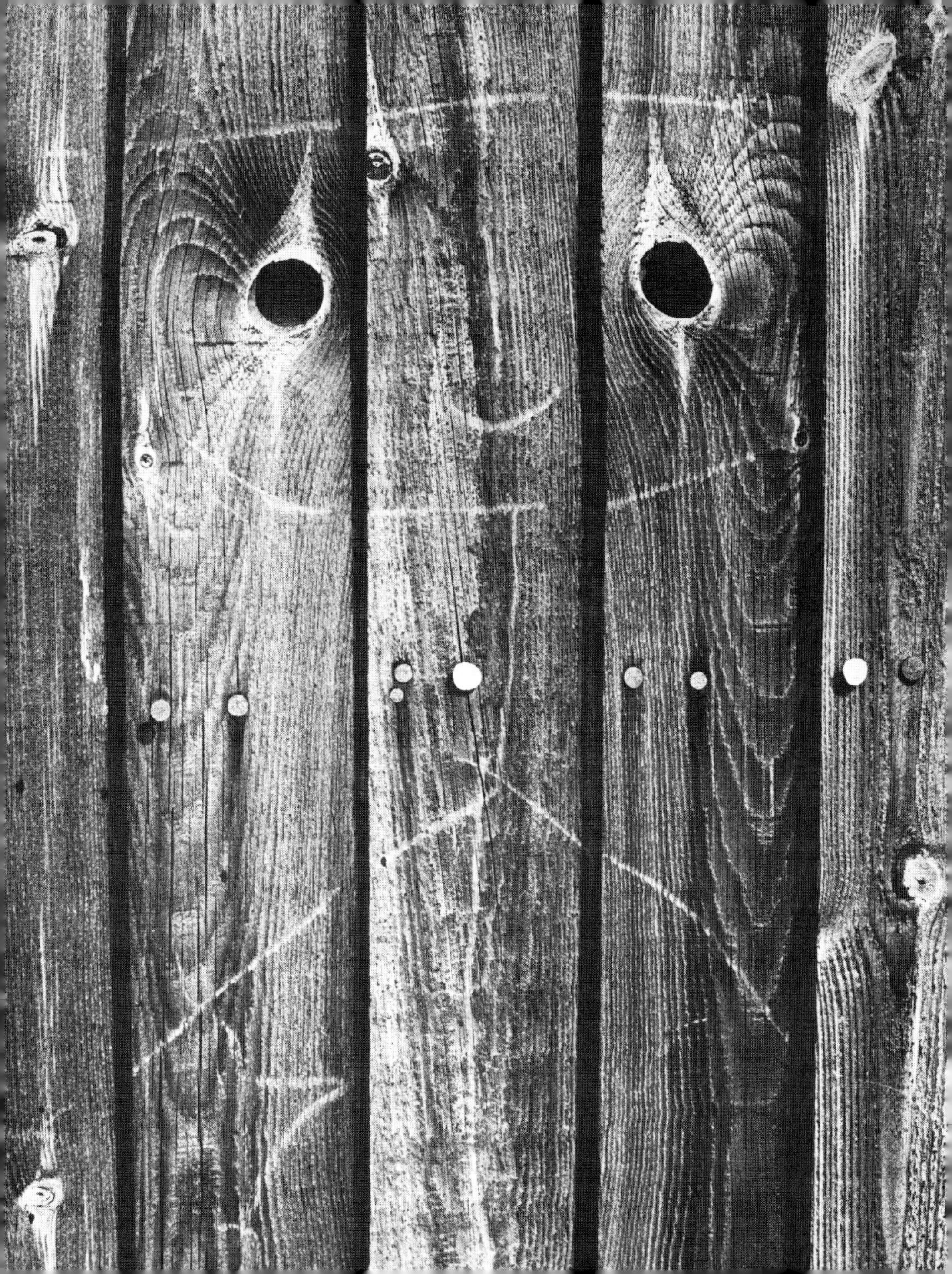

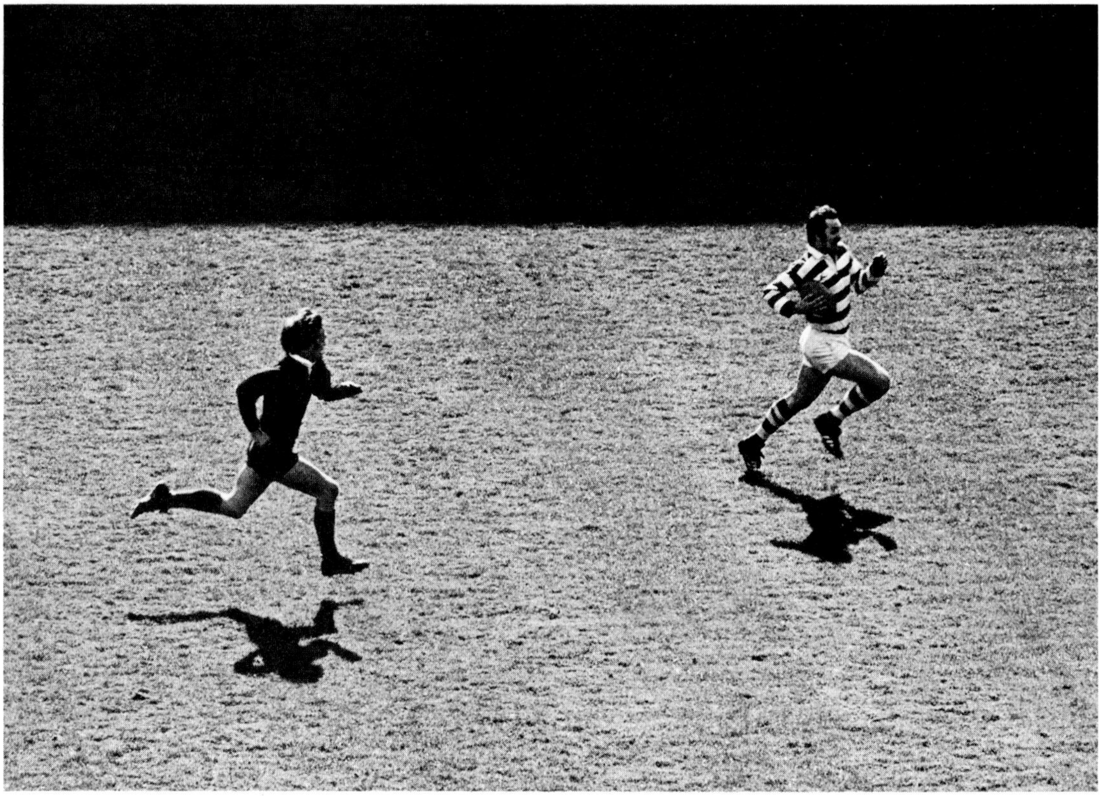

2 The strong graphic shapes of the rugby players, their shadows and the tone (dark to light) boundary running across the picture have far greater dramatic impact in black-and-white than the same subject would have if recorded in colour. Notice the textural quality of the back-lit grass, enhanced by black-and-white photography.

which breaks the rule and yields a superb photograph.

Definition

Although remarkable improvements in the quality of colour materials have been made in recent years, the black-and-white image still has considerable superiority where high definition is required. This is particularly true when small formats (35mm etc) and fast films are used. It is difficult to imagine an ASA 400 35mm colour negative enlarged to 40 x 50cm (16 x 20in) still retaining its impact, whereas an ASA 400 black-and-white negative on the same format can certainly do so.

Where very fine detail is required, for example in some landscape work, there is no better combination for producing quality of definition than the use of larger format cameras (6 x 6cm, 4 x 5in) and slow or medium-speed black-and-white films, as the superb work of photographers such as Ansel Adams, Wynn Bullock and John Blakemore testifies.

Tonal range

There is something magical about the range of tones in good black-and-white prints. From the rich blacks of shadow areas through subtle mid-greys to delicate highlights, the black-and-white print has an almost tactile feel about it. There is a beauty about a well-lit subject transposing itself into a full tonal scale in the print. It is rare for a colour print to have the same subtlety of feeling.

When more impact is required, it is possible to simplify the tonal range in a black-and-white print and produce a more graphic image. This treatment is often used when arresting images are needed, such as in posters or advertisements. The tonal control available in black-and-white photography is infinite, whereas in colour photography it is virtually non-existent, except through complicated masking techniques.

Texture and mood can be expressed more vividly in black-and-white terms by control of the

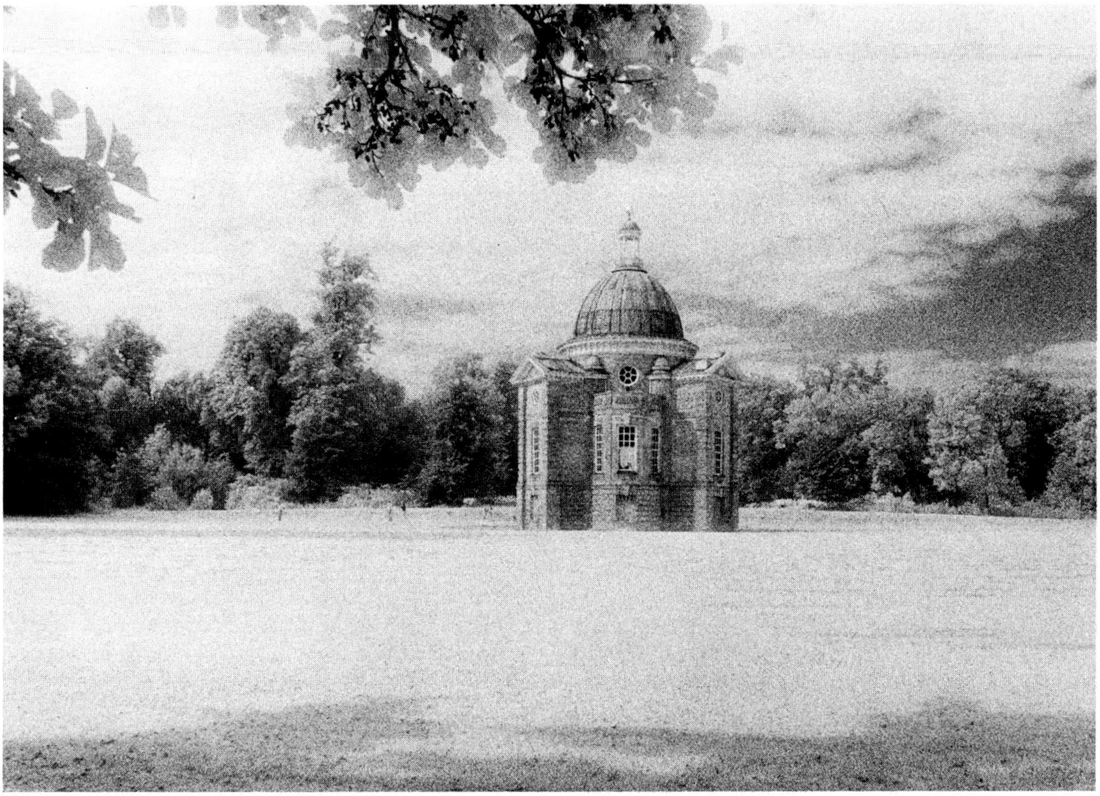

3 Much of the appeal of this infra-red photograph is due to the fact that the print resembles a fine ink sketch. However, it is difficult to imagine a sketch with the same tonal quality, which gives the print a tactile dimension. Photographs such as this are sought by collectors as examples of 'fine art' photography.

tonal range. This is especially true of more or less monochromatic subjects such as landscapes and desert scenes, where the lack of colour does not hinder the ability of black-and-white materials to extract the essence of the scene.

The tonality of one area of the subject in comparison with another can also be controlled by various techniques, such as the use of filters, specialist films, printing etc. All these possibilities are discussed at length later in the book.

Graininess

The 'peppery' appearance of a print (particularly noticeable in mid-tone areas), caused by the enlargement of the silver particles in the processed negative, can itself add dramatically to the impact of an image. The coarse grain of fast films which have been 'push processed' can actually be used to enhance the appeal of low light subjects. For example, a musician playing on stage or in a club almost demands the gritty feel of a grainy print to suggest the special atmosphere. The large image 'blobs' suggest to the viewer the darkness of the original scene and that the photograph was taken candidly without intruding on the subject. The same subject taken with a slower film and electronic flash would exhibit a completely different ambience.

Conversely, the very fine grain characteristic of slow films and larger formats can produce a quality of smoothness which is impossible to match in colour prints. This 'velvety' feel is most noticeable in large image areas of mid- or light tone. Landscapes with substantial areas of one tone, such as sea, sky, sand and mountain, often need this smoothness to convey a feeling of peacefulness and serenity.

Cost

The fact that black-and-white materials are cheaper than those for colour work certainly encourages more experimentation; photographers are not so concerned about wasting shots. This is particularly true with the type of camera work where the black-and-white photographer can try several different viewpoints of the same subject and then also bracket exposures. The most pleasing images can then be selected at leisure when printing in the darkroom. Most colour enthusiasts are inhibited by the cost of materials and may only make one exposure of a particular subject, instead of continuing to explore new ideas.

Many black-and-white materials are available in bulk quantities, which certainly reduces the overall outlay for film and paper. If possible, always buy materials in batches, as this minimises any slight variations between one film coating and another.

Photographs as an art form

Most collectors of photographic art prefer to buy black-and-white work. There are several reasons for this, mainly connected with the permanence of the image.

Because colour dyes fade when they come into contact with air and light, the colour print or slide will change its colour and density after being kept for a while. The rate at which a coloured image fades depends on the material, how it is processed and, most importantly, how it is stored. If it is kept in near-ideal conditions (low temperature and humidity and in darkness) the colours should last for many decades. But they will not survive for centuries. When poorly kept, a colour image may deteriorate to an unacceptable extent in less than a year. This is very clearly seen when prints are left in shop windows.

The black-and-white image is composed of metallic silver. Correctly processed and stored it should survive for long enough for future generations to view. For this reason, collectors of black-and-white photographs make a much more secure investment, both from the financial and visual standpoint. There are materials and procedures

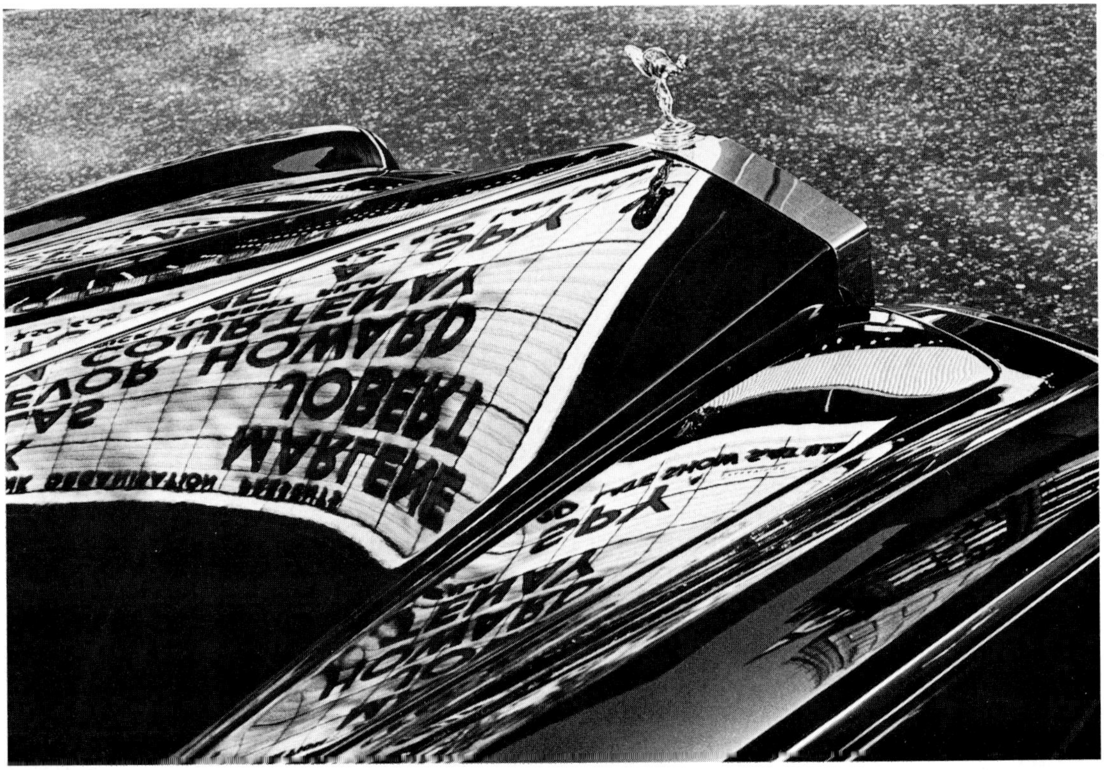

4 The composition here is simple and very graphic, and further enhanced by the reduction of the strongly coloured scene to black-and-white.

5 Very careful control of film exposure, film development and printing is needed to obtain 'surrealistic' images such as this. The original scene has been greatly dramatised to fit the photographer's own 'vision' of the subject.

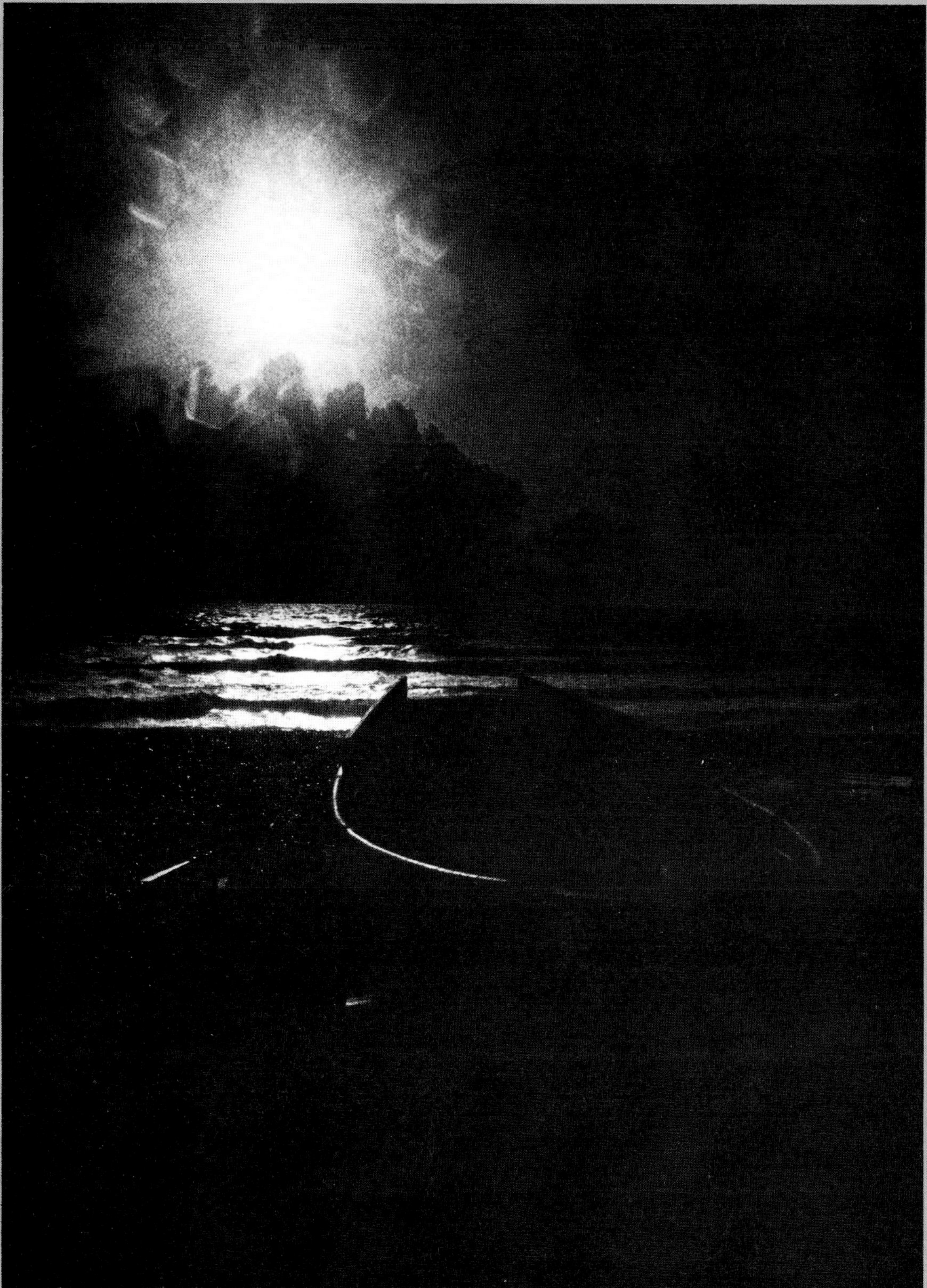

available to achieve this archival permanence and these are described later in the book.

Although image permanence does, of course, play an important part in deciding which photographs should be collected, most photographic critics and historians also believe that the best photography has been done in black-and-white. Almost certainly, the proportion of colour work collected will increase, especially as better storage systems, such as computer records, video images and colour separations, become more reliable and readily available.

Controlling the final print

The viewer only sees the final print and in most cases he is not aware of the many stages which may be necessary to produce the end product. To control the quality of the print the photographer must understand and be able to control all the intermediate stages of its production. This can only be achieved by a complete technical and creative mastery of the photographic process.

The most experienced photographers can look at a (coloured) subject and be able to 'pre-visualise' how the final black-and-white print will appear. This takes considerable practice, skill and mastery of technique. But without this ability the creative photographer will not be able to control his vision and will be frustrated by not achieving precisely what he wants. All the necessary techniques and theory are fully discussed in this book so that the reader can find the quickest route to achieving this mastery of black-and-white photography.

The variables within the black-and-white process are many, and it is worthwhile in this chapter to introduce the more important factors before they are discussed in greater detail in the main body of the book. The principal factors, in chronological order, are composition, exposure, film processing, printing and presentation.

Composition

The composition of the image depends on what the photographer decides to include and what to leave out of the picture. He must decide on the relationship within the image frame of one part of the subject to another, their tonal differences and their relative sizes and position. This selection process also includes the best moment to press the shutter–and even the choice of shutter speed and aperture.

Undoubtedly, composition is the dominant factor. The next two chapters contain guidelines for composing the black-and-white picture.

Film exposure and processing

At first, making the 'correct' exposure for the prevailing scene and lighting conditions and then processing the film, may appear to be a straightforward technical procedure; in fact, it is not that simple. Exposure and processing are interlinked; the quality of the negative and, thus, the quality of the print depend on precise control of both operations. To obtain image detail and tones which are predictable means that the photographer must understand precisely how these two variables are controlled.

Chapters 4 and 5 explain, in both technical and visual terms, how film exposure and development can be harnessed to give the picture you want. At all times, remember that good technical control of materials is very important, but that it is only a controllable means to an end; never allow yourself to become a slave to the technology.

Printing the negative

Many photographs never reach their full potential, because they are let down by poor printing. Some very good images are minimised because the printer fails to extract all the qualities that are possible from the negative. The really skilled printer can sometimes transform an 'ordinary' negative into a superb print. However, it is impossible for a poor negative to yield a good print; you cannot put into an image what is not there in the first place (for example, absent shadow detail). Nor can you put right such errors as poor focusing and incorrect exposure.

Chapter 6 shows you how to become a skilled printer and get the most out of your negatives, and also gives guidelines for presentation of photographs. The very precise Zone System for obtaining critical control of black-and-white photography is covered in Chapter 7.

For some photographers, the image only really takes shape in the darkroom; the original camera exposure is just a starting point. Chapter 8 covers many techniques which can be used to distort the tone scale and modify definition, and also describes how to combine more than one image in a single photograph.

Uniting the variables

For clarity, the various stages of the printmaking process are dealt with in separate chapters, but

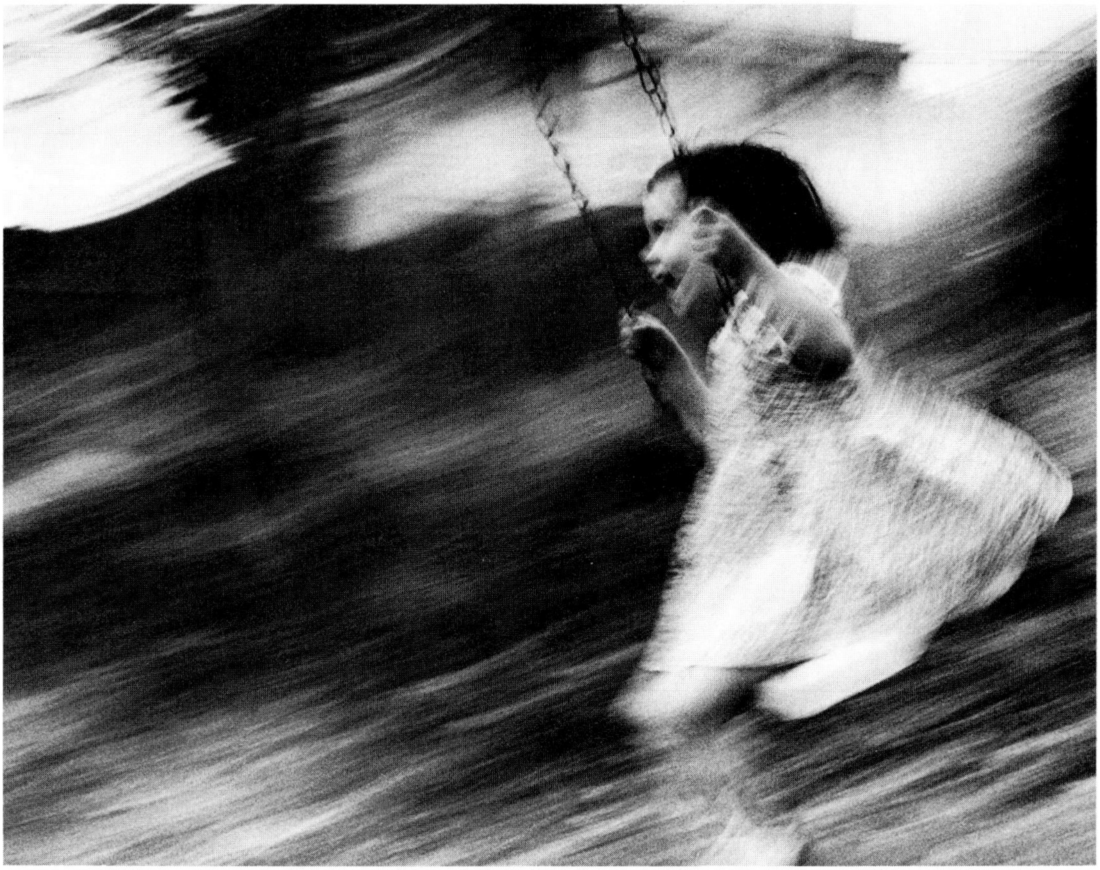

because most of the variables are dependent on one another there is necessarily some cross-over of information. This should help reinforce the more important aspects of black-and-white photography.

The final chapter gives some advice on how the variables can be united and used to produce effective pictures. Fortunately, there is no one best method of producing photographs but some general observations may help each photographer to find his own way to a more satisfying and meaningful pastime.

An extensive glossary covering all aspects of black-and-white photography should provide a helpful link with other relevant publications. The less experienced photographer may also find the glossary a useful source of basic photographic facts.

6 Many photographic variables can be controlled to create an image which could never have been seen by the photographer when the shutter was pressed. In this example, a slow shutter speed (about 1/8 sec) was used as the camera was panned with the subject.

2 COMPOSING THE IMAGE

It has often been said that photographic composition is an intuitive process which cannot be taught. You either have an eye for a picture or you don't. However, adopting this attitude does not help inexperienced photographers to find opportunities to explore their own visions and ideas.

This chapter, therefore, endeavours to break down composition into its basic elements so that each aspect can be studied and new possibilities tried out.

The main technical aspects of camera work (exposure estimation, choice of film, linking to development, etc) are explored in Chapter 4. Here, we concern ourselves only with 'seeing' the black-and-white image.

First thoughts

First and foremost, composition is a selection process. The edges of the picture are chosen by the direction in which the camera is pointed, the angle of view of the camera lens, ie. its focal length, and the distance of the camera from the subject. To change the composition, you must select a different lens (or zoom in or out), point the camera in another direction, or move nearer or further from the subject. These may appear obvious choices but it is very easy for the photo-

2.1 There are many possible edge boundaries to this photograph apart from the full frame area shown. The concentration on the woman, indicated by the tightest cropping, gives a restful photograph showing simply a sleeping peasant. The cropping behind the woman, which includes in the picture the road around the corner gives a less stable image, causing the viewer to ponder as to what might have happened after the picture was taken–there is some tension in the scene. The other example of possible cropping excludes the road and the viewer assumes that the wall extends for a considerable distance on either side of the figure–here the wall offers some 'protection' but because the camera includes more on the right of the picture there is a possible 'threat' from behind. These differences are best observed if you use paper to blank off parts of the picture.

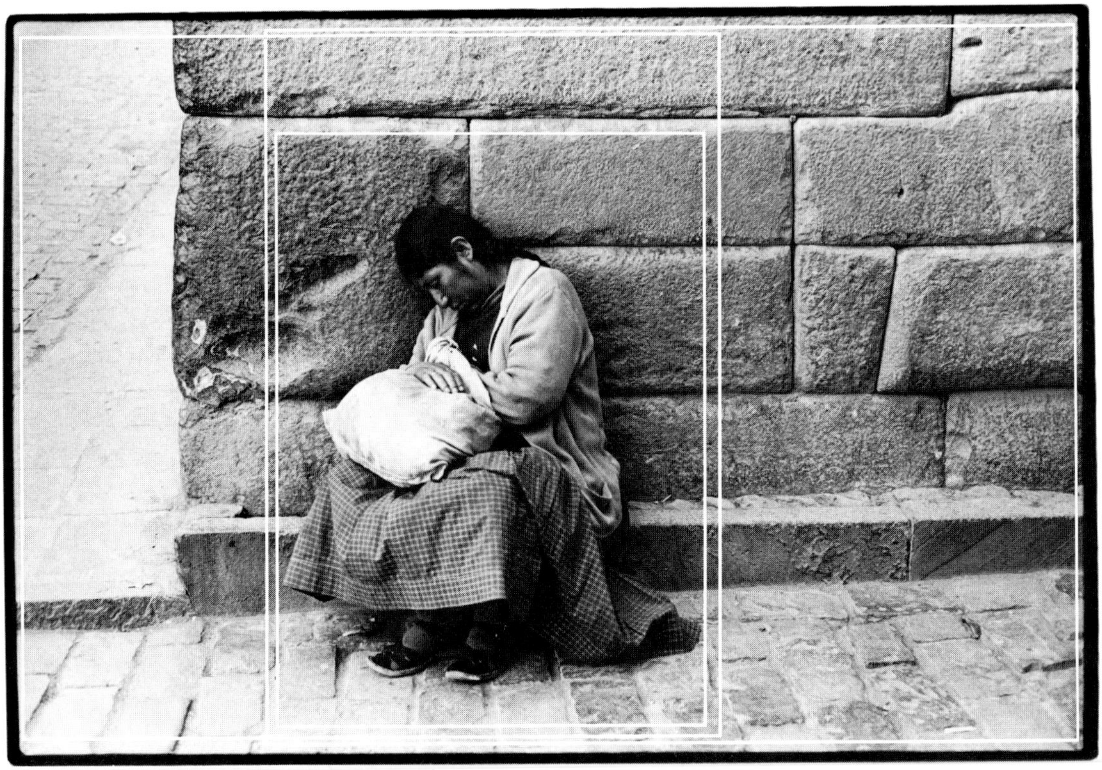

grapher to be seduced by the colour of the subject, work out the first idea that he has for a picture and then move on to something else.

When you first encounter a potential subject for a black-and-white photograph, it is a good principle to take one exposure immediately; this somehow frees the mind and removes any doubts as to whether or not it is worthwhile exposing film at all. Remember that black-and-white film is relatively cheap, so you should not feel bad about 'wasting' it. Once the shutter finger has been activated, you can spend time (if circumstances allow) examining the scene and visualising how it will reproduce in black-and-white.

Picture edges defined by enlarging

There has long been controversy over whether cropping during printing is a valid photographic technique. Some traditionalists, including the magnificent Henri Cartier-Bresson, are firm advocates of seeing a picture in the camera and retaining this vision through to the final print. They believe it is wrong to modify frame edges during enlarging by excluding parts of the original negative. This approach, puritanical in the author's opinion, is very restrictive and can only throw restrictions around final photographic composition.

At the other extreme, there are some photographers who crop almost every negative they project on to the enlarger baseboard. This practice does mean that image quality (in terms of definition and graininess) is reduced, especially where a high degree of enlargement is used and the original negative is of small format, eg: 35mm.

For many types of black-and-white work the quality of the image is crucial, for example, in landscapes where large areas of a single tone might need to be relatively free of graininess to convey a smooth, tactile feeling. The higher definition of black-and-white films compared with most colour emulsions is wasted if the photographer does not frame his subject carefully in the viewfinder but, instead, leaves his composing to the darkroom.

Most photographers probably adopt an intermediate approach and crop where necessary, but generally avoid excessive modifications to the composition whilst enlarging. This flexible standpoint does leave the image maker with more options but ensures that the creative process can continue in the darkroom.

In practice, many photographers print their negatives on standard sizes of paper; the more common aspect ratio being 4:5 eg 20 x 25cm (8 x 10in), 40 x 50cm (16 x 20in). This method is as restrictive as never cropping the negative in that it generates prints of uniform proportions.

Again, a middle-of-the-road standpoint is likely to be best. Let each picture dictate how it is to be presented as a print. Be prepared to be flexible about composition within the film format by mentally drawing frame lines where you want them, not necessarily letting the view seen by the camera dictate the final print boundaries. In addition, when printing your negatives do not always feel bound to fill the paper to the edges–there is a great temptation to use every inch to avoid wastage!

How much sharpness?

When we look at a scene, everything appears to be sharp. Our eyes are constantly scanning the subject in various directions and switching to different distances, changing focus automatically to give a totally sharp image. To the eye, even moving subjects appear sharp except if they are moving very rapidly. The camera, however, does not have this kind of flexibility and photographic sharpness is limited by a number of factors.

The main variables that influence the sharpness of the final black-and-white are depth of field, subject or camera movement, film type and size and lens quality. Apparent image sharpness, the phenomenon whereby some monochrome photographs look sharper than others, is affected by subject, lighting, print quality (eg: contrast, not, of course, colour contrast) and viewing conditions.

Depth of field

The amount, in depth, of a subject which is recorded sharply is controlled by the lens optics and is normally referred to as depth of field. It is defined as the distance between the nearest and furthest parts of a scene which are considered to be *acceptably* sharp.

The lens only gives one plane of *absolute* sharpness and this is (for all cameras without 'movements') the plane of the subject which is parallel to the film plane and on which the lens is focused. Any object nearer or further from the focused plane is less than perfectly sharp. In practice, because the eye has only limited resolving power, there is a range of 'unsharpness' which the eye can, nevertheless, accept as sharp, ie: depth of field. There is no sudden change from unsharp detail to acceptable sharpness; it is a gradual shift.

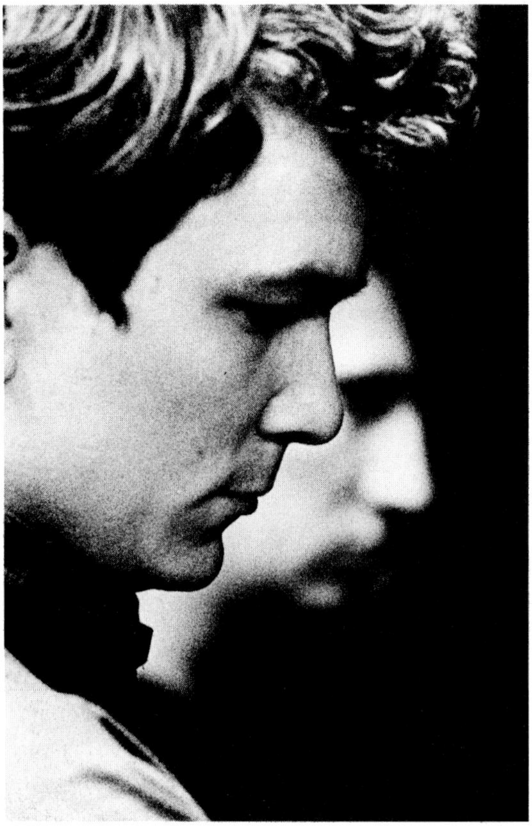

7 Because a relatively wide aperture (about f/2.8) has been used here, the background is very unsharp. However, we can still recognise a face there and this gives the photograph a kind of mirror image. It is doubtful if the 'sharper' background image given by the use of a smaller aperture (say f/11) would be as captivating–there would be less mystery.

Depth of field markings on the camera lens give only a *guide* to acceptable sharpness and have been determined by practical viewing tests with photographic prints.

Depth of field depends mainly on the focal length of the lens, the chosen aperture and the degree of enlargement (related, of course, to format). Because the factors which affect print definition are interrelated, you cannot separate depth of field from other sharpness variables, such as film type, subject, or print quality.

In practice, most photographers select their camera viewpoint (ie: perspective), determine what area of the visible scene is to be recorded, by choosing the most suitable available lens focal length and then use the lens aperture to control depth of field. To obtain the greatest depth of field the lens is 'stopped down' to the smallest workable aperture, eg.*f*/22; a lens set 'wide open' (at full aperture) gives the least depth of field. Often, the choice of aperture is a compromise because of other factors such as film speed, lighting, or shutter speed. For example, if you are photographing a soccer match on a dull day and you want the players to be recorded sharply and therefore have to use a relatively fast shutter speed, your choice of aperture is likely to be very limited and you will probably have to accept an equally limited depth of field.

When you are uncertain about the depth of field you need, you can either use the preview button on the camera to give you a visual idea of sharpness (in depth), or you can take several exposures at different apertures and select the 'best' when printing.

When you look through the viewfinder, the out-of-focus parts of the subject appear as 'blurred' colours and can look very attractive–many colour photographs rely on these defocused colours for much of their appeal. These same defocused colours appear in a black-and-white print as unsharp areas of tone; if they are close in tonal value and position they will merge into one another, often resulting in a 'muddy' background or foreground. The black-and-white photographer must constantly remind himself that tonal differences are paramount and he must not be seduced by the colours of the subject whether in, or out of focus.

To judge the 'best' aperture setting (ie. corresponding depth of field) for a black-and-white photograph, ask yourself the following questions:

1 Is the subject sufficiently strong to separate clearly from the foreground or background, irrespective of aperture and subject tonal values? This would certainly occur for many photojournalistic subjects, but, even here, a slight change of viewpoint may help separate the main subject from similarly toned surroundings, eg. people photographed against light or dark tones (sky, heavy shadows, etc) rather than mid-tones such as trees, walls.

2 Do very defocused subject areas produce interesting tonal patterns? Highlights of small irregular shapes, such as sunlight on water, recorded out of focus at large camera apertures can enhance a black-and-white photograph whereas the sharp recording when small apertures are used would make the same subject uninteresting and draw attention from the main subject.

3 Does the mood of the subject influence your choice of depth of field? For example, a tranquil landscape might need every detail to be recorded sharply so that the viewer can concentrate on tonal and textural differences within the photograph. On the other hand, if a 'disturbing' subject also has undefined areas of defocus this may add mystery to the overall effect; for example, an out-of-focus figure reflected in a dark puddle.

As previously mentioned, with difficult subjects you should, if possible, take several exposures at different apertures and select the most appropriate depth of field after carefully examining the contact prints.

It is interesting to note that many of the best black-and-white photographs are made with the lens set either at small apertures or at relatively large *f*-stops. Somehow, the 'compromise' middle apertures tend to produce unsatisfactory images, perhaps because the defocused areas are neither sharp enough to inform the viewer beyond any doubt of what they are, nor so unsharp that they wander undetected into the mind's unenquiring subconscious.

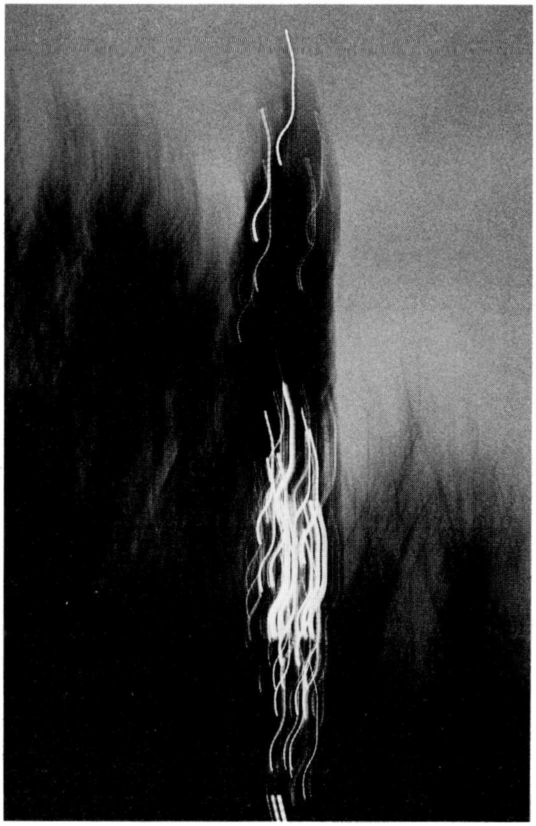

8 The combination of a long shutter speed (about ½ sec) and deliberate movement of the camera during the exposure has produced an abstract dynamic image out of this tall office block photographed at dusk. To increase your chances of success when attempting an effect like this, try several different shutter speeds and vary the direction of camera movement.

Subject movement

The recorded sharpness of a moving subject depends on the shutter speed and the speed and direction of subject movement relative to the camera position. To obtain maximum sharpness, use a high shutter speed and, if possible, photograph the subject as it directly approaches or retreats from the camera. This last technique does, of course, limit your choice of composition, so some sort of compromise between camera position and direction of travel may have to be found.

Sometimes, exciting black-and-white photographs are made by exaggerating movement and making this an important aspect of the picture. To 'freeze' a fast-moving car by using a short exposure does not give the impression of speed– indeed, the car may even appear stationary. So a common technique for this type of situation is to use a relatively slow shutter speed (1/8–1/125 sec) and pan with the moving object; you squeeze the shutter whilst continuing to follow the subject. The result is a relatively sharp main subject set against a 'streaked' background.

The same principles concerning the visibility of unsharp detail apply here as they did when discussing depth of field. The streaking can only be effective if the *tonal* differences between the relatively sharp main object and the background are sufficient not to merge into one another.

Camera movement

The problem of blur due to unsteady support of the camera when hand-holding varies greatly according to the individual – some people have a steadier hold than others. A rule of thumb for shake-free pictures is to use an exposure of 1/focal length in sec (approx) as the slowest possible speed to avoid camera shake. For example, a 250mm (or say, a 200mm) lens requires 1/250 sec. This 'rule' can only be a guideline; some photographers may be able to hand-hold slower

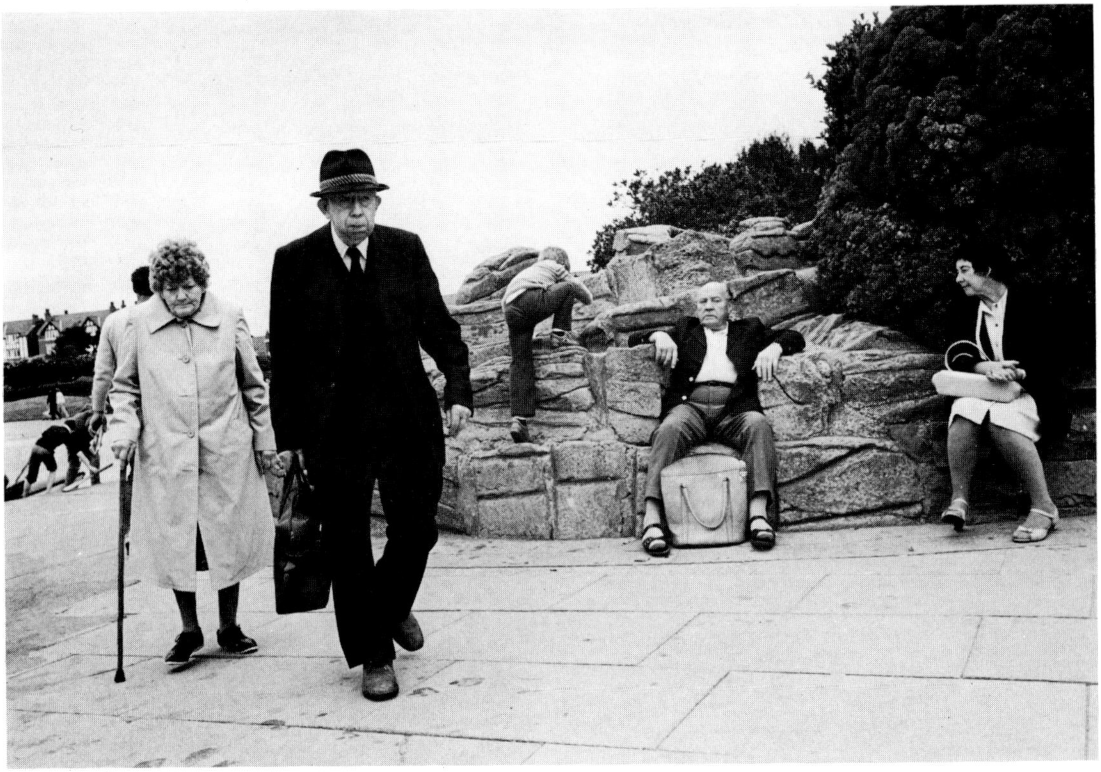

9 The 35mm format tends to force the photographer into relatively elongated compositions, in either portrait or landscape orientation. This full-frame image shows how many apparently unconnected elements can be united within the boundaries of the print. This type of photograph relies for its success on the quick reaction and observation of the cameraman. The minor background irritations on the extreme left of the frame are 'forgiven' because the decisive moment has been captured.

speeds while others need faster ones. However, never be dissuaded from taking a photograph simply because the only shutter speed possible is too slow, perhaps owing to low light levels. Seize the opportunity, take the photograph and hope for an acceptable result. If possible take several exposures to increase the chance of success.

You can remove any possibility of camera movement when using slower shutter speeds by employing a camera support. This need is likely to occur when small apertures are called for (eg. in landscape work) especially with larger format cameras. The quality necessary for much black-and-white pictorial work can only be achieved by using a rigid tripod. This 'static' approach also forces the photographer to examine his subject more closely, searching perhaps for interesting tonal variations or using longish exposure times to give flowing water an 'ethereal' look. Many of the masters of black-and-white photography place their camera on a tripod, view the potential picture through the viewfinder and then wait until they are happy with the composition and exposure, and feel 'at one' with the subject before they press the shutter. Photographers of the calibre of Minor White, Edward Weston and John Blakemore have considered photography a contemplative art.

So far, we have assumed that camera movement is a bad thing. However, there are subjects which are better captured using slower speeds and the inevitable camera shake may well add to the total impression. Photojournalistic studies often convey a more realistic feeling of involvement with the action if the photographer does not get too concerned with eliminating camera movement. This is particularly the case where lighting levels are low, and the viewer has become accustomed to expect technically 'poorer' photographs. The 'high quality' print with all its carefully separated tones, low graininess and high definition may appear so good that the viewer suspects its authenticity and may even believe that it has been

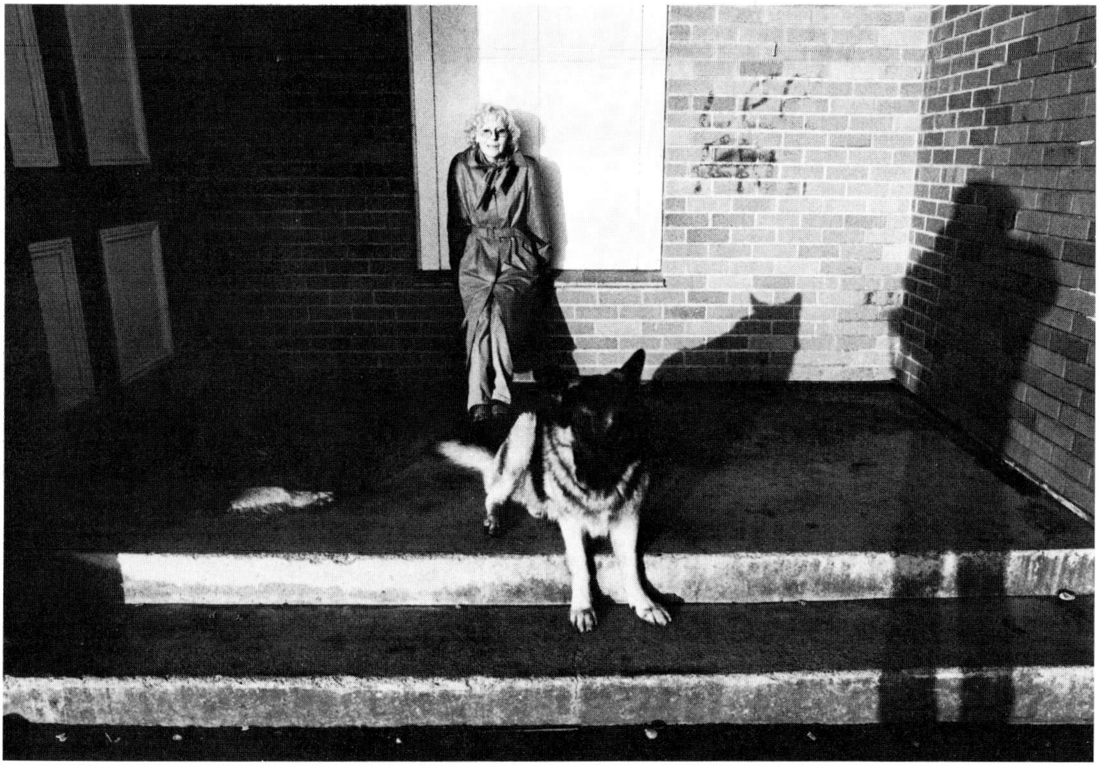

10 The effect of strong directional sunlight is the main element of this picture. A complex arrangement of subject elements and their shadows helps to keep the viewer's attention within the frame and gives the photograph a deliberately conceived 'confusion'.

carefully set up for the camera.

Deliberate waving around of the camera during a longish exposure can produce very attractive abstract photographs but this usually works more successfully with colour rather than black-and-white. The different colours can paint an exciting abstract image where abstract tonal variations are seldom interesting.

Film type and format

Maximum sharpness is obtained with slow films and larger formats. The quality obtainable with a 5 x 4in format camera and, say, Ilford FP4 film is magnificent; a 6 x 6cm camera and Kodak Panatomic-X (slow speed) film also produces excellent results. When the available conditions (light level, subject movement, tripod, etc) permit use of these 'ideal' camera and film combinations, maximum print quality is likely, although this does also assume correct exposure, development and printing (see later chapters).

The basic guide is to use the slowest film and largest format suitable for the subject. Well lit landscapes can be photographed in this manner to yield prints of superb quality, but the resulting pictures may not necessarily convey your *feelings* on the subject. Perhaps grainy high-contrast pictures are more in sympathy with your ideas. In this case a 35mm high-speed film (such as Tri-X) would probably be more suitable.

Never let the technical quality of photographs cloud your vision. It is important that you establish your ideas first and then apply the most suitable techniques. The good photographer is capable of extracting the right kind of image quality from the selected materials because he knows precisely how the materials respond in different conditions.

Lens quality

It goes almost without saying that the best quality lenses are capable of producing technically superior negatives and therefore better prints. If you want to produce the kind of picture where high technical quality is an important ingredient, it is obviously common sense to buy the best lenses you can afford. This also gives the psychological

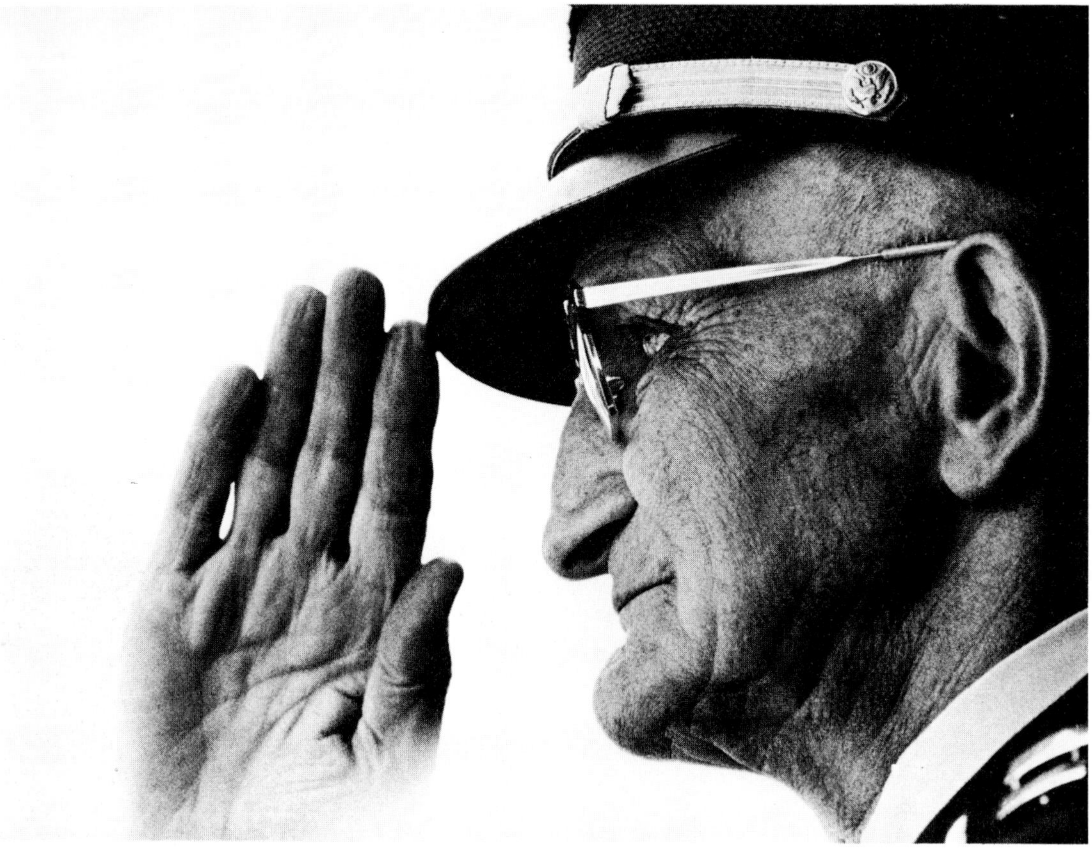

11 A high quality 300mm lens on a 35mm camera was used to portray this old soldier at a remembrance day parade. Even though the lens was used at maximum aperture (f/4.5) the image quality is excellent–the use of a poor quality lens would have detracted greatly from the overall effect.

advantage of knowing that your equipment will always give you excellent results.

Black-and-white films are capable of recording considerably higher definition than colour and the differences between the best and 'fair' lenses is much more noticeable in black-and-white work than in colour photographs.

It is therefore a worthwhile exercise to test your lenses soon after you buy them, especially if they were purchased secondhand. This will show you their real capabilities, and has the added benefit of ensuring that you get the lens quality you expect for your outlay. If you have paid for the best, you are well within your rights to return an unsatisfactory lens. The following method is suitable for testing a lens:

1 Photograph a subject containing a range of tones and some fine detail, such as a well-lit building, and use a tripod and slow speed film.
2 Make exposures at all apertures and keep detailed notes.
3 If possible, repeat the exposures using another lens, one which is known to give good results, and preferably one which fits the same camera body as your new lens. The second lens can come from a friend, or might be one of your own with a focal length near to that of the lens being tested; in the latter case move the tripod so both lenses cover the same subject area and therefore give approximately the same subject information.
4 Evaluate the processed negatives on a light box and look at the images with a magnifier (x5 to x10); any gross faults will immediately become obvious. In particular, compare the quality of the image at the centre with that achieved at the corners.
5 To reveal minor faults you should enlarge the full negative up to about 50 x 40cm (20 x 16in) and make small prints of the centre and one corner. To

ensure that the enlarger optics do not influence results (page 86), use a high quality enlarging lens stopped down by at least two stops from maximum aperture.

Once you have tested your equipment and are happy with the quality attainable, you should no longer worry about it. The camera is only a tool and should be thought of in the same manner as a painter regards his brushes, or a musician his instrument. Unfortunately, the equipment-minded photographer is often never capable of concentrating fully on picture making, but blames his equipment for not being able to produce satisfactory images.

Apparent image sharpness

So far, we have discussed the aspects of photography which can be easily identified as contributing directly to image sharpness. There are, however, a number of factors which have an influence on how sharp the image *appears*.

The nature of the subject and how it is lit have an effect on apparent image sharpness. Subjects consisting of fine detail seen in high contrast appear sharper than other subjects, especially if the lighting accentuates the detail. For example, a cross-lit textured surface, such as a brick wall or sand, always appears very crisp.

The quality of the print also has a bearing on apparent sharpness – high-contrast prints look sharper than low-contrast photographs. But the difference also depends on how the prints are viewed and the quality of the light shining on them. A spotlight always gives a print more sparkle, provided it is adjusted so that it does not cause reflections direct from the print surface.

There are some other smaller factors which influence apparent image sharpness. These include the way in which the print is mounted, especially the surrounding tone or colour, the viewing distance, the nature and quality of adjacent prints and the psychological frame of mind of the viewer–which affects overall perception of photographs; this last factor accounts for the fact that photographic exhibitions are often accompanied by music and wine.

Lighting

When interviewed, many master photographers attribute much of the success of their best pictures to the 'right' lighting; the black-and-white photographer has no colour contrast to stimulate the viewer but must rely on the light falling on the subject to produce exciting tonal relationships, subject texture and detail. The master photographer may have a particular scene in mind to portray, but has to wait for precisely the right lighting to make it a worthwhile photograph. This is especially true of architectural and landscape subjects.

Controlling light

It is beyond the scope of this book to cover lighting in great detail but it is a convenient place to mention some of its more important aspects.

At first, it may seem that when working outdoors, the photographer has no control over lighting. He simply uses the conditions that prevail. Although this is largely true, there are one or two techniques (besides the use of filters etc, which are discussed in Chapter 3), that can slightly modify existing lighting. The most obvious control, though often ignored, is to wait until the lighting is just as you want it; this applies particularly in countries where weather conditions are constantly changing.

To take advantage of this, examine a potential subject very carefully and note how the tones change as the sun disappears slightly behind the clouds. Notice also how the edges of shadows soften as the light becomes more diffuse and how much more detail is now visible within the shadows. Try to estimate the difference in the light reflected from the highlights and the shadows in the two different lighting situations. Detailed information on how to handle these exposure problems is given in Chapter 4.

Auxiliary lighting is difficult to arrange in outdoor work, but it is possible to employ electronic flash as a fill-in for shadows, or even as a main light for smaller subjects. Fig 2.2 gives some guidance to the use of fill-in flash. If you are planning to photograph small wild plants, you should find a small reflector a very useful item to carry with you. By positioning this at the correct angle, you can reduce contrast quite satisfactorily by filling in shadows in the subject.

The best position for a white reflector is found by trial-and-error but the following guidelines should be helpful:

1 Place the reflector as close as possible to the area to be lit, without letting the reflector itself intrude into the picture area.
2 Rotate the card about a horizontal axis until

maximum lighting is obtained in the shadow.
3 Next rotate the card about a vertical axis until further lightening is obtained.
4 If the dark area is now too light, move the card away from the subject until the tonal range appears about correct. Because the eye, though not the film, has the ability to penetrate the shadows, it is a common mistake to reflect insufficient light into the dark areas.
5 For difficult subjects, expose several frames with the reflector at different positions.

The studio photographer has, of course, infinite control over lighting and most of his photographs depend for their effectiveness largely on the skilful use of lamps. There are a number of excellent books which deal specifically with lighting technique including *Photographic Lighting in Practice* by John Evans, in this series.

2.2 Example of fill-in flash

Daylight meter reading 1/125 *f*/8 (125 ASA)
*Flash calculator dial indicates *f*/11 at subject distance of 3m.
Lighting ratio (daylight: flash)

	Flash Power				
Camera settings	Full	1/2	1/4	1/8	1/16
1/15 *f*/22	4:1	8:1	16:1	32:1	64:1
1/30 *f*/16	2:1	4:1	8:1	16:1	32:1
1/60 *f*/11	1:1	2:1	4:1	8:1	16:1
1/125** *f*/8	1:2	1:1	2:1	4:1	8:1
1/250** *f*/5.6	1:4	1:2	1:1	2:1	4:1
1/500** *f*/4	1:8	1:4	1:2	1:1	2:1

2.2 The left-hand column shows some *equivalent exposures* to 1/125 *f*/8. Flash power is most conveniently altered by replacing the automatic control sensor of the flash unit with a normally-set control. If your unit does not have this accessory, increase the ASA setting (eg. ASA 100 to ASA 200 for half power, to ASA 400 for quarter power, etc). The latter technique should be tested on your own equipment as some sensors may also take available daylight into account and therefore give inconsistent output. For most black-and-white work a lighting (daylight to flash) ratio of 4:1 or 8:1 is ideal as it increases shadow detail without giving the picture an artificial appearance.
* Set calculator at ASA 64 for outside work, as most units are calibrated for average-sized rooms where reflection off the walls increases the light reaching the subject.
** Remember, the higher speeds of most focal plane shutters do not synchronise with electronic flash and cannot be used for fill-in lighting.

Brightness range

The range of tones found in a subject depends on both the reflectivity of the various parts of the subject and the nature of the lighting falling on it. For successful black-and-white photography, it is important to be able to recognise this subject brightness range and know how to modify film exposure and development accordingly.

Subject brightness range is discussed in a more direct context in Chapters 4 and 5, but it is important for the reader to realise the interrelated nature of subject reflectivity, lighting, film exposure and development.

Seeing in black-and-white

We have already discussed the fact that the black-and-white photographer is concerned with translating a 3-D 'real' colour scene into an unreal 2-D representation of the subject in terms of shapes and tones only. It takes considerable practice and experience for a black-and-white photographer to be able to visualise the final print simply by looking through the viewfinder. Although there is no substitute for practice, some guidelines can help the inexperienced to 'see' in black-and-white.

It is very easy to be seduced by the colours of a potential photographic subject and then make exposures in the camera which result in unsuccessful black-and-white prints. You must try to mentally eliminate the colour in the scene and, instead, endeavour to see areas in terms of tone. For example, green grass becomes a mid-grey, 'white' skin is light in tone, and the sky also normally becomes light in tone, unless filtered. A technique practised by some photographers is to look at the scene through half-closed eyes. This has the effect of darkening the subject, making it appear almost monochromatic and showing more clearly the main areas of tone and shadow.

Obviously, lighting is a major influence on the tonal range. To gauge if a subject is suitable for black-and-white photography, study how the light falls on it, examine where the highlights (light tones) are and if they are attractive. Remember, most pictures rely on highlight detail for their main interest. Look into the shadows and see if there is subtle detail which is important to record. Compare how the middle tones are spread across the subject and how they tonally balance the highlights and shadows.

Recording ability of the film

Because of its 'adjustable' sensitivity, the eye is able to perceive a wide brightness range within a subject. A scene is scanned by the eye at a very

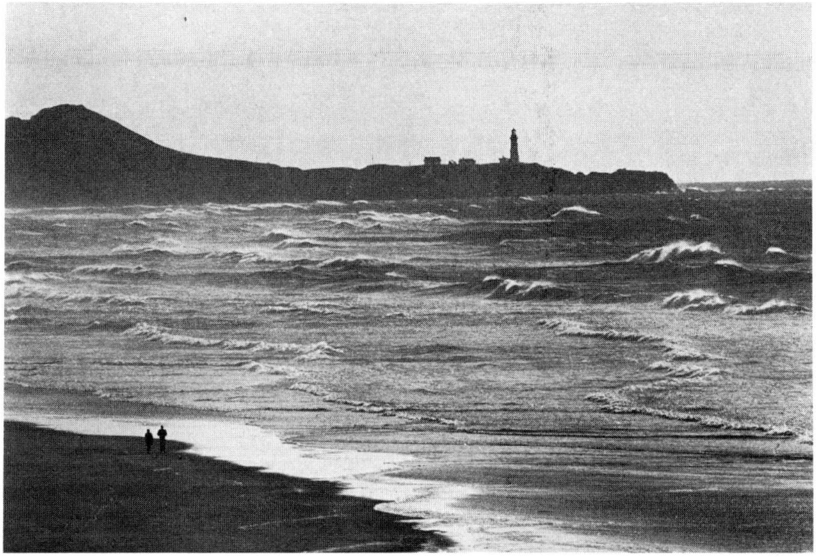

12 Because of the 'flat' lighting and large areas of single colour it is relatively easy to visualise this seascape in black-and-white tones. The greatest concentration has gone into capturing the two figures at exactly the desired position within the composition and waiting for the sea to produce the best wave patterns and tide boundary with the sand.

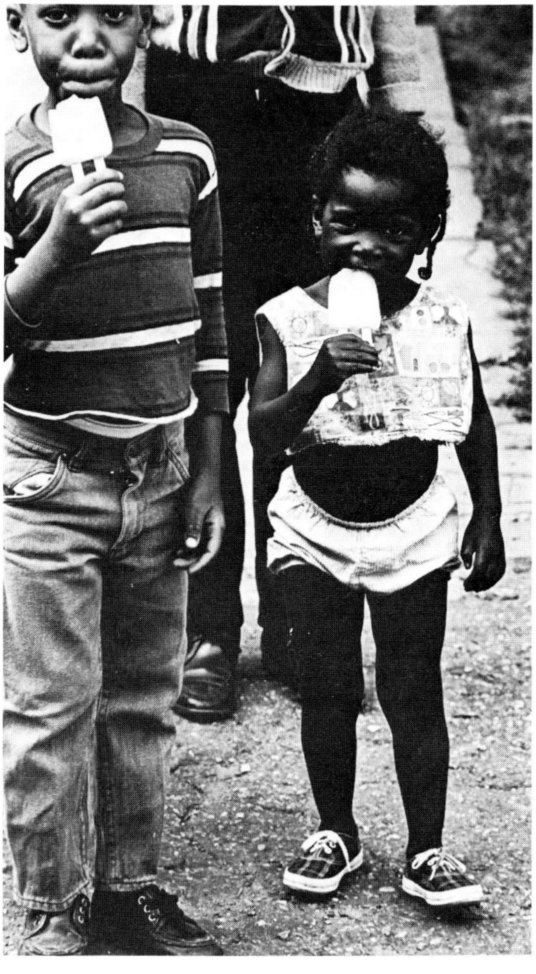

13 Subjects which have a large difference between the light reflected from the light tones (highlights) and that reflected from the dark areas (shadows) must be photographed carefully so that a maximum of subject detail is retained. Precise control of film exposure, film development and print making is essential.

rapid rate, and the 2° angle of dominant vision searches the subject to find interesting detail for the brain to interpret. The eye can look at a bright highlight and then almost immediately search shadows for information. During this scanning process the sensitivity controls of the eye are adjusted so that the brain can cope with a wide brightness range. Photographic film does not have this variable sensitivity but can record only a limited range of brightnesses.

The brightness range that a specific film is capable of recording depends mainly on the amount of development it receives. Longer development times reduce the brightness range that can be recorded by the film, while shorter times increase this range of tones. This subject is examined in greater detail in later chapters.

The net result of the limited ability of a film to record different subject tones is that the photographer must often select the subject tones he wishes to record. As previously stated, film development offers some control over the recording of subject brightness range.

When lighting is very direct, for example on a cloudless day, the subject brightness range is likely to be too great for the film to handle, and the photographer must make a few decisions. He may

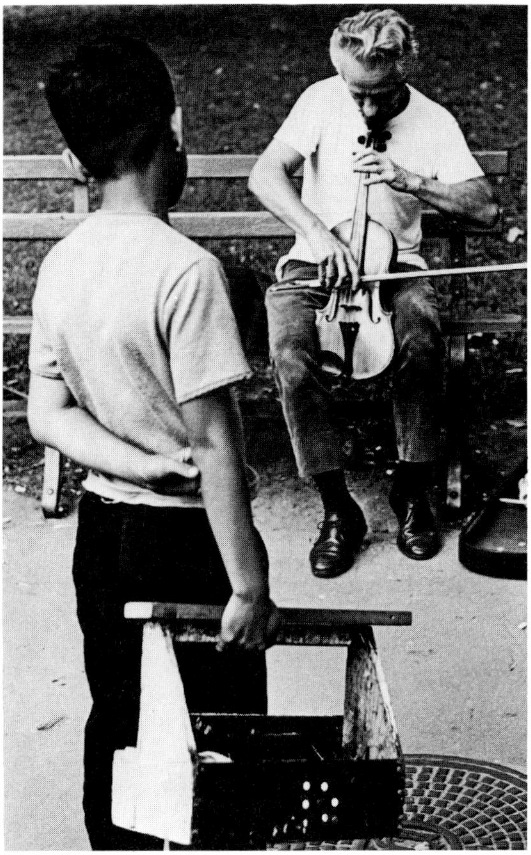

14 The camera has not disturbed this situation but simply recorded it unobserved–an example of the 'voyeur' approach to photography. The use of a standard lens rather than a long lens ('telephoto') involves the viewer more with the event.

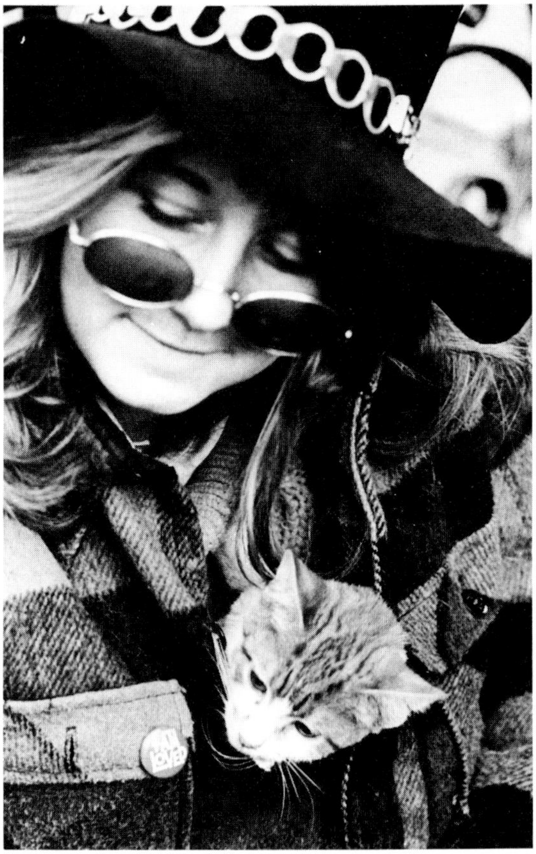

15 The three strongest elements here, the cat, the girl's face and the 'I am loved' button, form a strong triangular shape which keeps the viewer's attention within the photograph. Neither the 'busy' jacket nor the defocused face disturb this composition.

elect not to record some tones, which means sacrificing either shadow or highlight detail or part of both, or he might reduce the brightness range of the subject by using fill-in lighting (flash or reflector). Or, he can reduce development time to ensure that the maximum tonal range is recorded. The photographer can, of course, use all three possibilities at once.

When the nature of the subject and/or lighting is such that there is only a relatively small tonal range, the film is able to reproduce all subject tones. This is the case for most subjects on dull, overcast days.

Try to develop the ability to 'see' in black-and-white and to judge how the subject tones record on the film and subsequently transfer to the printing paper.

Involvement with your subject

There are two extremes of approach when photographing a subject. On the one hand, the photographer can view the scene from a distance as an observer; this is often referred to as the 'voyeur' approach. At the other extreme, the photographer becomes completely involved with the subject. So, you can either stand back and observe, or get into the action. Between these two extremes there are, of course, compromise approaches.

The type of approach you select will depend on the subject matter, the equipment you have available, and your own personality. Remember, no one approach is any more valid than another–what matters is the result.

The 'voyeur' approach

To photograph a scene unobserved means that you are able to record what is going on without in any way influencing the action. The most common example of this approach is the candid photograph.

To obtain a candid picture you can either take photographs at a reasonable distance from the subject, which normally involves the use of long focal length lenses; or you can adopt techniques which will enable you to photograph close to the subject, undetected.

The 'long lens' technique is most convenient for subjects which are not particularly accessible, such as sportsmen or animals. You will often need fast films, because long lenses require high shutter speeds for hand-holding and usually have relatively modest maximum apertures. You can use a tripod, although this does tend to inhibit the style you adopt.

Pictures taken with long focal length lenses also usually exhibit flattened perspective so that the different parts of the subject appear 'squashed' together. This can, however, be used to good effect on a number of subjects, for example, parades, or where a sense of isolation is needed. In the final sequences of the movie *The Graduate,* Dustin Hoffmann was 'suspended' in his chase to the church by the use of a long lens. The tension was held because he appeared to be going nowhere very fast. The same feeling can be engendered in still photography by the use of long focal length lenses.

In black-and-white work, long focal length lenses may 'force' certain subject tones closer together, so you must be careful to prevent such tones merging, with the resultant loss of subject detail. The perspective may be further flattened by the juxtaposition of similar image tones and this is likely to produce a lifeless picture. Search carefully for a dominant subject that will separate clearly from defocused tones by virtue of its strong visual impact. The use of fast film with its increased graininess does, in fact, help to break up similar tones and avoid such flattened tonality.

The interactive approach

In recent years, many young photojournalists have favoured a style whereby the photographer seems to actually get involved with what is going on. This usually means getting in close to the subject with wide-angle (short focal length) lenses. Often, as a consequence, the subject responds to the presence of a camera.

16 Even though a medium long lens (135mm on a 35mm camera) has been used here, there is strong involvement with the subject. The camera has confronted the subject and 'forced' him to interact with it.

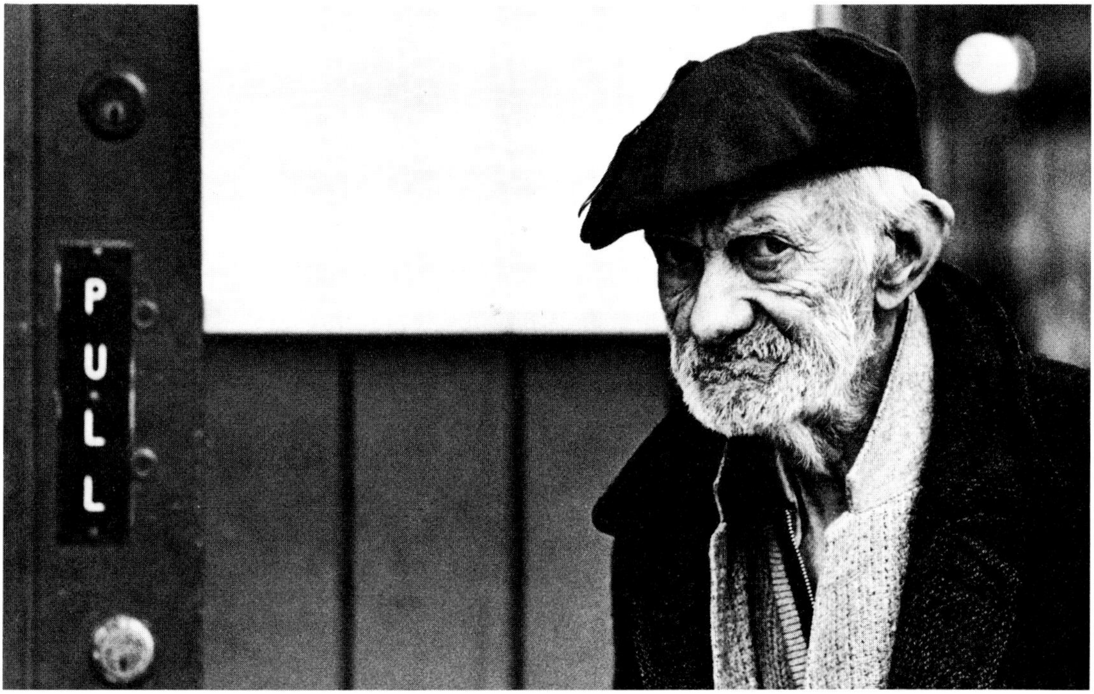

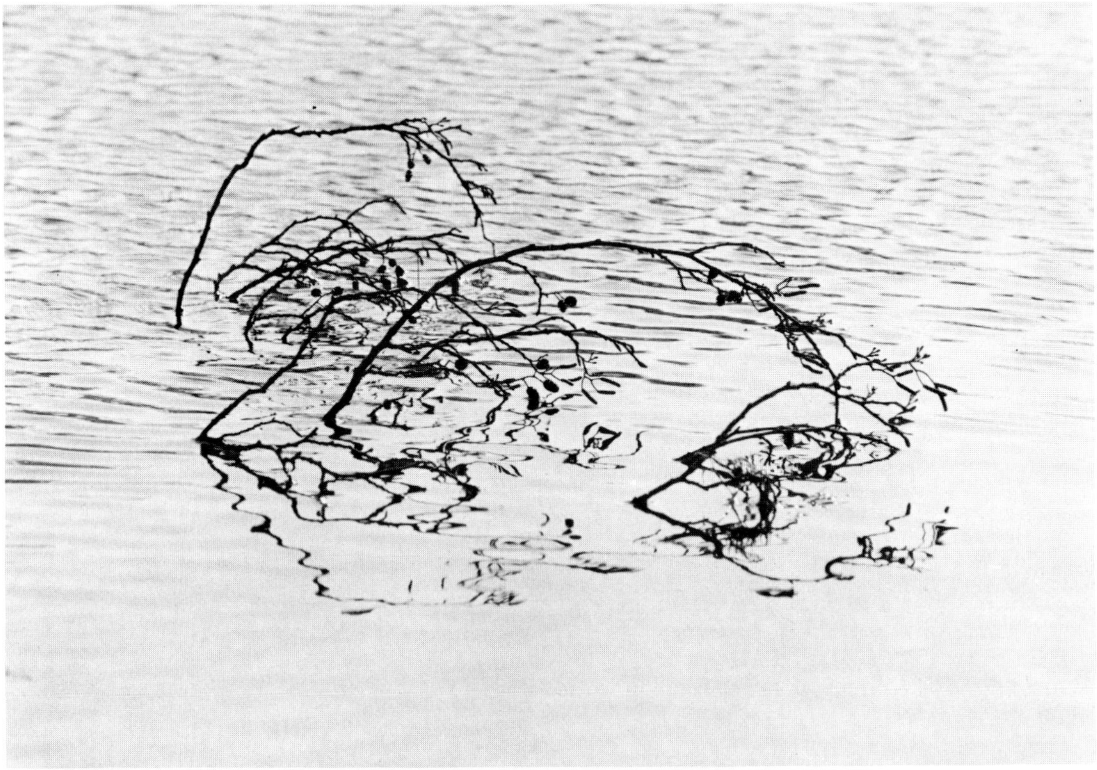

There are, of course, a number of drawbacks to this method. You can destroy the naturalness of the scene, or risk getting hurt if someone takes exception to your intrusion. The main reward of the 'involved' style is that the pictures convey a strong feeling of 'being there'–everything appears much more immediate and exciting.

In contrast to the use of lenses of long focal length, wide-angle lenses have relatively large maximum apertures (*f*/2.8 or larger) and therefore allow longer shutter speeds (about 1/30 sec.) to be used without the fear of getting camera shake. Combining these two facts means that medium-speed or slow film can be loaded into the camera or, if great depth of field is required (eg. *f*/16), a fast film should be used.

Lenses of shorter focal length exaggerate perspective and 'stretch' the different parts of the scene away from each other. As normally used, the foreground appears closer and the background recedes rapidly to infinity. Some people feel that this steep perspective destroys the sense of reality in a photograph because the photographic device is all too obvious. However, it can be argued that the obviously photographic character of the wide-angle image makes the viewer more aware of the fact that the person taking the picture is intimately involved with the subject.

Where there is this exaggerated perspective, the subject tones in a black-and-white photograph are more likely to be clearly separated, ie: there is less likelihood of tones merging to give a muddy appearance, and the probably large depth of field also helps to give distinct subject detail.

The 'rules' of composition

There has been much debate, especially in the earlier days of photography, as to the 'correct' way to compose an image in the camera. The traditionalists have always given the beginner a set of rules which should be followed while arranging the photograph. Fortunately, rules of composition are no longer drummed into photographers.

Nevertheless, a discussion on the arrangement of subjects, and the key compositional decisions which the photographer has to make, should prove helpful.

17 The gentle curves of the branches coupled with the soft tonal gradation give this photograph its peaceful feeling. The viewer's attention is prevented from wandering out of the top of the photograph by the presence there of rougher water, which produces an overall darker tonality than the foreground.

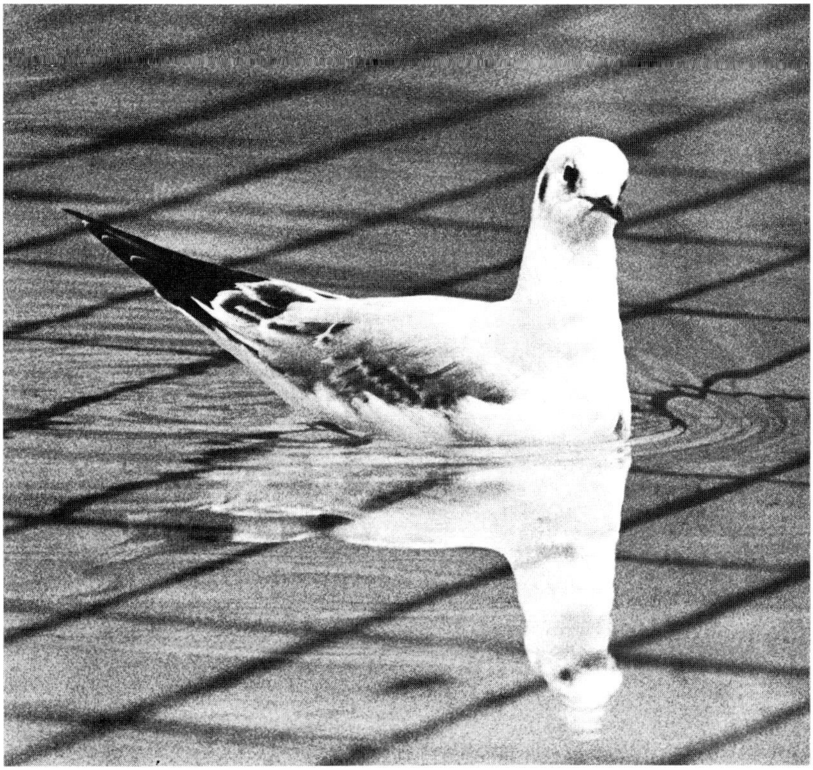

18 Simple subjects need strong compositional elements if they are to be effective. The dark diagonal lines help to lead the viewer's eye towards the main subject, which is itself reinforced by the reflected image. Also, the relatively dark surroundings make the light-toned gull more dominant (much of this effect was achieved by local printing control–see Chapter 6).

Main subject position within the frame

If paintings and photographs are analysed, it is surprising how many obey the 'law of thirds' (see fig 2.3). This law states that the main subject interest should be near one of the four intersections created when a picture is split into thirds along both edges. Many photographers unconsciously compose their pictures according to this law, but it would be a mistake to try, deliberately and artificially, to place your main focal point at one of these intersections. Nine times out of ten the result would look contrived.

Placing the main subject centrally within the frame seldom produces a pleasing photograph. It creates an unsettling effect which can be attributed to the eyes (and brain) not being able to rest in one particular place. Occasionally, a deliberate halving of the image space–achieved by placing the main subject in the centre–is successful, and in this situation the photographer has *deliberately* caused the brain to be unsettled. A state of tension created within a photograph can have

2.3 Dividing a picture into thirds gives four intersecting points (A,B,C,D). The 'law of thirds' states that the strongest part (focal point) of the subject should be placed at one of these intersections to give a pleasingly balanced picture.

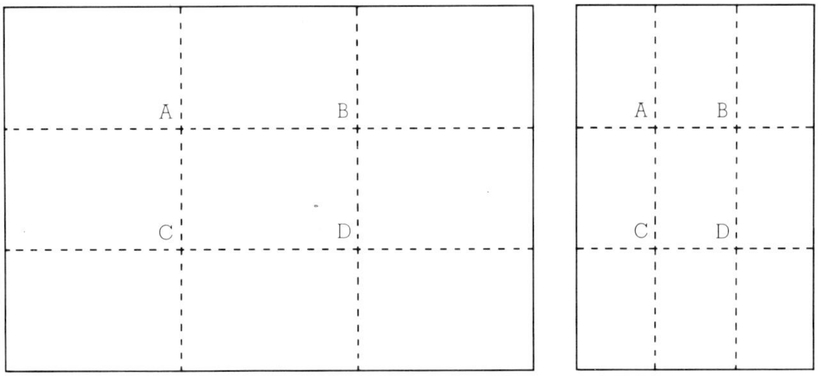

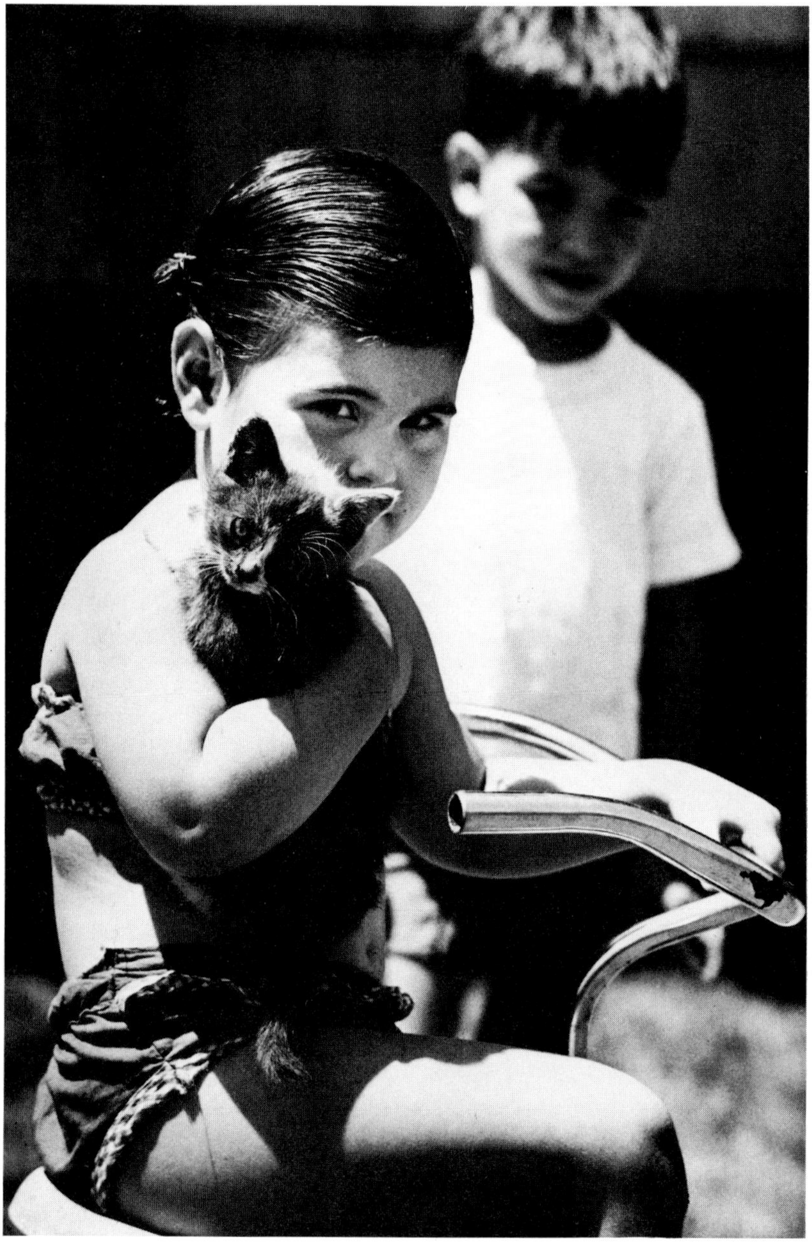

19 The decision to include the boy, especially as he is defocused, in this composition can be considered 'against the rules'. However, it does direct the viewer's gaze back to the main subject of girl and cat. This is achieved mainly by a 'circle' of important compositional elements, ie. cat, girl's face, boy's face, white tee shirt, hand, handlebars and arm, which retain the interest within the picture area.

an extremely powerful effect. This tension is most noticeable in a black-and-white photograph because the emphasis is principally on the subject content. In fact, this device is more likely to be successful in black-and-white rather than in colour where it may simply annoy the viewer.

Space within a picture

Just as silence may be used in music to accentuate the melodic theme, space in a photograph can provide the perfect balance to the main image. It is not essential to fill the frame with interesting matter. It is often more pleasing to allow your main photographic message to be stated simply, among uncomplicated surroundings. Simple images are often the most successful.

Space within a picture can be used to direct the viewers' eyes to the main subject and prevent his attention from wandering to the frame edges and outside the picture. Many good landscape photographs contain large areas of a single tone which gives the picture a degree of relaxation; the eye finds these tones restful while scanning the image. A smooth tonal range, ie: flowing easily from one tone to another, and a lack of grain also help to promote this contented feeling. This is why so many landscape photographers work with large format cameras.

The space within a picture should have a pleasing shape. This will occur where the boundaries of space are gradual and curved, while sharp, straight edges between the main image and surrounding spaces can cause tension. But, as we have already noted, tension within a photograph is not always a bad thing.

Lines and curves

The viewer's attention can be directed towards the main picture content by the use of strong lines and/or curves. A classical example is the path which leads up to a house, or the stem which finishes with the flower–there are many instances of lines and curves in nature that direct the viewer's eyes in this manner. Black-and-white photographs tend to accentuate lines and curves within the subject, whereas colour in a photograph is likely to considerably reduce the impact of these design elements.

Most photographers with a 'natural eye' employ lines and curves in their photographs to help the viewer find the main interest and to connect unrelated parts of the picture. A few photography books even go as far as to draw these strong lead-in lines and curves over the photograph to indicate compositional elements. If you are trying to improve your 'seeing', a useful device is to carefully observe a potential photographic scene and decide how best the existing lines and curves can be incorporated in the final design. Perhaps a change of viewpoint (ie: perspective) may improve the arrangement of lines and curves, or a different lens may concentrate or expand them.

Tonal balance

The distribution of tones within a black-and-white photograph has a significant effect on the overall 'feeling' perceived by the viewer. The tonal balance, from whites through greys to black, can be evenly distributed, or concentrated at one end of the grey scale.

An even distribution of tones in a photograph often produces a very relaxing and peaceful effect–especially when the tones gradually blend into one another. In practice, most subjects reflect an even distribution of tone, which is why lightmeters are so successful in gauging exposure. (Lightmeter readings are based on an 18% reflectance from the 'average' subject – see Chapter 4.)

A subject with a preponderance of lighter tones is referred to as *'high key'*, and suggests lightheartedness, a feeling of well-being. For example, blonde women are generally considered to be more fun-loving and carefree than brunettes and sports cars are often lighter in tone than stately 'official' limousines, which are usually dark.

In contrast to high key subjects, the *'low key'* image consists mainly of darker tones and is a more 'serious' subject. Here, the tonal balance is shifted towards the dark end of the grey scale, and detail in the shadows is often very important. Again, pursuing the musical analogy, low key images equate to the deeper and often louder passages of a symphony. Some photographers, like some composers, have a preference for low key 'serious' images, which are sometimes associated with melancholy feelings.

Overall picture mood

The mood that a photograph conveys depends largely on content and tonal balance. It might at first seem that the photographer has no control over the mood once he has selected his subject; he simply takes a reading, and makes the exposure. However, this is not so, because the photographer working in black-and-white can manipulate the depth and range of tones during the processing of the film and the printing of the negative. Even the original camera exposure can be chosen to suit the visualisation of the photographer.

Breaking the rules

The discussion above is only intended to give rough guidelines to composition. These should never be considered as unbreakable rules. Often, the photographer who disregards the rules produces the most exciting images, although he would probably concede that he needed to understand conventional composition before he could ignore it. The unconventional approach is adopted in full knowledge of the conventional.

Some styles of photography thrive on disregard of the rules and enjoy challenging the viewer, while others are successful because they do not break new ground. Most portraiture is conventional, but anyone who has seen Diane Arbus's unique style cannot fail to be moved towards strong approval or disapproval. The landscapes produced by Ansel Adams, Bill Brandt, and Jerry Uelsmann could not be more different; yet the conventional style of Adams is just as valid as the more individual approaches of Brandt and Uelsmann. Inevitably, what is considered avant-garde today may find its place in the rule book tomorrow.

Analysing the viewers' reactions

It is very constructive to analyse ways of looking at photographs to determine which approaches are 'successful' and which are 'failures'. Try to look at photographs critically; how do your eyes react to the various parts of the image? Try to determine the path your eyes take while 'reading' the photograph. Do they go immediately to the main subject interest? What happens when you find the focal point? Does your attention wander out of the picture or return to the main interest via a different route? Which elements of the image are aggressive and which parts are passive? Are the highlights more important than the shadows? How does the tonal distribution affect the mood? What would happen if the contrast were increased or reduced, or the graininess changed by the use of a slower or faster film? Would an (overall) darker or lighter print be more effective? Does the frame line of the photograph play an important part in your perception of the image?

These are some of the many questions you can ask about a photograph. Try to make your analysis objective, and determine how you can use the answers to improve your photography. Consider what black-and-white variables could be changed to improve the picture. Get as many picture books as you can find from your local bookseller or library, and try to 'understand' the more successful photographs.

There is, however, one danger in devoting too much time to evaluating other people's photographs, and that is believing that their approach is the best one. To avoid this emulation of the great, thereby suppressing your own style, look at a wide variety of images (photographic and non-photographic) and do not take the whole matter too seriously. Above all, try to please yourself and do not seek public approval, as this will dilute your vision and lead you to accept the unexciting compromise.

3 CAMERAWORK IN PRACTICE

So far, we have discussed the composition of the image and the photographic controls that can be used to change the picture. This chapter examines certain practical aspects of camera-work as far as they concern a photographer working in black-and-white and gives some advice on choice of equipment and materials.

Getting the picture

Every choice you make of equipment or materials has a very definite influence on the type of photograph you are likely to produce. It is important that you understand the abilities and limitations of your photographic gear and chosen film. Good technical knowledge is extremely useful to a photographer, but always remember that the image must come first, and that the technology is only there to make it all possible.

Because of the high levels of design skill that go into producing photographic equipment, it is easy to be seduced by the sheer wonder of it all. By all means read the magazines and get as much advice as you can before investing in hardware, but once you have made your purchase, get to know it quickly and then start searching for satisfying pictures.

When embarking on a photographic trip there is a great temptation to take every piece of equipment you own to cover every eventuality. This will soon tire you out physically and will also encourage you to attempt an unmanageably wide range of subject matter. Instead, concentrate your efforts by carrying only essential gear, and try to start out with a specific project in mind. It is surprising how much can be achieved with, say, just one camera and one lens–this method is amazingly effective in

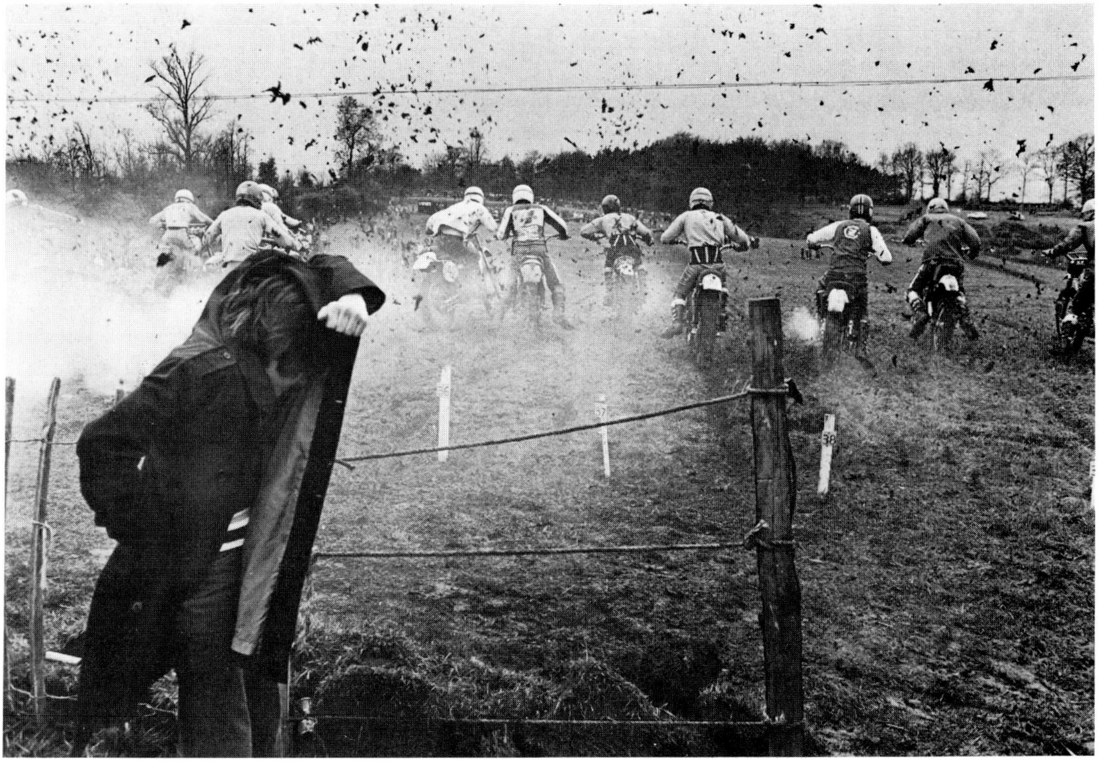

20 To produce this type of picture successfully, you need quick reactions, the ability to foresee the unexpected and to sense when to press the shutter! It might be argued that photographic technicalities are relatively unimportant, compared with getting the picture but a good photojournalist must have a sound grasp of such matters as depth of field and exposure, to ensure that his photographs are not marred by poor technical quality.

clearing your mind, and encourages a freer, less cluttered approach to a subject.

Choice of lenses

When buying a lens you should consider it as one of a set of lenses, and aim to own lenses that complement, and do not in general duplicate one another. As noted previously, the choice of lens(es) could depend mainly on your approach to a subject–whether you favour the 'voyeur' or 'involved' technique.

For 'general' photography, a good set of lenses to use would be a standard, a medium-long focal length, and a moderate wide-angle lens. For the 35mm camera, this set would comprise lenses having focal lengths of about 50mm, 105mm and 28mm; the equivalent set for 120 film users would consist of 80mm, 150mm and 40mm.

Standard lenses

Most cameras come supplied with a standard lens, which gives an impression of 'normal' perspective. In other words, as normally used it does not exaggerate the proportional relationship between one part of the scene and another part. It 'sees' the subject in much the same way the eye does. Because they are made in much larger numbers, standard lenses are less expensive than other focal lengths and offer the best value for money.

Most standard lenses have a maximum aperture of about *f*/1.7–*f*/2 but if you are intending to take photographs at low light levels, then the extra money for an *f*/1.4 lens is probably well spent. There are a few *f*/1.2 lenses available but these are disproportionately expensive and, for most photographers, quite unnecessary. They may also be relatively cumbersome.

If you are in the habit of carrying a camera most of the time to be ready to capture the unexpected picture, the best lens to fit to your camera is generally considered to be the standard lens. It can cope with most lighting conditions, especially if fast film is loaded, it has a moderate angle of view and it allows a reasonable camera-to-subject distance for most subjects. For the black-and-white photojournalist who wants to carry a camera at all times, the small fixed-lens rangefinder camera that can easily be slipped into a pocket or briefcase is a good choice.

Wide-angle lenses

Lenses of short focal length (wide-angles) are popular with landscape photographers and for the interactive style of photojournalism; they are also necessary when you are working in confined surroundings, such as alleyways or small rooms. As noted, the steep perspective impression associated with wide-angle lenses exaggerates the effect of distance.

When a lens is pointed upwards or downwards any vertical parallel lines in the scene are recorded as non-parallel (converging). This occurs most noticeably with wide angle lenses – typically when a tall building is photographed from below. If you wish to avoid this convergence of parallel lines, you must either keep the film plane (camera back) vertical and, perhaps, accept less than ideal framing and coverage of the subject, or correct a slight degree of convergence when printing the negative (page 101). A characteristic of the large format camera with movements is the ability to change the shape and also the focus of the image and thus control or remove converging lines.

However, the convergent effect can also be used to increase the impact of your photographs and produce the dynamic lines and shapes which can be so important in black-and-white compositions. For example, a pole vaulter photographed from below with a wide-angle lens can look very dramatic, especially if the sky is darkened by the use of a filter or by local printing controls.

21-22 The 'normal' perspective given by a standard lens has helped this pair of photographs to appear very real and not obviously 'photographic'. The viewer is able to concentrate on their content and compare one image with the other–near-identical framing of sequence pictures is essential to maintain continuity.

Longer focal lengths

With lenses of longer focal length a photographer can observe the subject from a reasonable distance yet still obtain relatively large images of the scene. For situations where it is impossible to get close to the action, such as with many sports for example, the use of long lenses is pretty well essential. Long focal length lenses are also used by photographers who favour a more detached style of recording their subject.

We have already discussed how long focal length lenses are usually associated with a reduced tonal range and a 'flattened' perspective, ie, the space between foreground, subject and background appears greatly diminished and

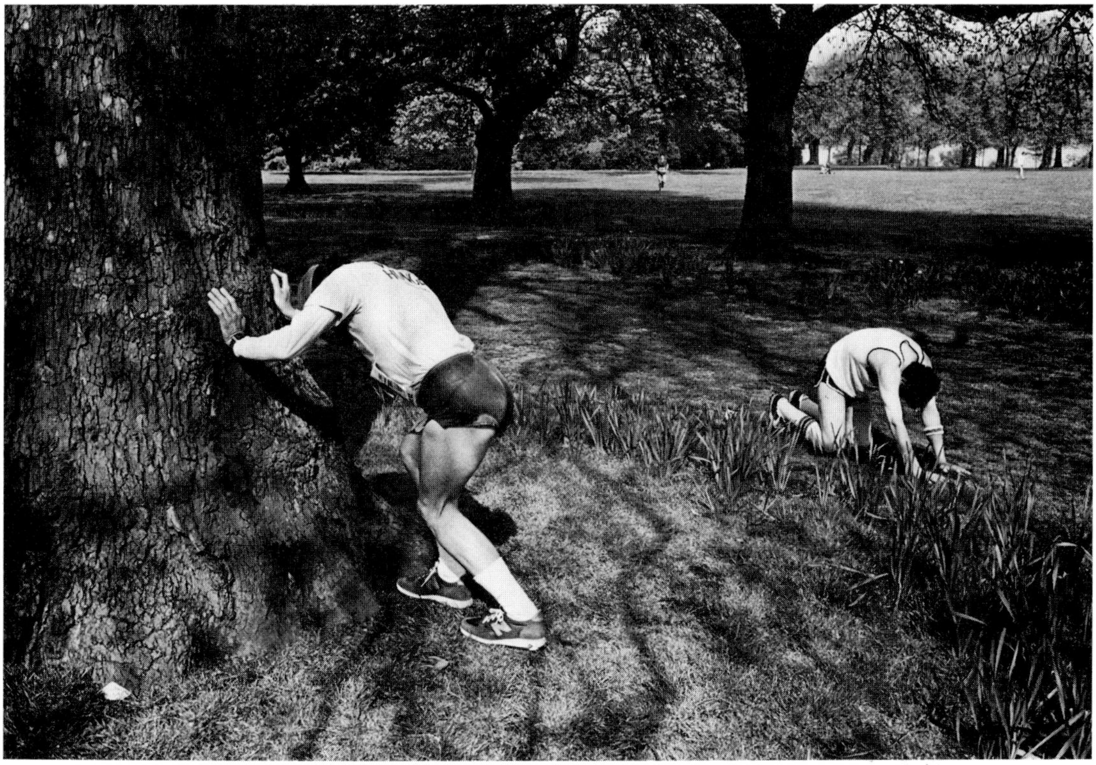

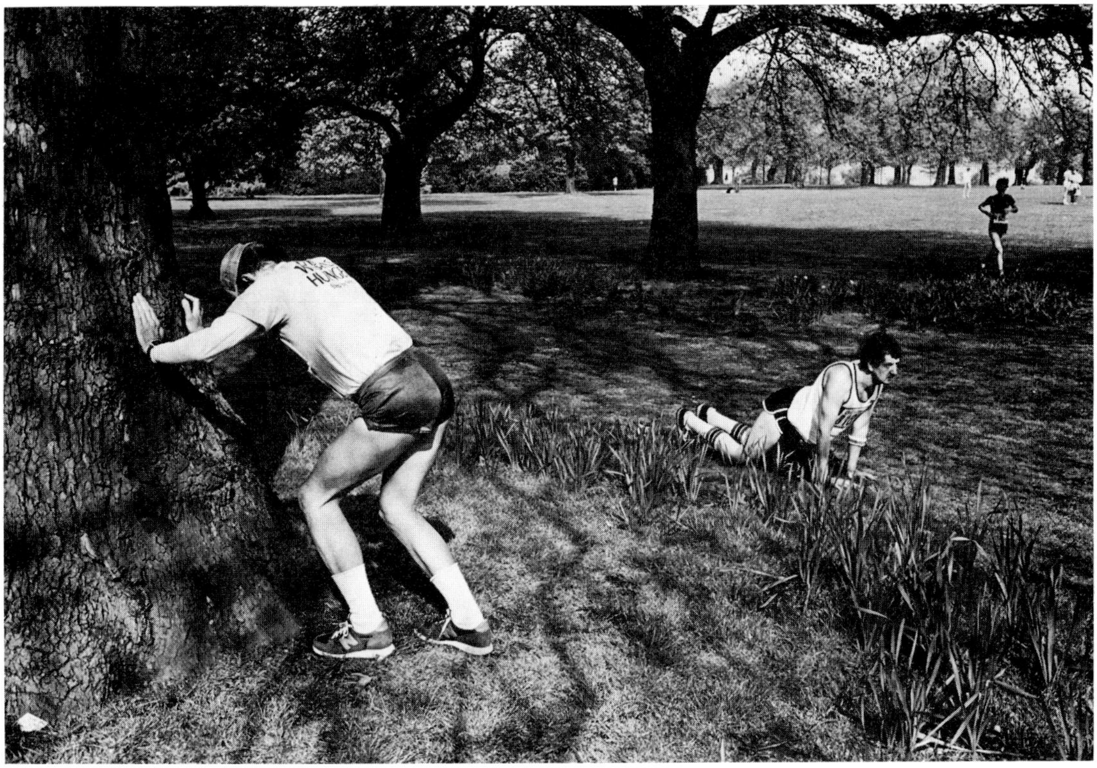

subjects within the field of view appear closer together than normal, and contrast range is also reduced. This compression of subject elements and tones can be employed to give an intentionally crowded or congested feeling to the scene, for example, when photographing a crowd of people head-on to suggest the crush of city life in the rush hour.

Very long focal length lenses (eg. 500mm) are available as conventional optical designs or as mirror lenses in which glass elements are substituted by reflecting surfaces. The disadvantage with the longer focal lengths of ordinary design is their sheer physical length and bulk. By comparison, mirror lenses are considerably lighter and less cumbersome but have only one working aperture (usually about *f*/8). If you are unable to adjust exposure sufficiently for the prevailing light conditions by changing the shutter speed, then you can either use a faster or slower film or (to reduce exposure) insert neutral density (ND) filters in the lens for which purpose the lens is provided

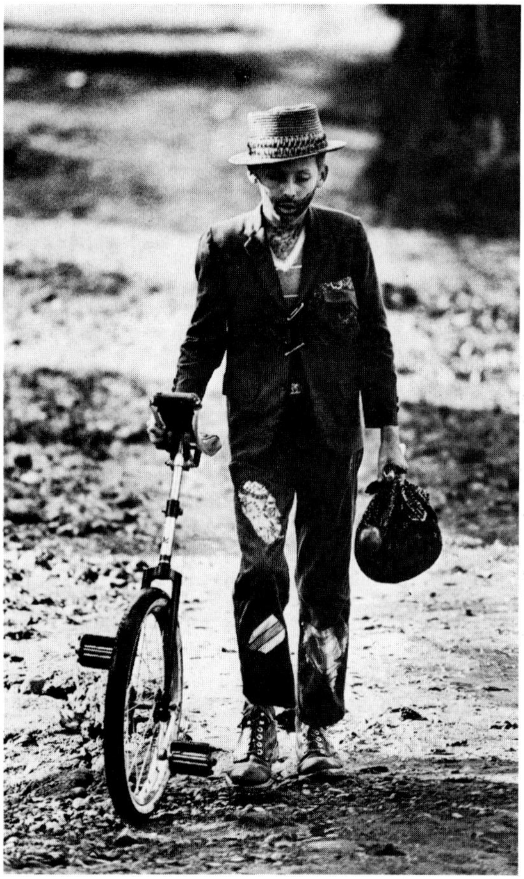

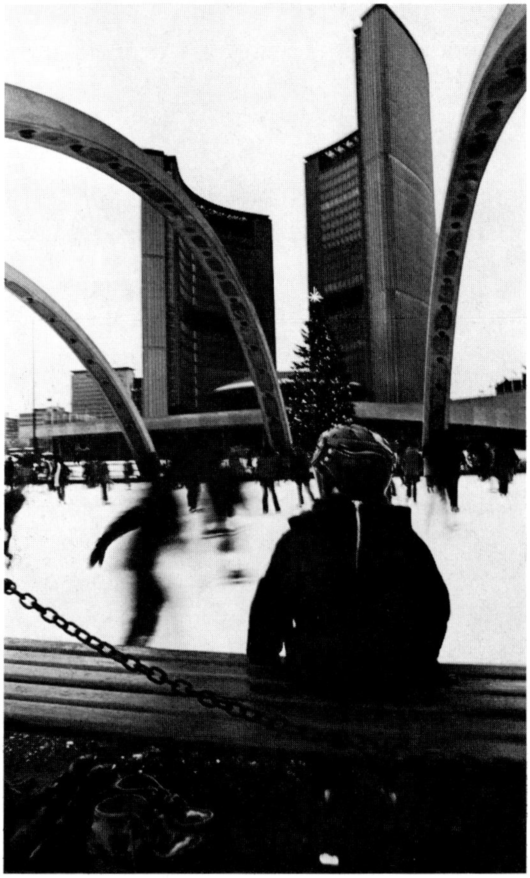

23 The isolation of the boy returning from a parade has been emphasised by the choice of a long lens (300mm on a 35mm camera). The 'flattened' perspective causes the foreground and background to be squeezed closer together.

24 The use of a wide-angle lens (24mm on a 35mm camera) has allowed the boots and tops of the buildings to be included in the picture, while ensuring that the main subject is still close to the camera. To avoid the lens causing excessive convergence of the tall buildings, the camera was kept fairly level. A slow shutter speed (about 1/15 sec), which is relatively easy to hand-hold when using a wide-angle lens, has ensured adequate depth of field and some blur of skaters.

25 For obvious reasons a long lens (300mm on a 35mm camera) has been used to photograph these large cats at an open zoo. To inject some compositional structure into what might otherwise have been just another animal photograph, the pair have been framed to appear as mirror images.

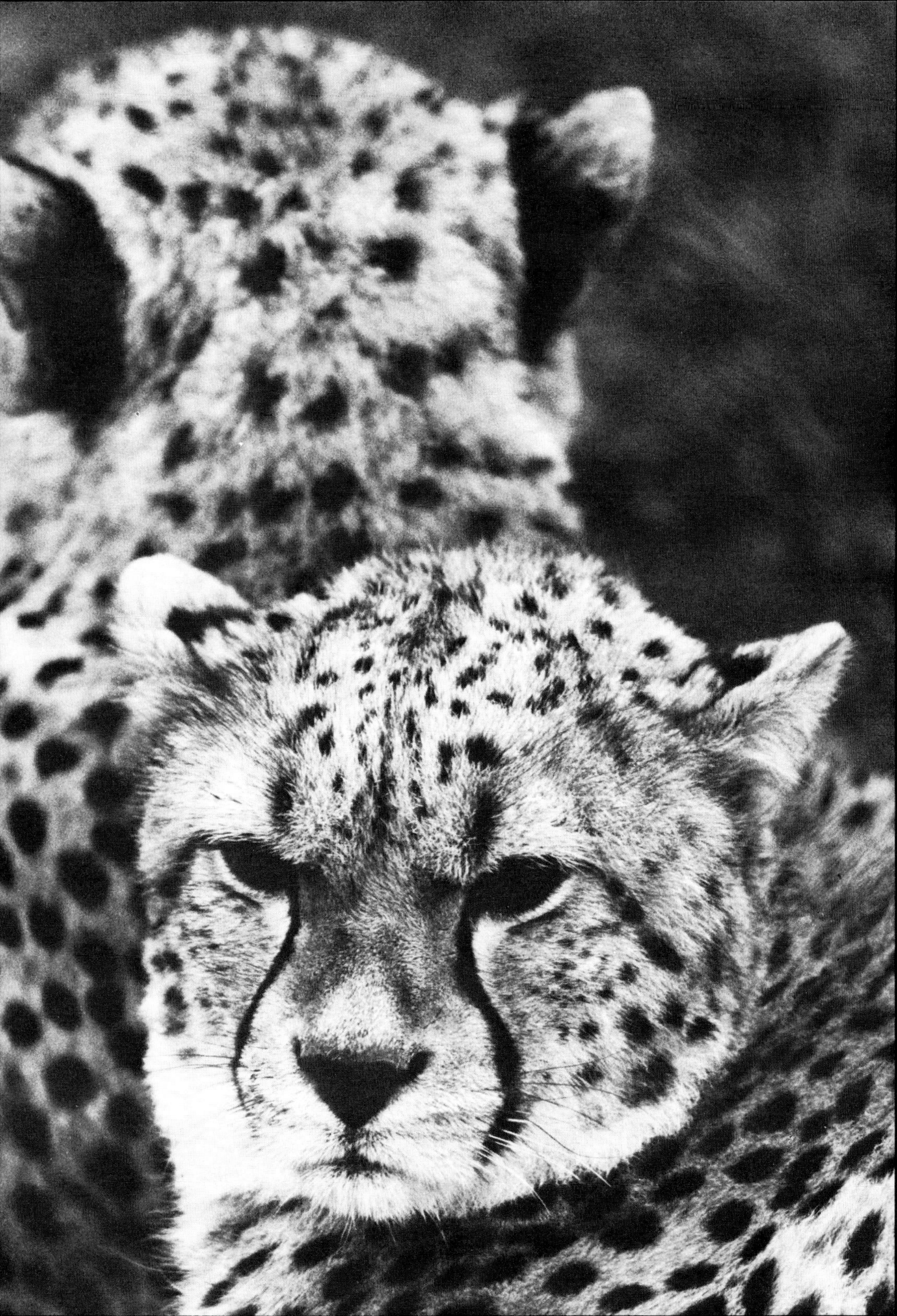

with the appropriate slot at the rear end.

Mirror lenses produce characteristic 'dough-nut' rings in some areas of the subject which are recorded out of focus – particularly highlights. Some people consider this 'distortion' of the image to be unacceptable, and prefer the more usual 'blur' of conventional lenses.

Zoom lenses

Zoom lenses allow continuous adjustment of focal length between certain designed limits. They take the place of two or more separate lenses of fixed focal length. When buying a zoom lens do spend as much as you can afford and do not expect the lens to do too much. The cheap close-focusing ('macro') lens with a largish zoom ratio is very likely to produce low quality (poor definition, image distortion) results. Good zoom lenses cannot be bought cheaply.

Because of the potentially higher image definition of black-and-white materials over colour films, you should choose your zoom lens carefully. If possible, buy the lens on approval and test it for image definition and distortion. Common weaknesses are barrel or pincushion distortion – lens aberrations which cause a lens to image a rectangle as a barrel or pincushion shape. These failings are particularly noticeable at the extreme ends of the zoom range (most zoom lenses give their best performance in the mid-range of focal lengths) and are particularly marked when photographing architectural subjects.

Zoom lenses are available in a wide variety of focal length ranges. Some examples are: 24–50mm *f*/4, 35–70mm *f*/4, 75–150mm *f*/4, 80–200mm *f*/4. 100–500mm *f*/8.

Using zoom lenses

The main advantage of using zoom lenses is the speed at which you can adjust the size of the image in the frame area without changing the camera position, or changing the lens. The main disadvantages with zoom lenses are cost relative to image quality and the modest maximum apertures available for most.

The best method of using a zoom lens is to first select your viewpoint (which governs the perspective) and then adjust the zoom control to give the required framing of the subject, thus giving yourself total control of the perspective *and* picture content. Unfortunately, it is very easy to become lazy when using a zoom lens, and simply take pictures from the most *convenient* camera position (or wherever you happen to be standing) and then zoom in or out as required. This method discourages examining the subject critically and selecting the best camera positions.

One technique which is unique to zoom lenses is the ability to change the lens focal length during the exposure. This zooming in or out causes a streaking of the subject from the centre towards the edges of the picture; the precise appearance of the subject depends on the rate of zooming, shutter speed, and whether the focal length control is kept stationary for part of the exposure. (The technique is however usually more successful in colour photography because the *tonal* streaking in black-and-white may only give a confused muddy impression.).

More than one camera body

It is surprising how many photographers buy several lenses before they consider purchasing another camera body. But for the relatively modest outlay, an extra camera body does offer great benefits. For example, you do not have to interchange lenses quite so frequently, so you increase operating speed and can have two lenses of different focal lengths available for immediate use. Indeed, two cameras equipped with zoom lenses (eg 24–50mm and 70–210mm) would enable you to cope immediately with virtually any photographic situation.

Alternatively, a different type of film could be loaded into each camera body, for example, slow and fast film, black-and-white and colour film, panchromatic and infra-red film. This would allow you to use the most appropriate black-and-white film for the subject and desired treatment–greater choice of tonality, graininess, and image sharpness.

Although it is rare for a camera to break down, it does happen occasionally and it is reassuring to know you will always be able to get your picture if you carry an extra camera body. Any good professional photographer always has at least one back-up camera in case of accidents.

Modifying reality

A great number of camera techniques can be used to produce a rendition of the scene that differs from the 'straight' black-and-white photograph. These alternative methods may be broadly divided into optical, exposure and film modifications.

The techniques described below can either be

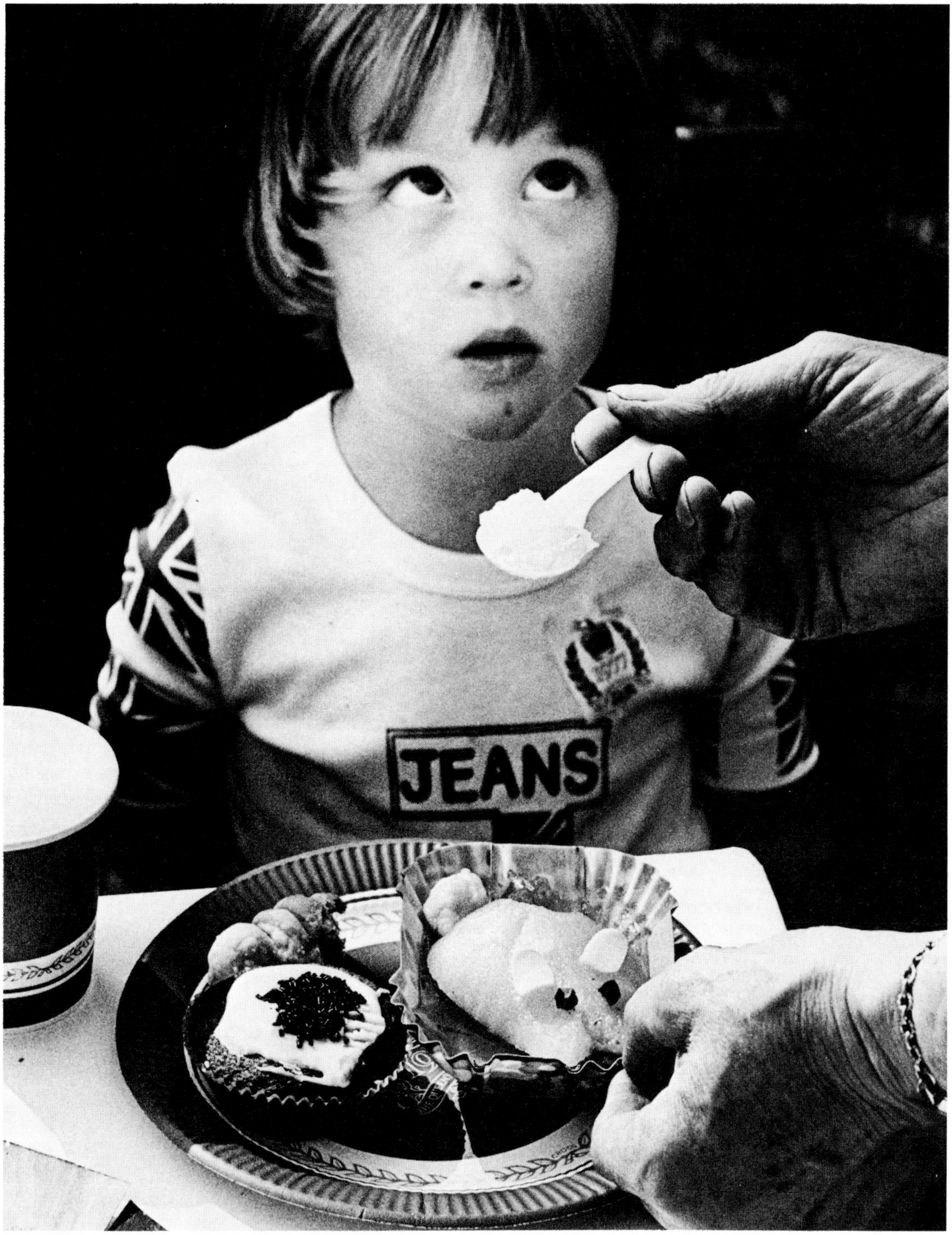

26 To give maximum flexibility and speed of operation, a zoom lens was used at this children's street party; for this particular picture the lens was set at a focal length of about 80mm.

used on their own or applied in conjunction with printing techniques (Chapter 8). Whatever the method, it is helpful to try and previsualise the final result and thus make the best use of the camera exposure.

Colour filters

When placed in front of the camera lens, a colour filter affects the black-and-white tonal rendition of colours in the original scene. A colour filter can be used to darken certain colours while lightening others (see fig 3.1) relative to one another. It is generally said that a filter lightens its own colour and darkens all others–this refers to the effect on the final print. For example, a red filter lightens reds and colours containing red (eg. yellow, purple), and darkens blues and greens.

3.1 Common filters for black-and-white use.

Filter colour	Lightens	Darkens	Main uses
Yellow	Green, red, yellow	Blue	Emphasising cloud formations.
Orange	Red, yellow	Blue, blue-green	Emphasising cloud formations — effect stronger than yellow filter. Accentuating wood grain.
Red	Red	Blue, green	Dramatic emphasising of clouds — 'storm' effect. Haze penetration.
Green	Green	Blue, red	Lightening foliage.
Blue	Blue	Green, red, yellow	Emphasising haze.

Landscape photographers often use yellow, orange or red filters to darken the blue sky and make the white clouds stand out from their background. A yellow filter gives the least effect and a red filter the most striking result. Sometimes a green filter is used to lighten foliage.

Do not forget that a filter absorbs light and you must therefore give extra exposure to compensate for this loss of light. All filters are given a filter factor which is usually engraved or printed on its mount. You must multiply your calculated exposure by this amount. For example, a yellow filter might have a filter factor of X2 and you should therefore either double the exposure time (eg. 1/250 sec becomes 1/125 sec) or open the lens aperture by one stop (eg. *f*/11 becomes *f*/8). A red filter with a factor of X6 changes a calculated exposure of, say, 1/125 sec *f*/8 to 1/125 sec at a setting halfway between *f*/2.8 and *f*/4 or to 1/30 sec *f*/8–5.6.

If you use a camera with TTL (through-the-lens) metering, the built-in exposure meter reads the light level after it has passed through the filter and lens, and therefore automatically adjusts the camera settings to compensate for the light absorbed by the filter.

This is reliable enough in most cases.

Altering subject tonality with colour filters

Besides the more common applications of colour filters to black-and-white photography just described, there is the subtle use of filters to control the tonal scale of the subject. Many advocates of the Zone System (Chapter 7) use filters to adjust tonal rendition in specific subject areas.

The most thorough (and in the end the only technically sound way) to understand colour filters and their effect on the final black-and-white print is to go back to basic light theory, best achieved by a step-by-step examination (see also fig 3.2):

1 Light is visible electromagnetic energy and is positioned within the electromagnetic spectrum between UV and IR energy. The visible band of energy can be characterised as having wavelengths between 400–700 nanometres (nm) – this band of 'white' light can be split into its component wavelengths (colours) by devices such as prisms and diffraction gratings; a rainbow is an example of this white light separation.
2 Different white light sources, such as daylight, electronic flash, tungsten lamps, fluorescent tubes, have various proportions of the component wavelengths of white light. Tungsten lamps emit more red light than blue whereas daylight has a larger proportion of blue light.
3 The colour of a specific area of a photographed scene depends on the 'colour' of the light falling on it and the absorption characteristics of the area. A red sweater appears red because the other colours of the light falling on the sweater are absorbed by the dyes in the wool–the eye sees only the reflected red light.
4 A colour filter is a clear material (gelatin coated on to plastic base, plastic itself, or glass) containing a dye, which absorbs certain wavelengths of light and transmits the rest. Strange as it may seem, a blue filter is so called because it absorbs all light except blue. It is known as a blue filter because it appears blue and filters out other colours.

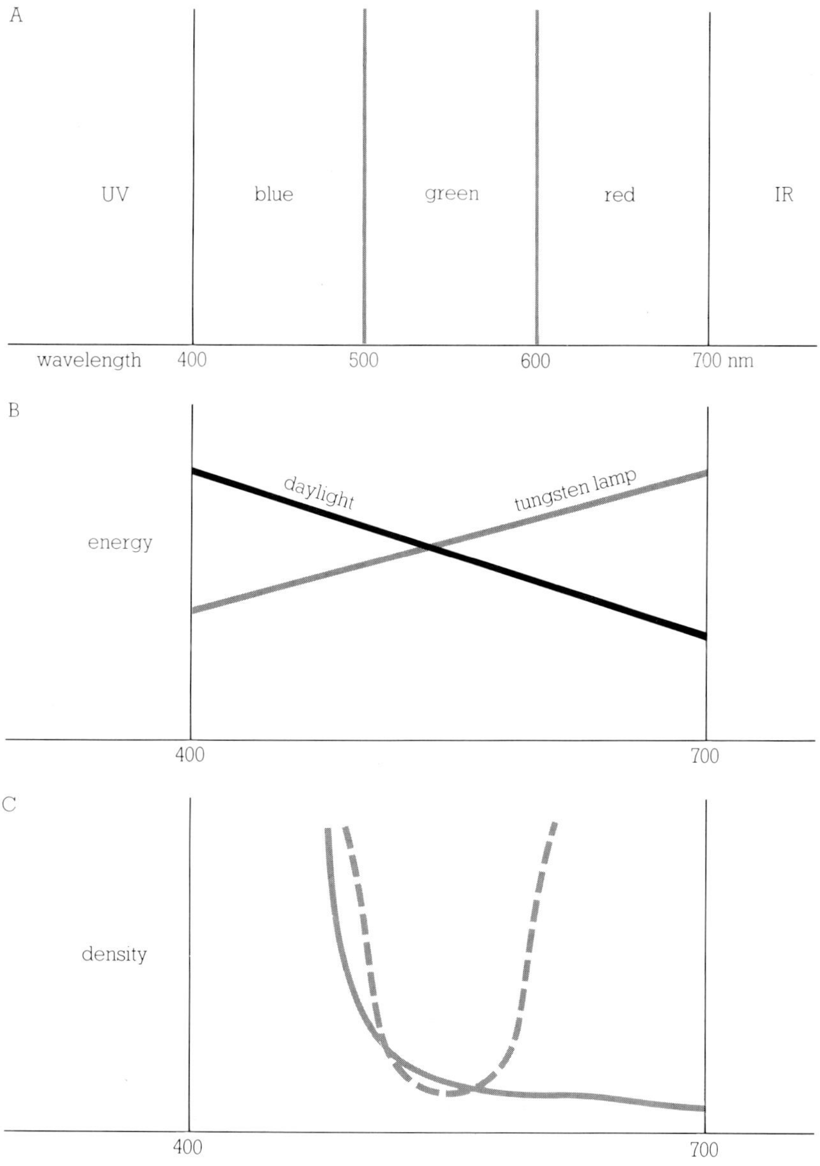

3.2A White light can be considered to be composed of three basic colours blue, green and red.
B The relative proportions (approximately) of colours in daylight and tungsten light. Notice that daylight is rich in blue, while tungsten contains relatively more red light.
C Absorption curves of two filters. The yellow filter (unbroken line) transmits green and blue, but has a high absorption of blue light. The green filter (broken line) transmits green but absorbs blue and red.

The precise absorption of a colour filter can be determined for each separate wavelength of light and this data can be plotted as the absorption curve of the filter.

5 The precise tonality of any part of a scene recorded by a panchromatic black-and-white film depends on the light reaching the film in this image area. Without the use of a colour filter the pan film records all colours equally; a mid-tone red and mid-tone green give the same mid-tone in the final black-and-white print. However, if a red filter is placed over the lens, a large proportion of the light reflected from the green area is absorbed by the filter, whereas the light from the red object is passed by the filter. The net result is that the film receives less exposure from the green area and therefore a lighter density results on the processed negative–and a corresponding darker tone on the print. Thus, the red filter darkens all colours except red; or, in other words,

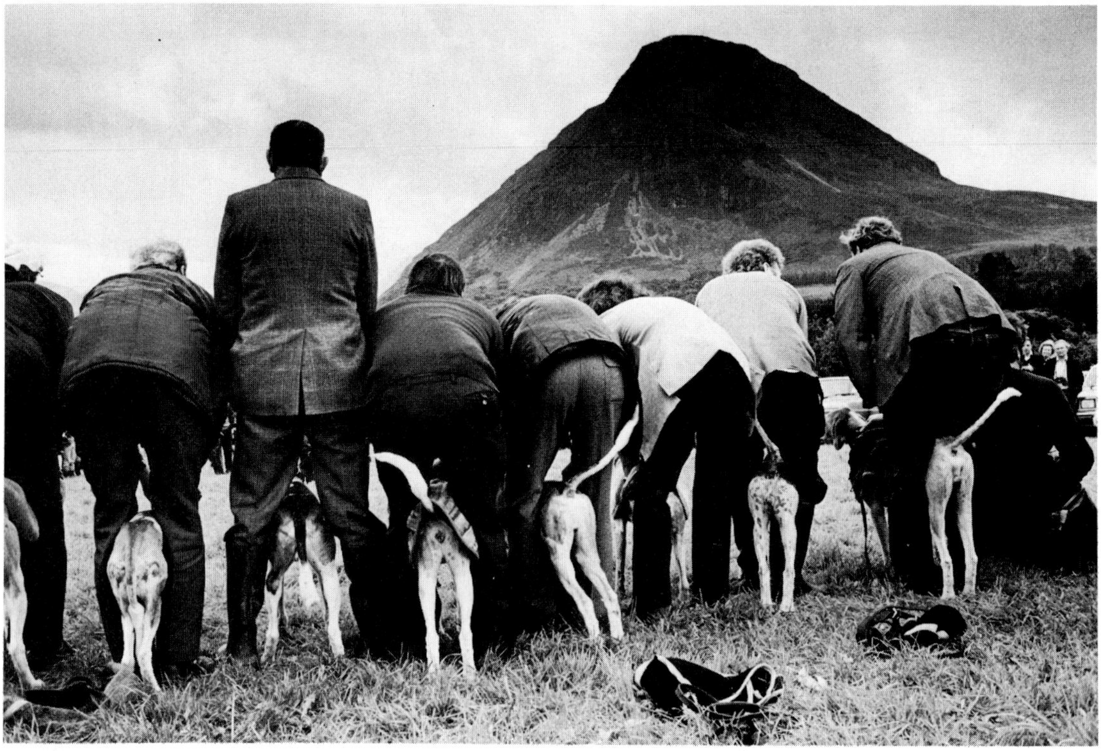

27 This type of picture will always have the kind of universal appeal that is certain to 'lighten' any photographic exhibition. A yellow filter was used to slightly dramatise the sky and extended film development was given to increase the negative contrast on this overcast day–see Chapter 5.

the reds of the subject are lightened *relative* to the other colours of the scene.

6 Thus, the tonality change caused by a colour filter depends on the colour of the light source, the absorption of the object and the absorption of the filter.

Colour filters in practice

It is not possible, in practice, to make absorption measurements of light sources and objects and then be able to relate these to published filter curves. However, the following guidelines can help you decide if a colour filter will be of use in black-and-white photography:

1 Examine the various tones of the scene and, if necessary, take lightmeter readings of separate areas (see Chapter 4). Decide if it is beneficial to change the relationships of these tones. For example, a light-toned green shrub may be positioned in front of a light-toned red brick wall. If photographed on unfiltered pan film the shrub and wall might well reproduce as similar tones and, in the black-and-white print, they would merge.

2 Having decided to separate certain subject areas tonally from others, you should select a filter carefully. In our shrub and wall example, a red filter would darken the shrub in the final print relative to the wall and a green filter would darken the wall relative to the shrub. The amount of tonal separation depends on the strength of the filter. For example, a lightish filter effects less of a shift than a darker one, eg. an orange rather than a red filter.

3 Because of your concern with, perhaps, only one problem area of the scene, you should not forget that the filter also changes other parts of the picture. Improving the tonal separation of one area may cause tones to merge in another.

4 As a guide, look at the scene through a filter and half-close your eyes to get an idea of tonal changes (for SLR cameras use the preview stop-down button). Because our eyes adapt to changes of colour and brightness fairly rapidly, you should never just stare through the filter but flick it quickly in and out of the line of sight. Also, with ex-

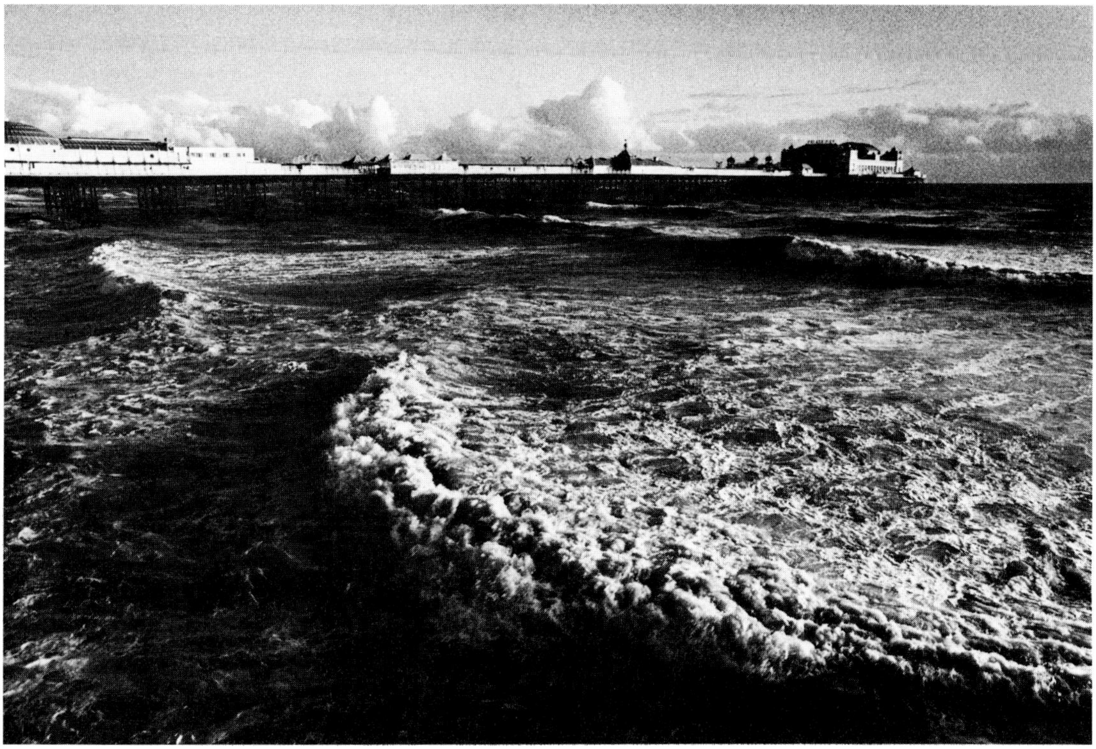

28 The stormy conditions were emphasised by placing a red filter over the camera lens, mainly to make the clouds more visible against the sky. The striking surf patterns in the foreground were the result of a patient wait.

perience, you will soon be able to 'guesstimate' the effect of a particular colour filter. Do not forget to allow for the filter factor in your exposure determination.

Polarising screens

Although polarising screens may be most often used by colour photographers (mainly to darken blue skies), they can also be useful in black-and-white work. In practice, a polarising screen is attached to the front of the lens and is rotated while the photographer looks through the camera lens until the desired image is obtained. The screen absorbs 'invisible' polarised light and thus darkens any part of the subject which reflects polarised light.

The most common uses of a polarising screen in black-and-white photography are: to darken the sky and thus make clouds more distinctive (maximum polarising of skylight and therefore maximum darkening occurs at 90° to the sun); to 'remove' glare from surfaces such as water, roads, glass; to act as a neutral density filter so that a slower shutter speed and/or wider aperture may be used.

It can be difficult to judge precisely the best rotational position for the polarising screen to obtain the desired darkening of a part of the scene. It is a good idea to take several exposures of the subject with the screen in different positions and select the 'best' result at leisure when the negative is printed.

Graduated filters

Filters which do not have an overall even density but change their density gradually from top to bottom (or side to side, depending on filter orientation) are referred to as graduated filters. They are used to darken the scene from top to bottom (or vice versa) or side to side. Graduated filters are similar to the colour filters described previously in that they darken colours which are complementary to the filter colour, eg. yellow filters darken blues.

Graduated filters are available in several colours, such as orange, tobacco (desaturated red), and neutral and also in more than one strength. The stronger filters have a larger density range from top to bottom than the weaker types and have a more dramatic impact on the scene.

The most common application of a graduated filter is to darken the sky in a landscape; the sky will appear darkest at the top of the photograph when the darkest section of the filter is uppermost. The precise effect of the filter can be observed through the viewfinder of an SLR camera and the filter can be manoeuvred to give the desired effect.

Some graduated filters show a fairly distinct transition from clear filter to the first density and it is usually important to position this dividing line within the image so that use of the filter is not apparent. For most applications this dividing line is best placed close to the horizon or on any other strong visual line in the scene, such as the break between the sand and sea.

Special effects filters

There are many filters which can be used to optically modify the 'straight' scene. Some of the special effect filters (eg. slight diffuser) cause only a small change in the observed subject while others (eg. multiple image) produce a dramatically altered image.

These special effects filters need to be used with caution and not too often, otherwise they merely produce rather clichéed photographs. A number of these filters, for example the 'starburst' type, have been excessively overworked and are now difficult to use without the resulting photograph looking very contrived. However, if used with discretion some of these filters can enhance a photographed subject. Unless you wish to be deliberately provocative, use them with subtlety.

Your own lens attachments

Instead of buying commercially-made filters you can make lens attachments to suit your own specific needs. The main advantages of doing it yourself are the total control you have over the final image and the fact that you will produce images which do not resemble someone else's optical effects.

One possible approach is to try various translucent or transparent materials in front of the camera lens, perhaps with a central hole punched clear to give a 'normal' image edged with optical distortion. Materials that are worth trying for this include acetate (with or without integral pattern), textured glass, thin cloths (eg. stockings, nylon, cheesecloth, silk), plastics (perhaps crumpled up). You need to experiment with various lens apertures and positions of materials in front of the lens – an SLR camera is essential to see what result you get. (Remember, however, that the effect will be different when the lens is stopped down in shooting.)

Because the total effect will only be completely revealed after printing, it is necessary to make careful notes as you go along. Be careful always not to be seduced by colour variations but concentrate on what is happening to the subject's *tonal values* and *image shapes*.

If you have an interest in optics, you may like to try glass or plastic objects in front of the lens which diffract or disperse light. Optical items such as mirrors (flat or curved), prisms, glass blocks, and diffraction gratings are available from specialist suppliers, many of which equip school science laboratories.

It is great fun to find new ways of optically modifying the 'straight' scene in front of the camera but, as with all derivative techniques, it is important never to let technique come before the image; the final print must be worthwhile. You should always apply a technique to a subject or idea, and not the other way round, ie. avoid looking for a subject just to accommodate your latest technique.

Multiple exposures

More than one exposure can be made on the same piece of film to build up a composite image. To be successful it is esssential to previsualise the final result, so that you place the various subject elements in the correct position within the frame.

Try to keep your image simple. Also, remember that very light areas of the scene 'burn-out' the parts of the film where they are recorded, so you cannot add another image to this area. It is best to photograph subjects which are surrounded by dark tones, so that the subsequent exposure(s) can be placed in these unexposed parts of the film. For ultimate control, it is worth considering the use of a studio and a black backdrop for at least one of your exposures.

Only a few 35mm cameras are truly capable of multiple exposure. Many books suggest moving the film advance lever while depressing the rewind button, but this usually causes the camera or the film to move slightly although the latter is less likely when it has been tightened by the rewind crank. For multiple exposures, larger format cameras (eg. 120 rollfilm, 5 x 4cm) have the great advantage of allowing you to draw on the focusing screen with a grease pencil and therefore to accurately compose the various subject elements. Also, with them the shutter can be cocked easily without having to disturb the film.

More than one subject can be combined in a single print by multiple printing techniques (Chapter 8) and you should consider which of these two methods best suits your intentions. Of course, you can employ both (camera and printing) multiple exposure techniques together to produce a complex image.

Close-up photography

This specialist section of photography merits discussion in its own right. There are several good books on close-up photography, such as Axel Brück's *Close up Photography in Practice* and anyone wishing to study the subject in detail should consult these books.

Most people are unaware of the fascinating images which can result when objects are examined critically at close range. Exciting and abstract photographs can be produced by close-up photography, either in colour or black-and-white. In fact, many textile designs are based on close-up photographs. The three main classifications are simple 'close-up' photography, photomacrography (or macrophotography), and photomicrography.

Simple close-up photography

Many lenses are now sold with a 'macro' facility. This is the advertiser's way of telling you that a particular lens can give an image of higher than normal magnification. As described below, a truly macro lens is able to produce a high-quality image on film which is life size (magnification = 1) or larger, but most so-called macro lenses do not

29 Close-up photography is never easy, especially with mobile subjects. To ensure adequate depth of field and no blur resulting from a sudden movement of the cat, an automatic electronic flash with diffuser was used. An 85mm lens with automatic extension tubes was fitted to the 35mm camera because it gives reasonable working distances from the subject; a fast (ASA 400) 35mm film was necessary to ensure a small working aperture (*f*/22).

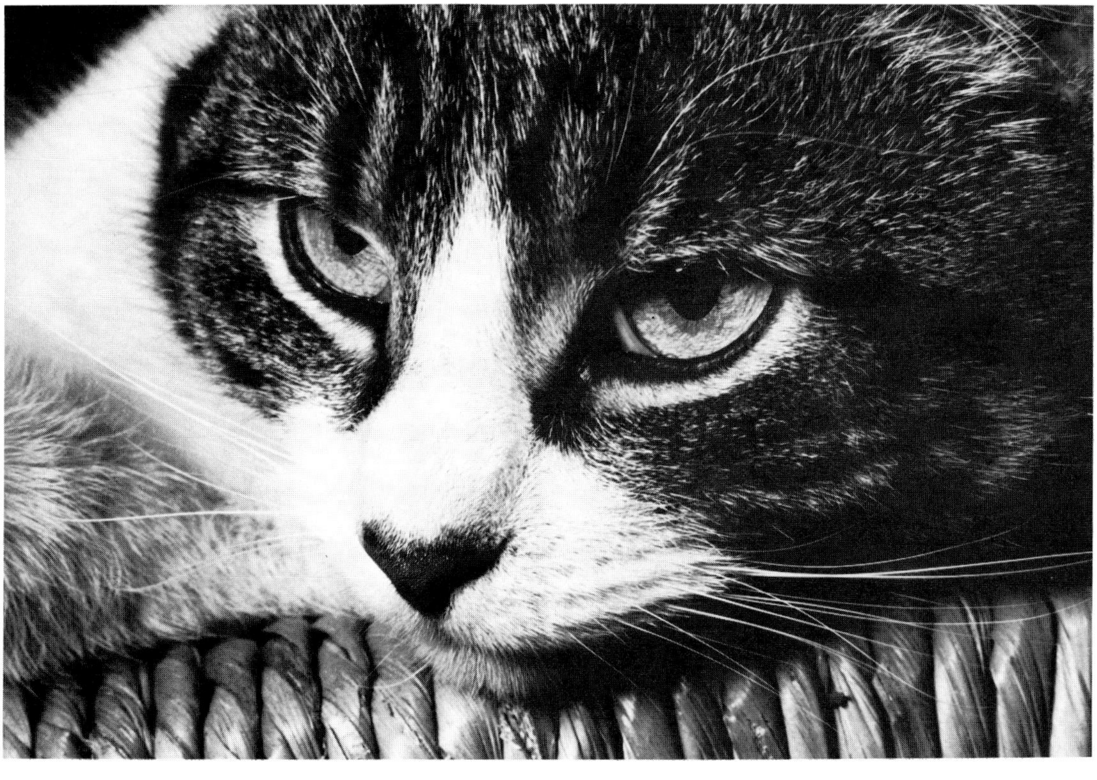

magnify as much as this. Nevertheless, they are useful for moderate close-up work.

Beware the lens manufacturer who offers you a lens, especially a zoom lens, which he claims can produce superb quality images for all possible uses, ie. focused on infinity, close-up, at all apertures, etc., and which costs a modest sum. There is a strong probability that the lens in question will produce unacceptable results, because here, as in any other type of purchase, you only get what you pay for.

In black-and-white photography you need high quality optics, and if you intend to specialise in close-up work you should consider buying special macro lenses of fixed focal length.

Depth of field in close-up work is extremely limited, even if the lens is stopped down to small apertures, and what might look attractive out of focus in colour may be uninspired in black-and-white. One solution to muddy, defocused backgrounds is to photograph against plain backgrounds; some photographers carry small white, black or grey cards to place behind close-up subjects.

Photomacrography and photomicrography

The general name photomacrography is given to close-up photography in the magnification (on the film) range of x1 (life size) or larger, which uses conventional photographic devices and does not involve microscopes. In practice this might be up to a limit of about x10. To obtain this degree of magnification it is necessary to increase the distance between the camera lens and film (by using extension tubes or bellows).

Because a consistent amount of light enters the lens from the subject for any given aperture, and this is then spread over a relatively larger area than with normal lens-film distances, it is evident that the greater the magnification, the less bright the image. Therefore, either the exposure time or the aperture must be increased as the image magnification increases. Fig 3.3 indicates by how much the exposure must be increased to compensate for the magnification. This so-called 'bellows extension' is automatically allowed for if your camera has TTL metering.

Photomicrography, the technique of photographing through a microscope, is a highly specialised skill. It is possible to adapt ordinary microscopes for photography but the best photomicrographs are obtained through the use of microscopes designed specifically for photographic purposes. Image magnification on to film is usually in the range of about x10 to x100.

3.3 Alternative methods of calculating exposures for close-up photography. The magnification formula (**A**) is generally quicker to use, especially if an easy table (**C**) is memorised or consulted.

Formula A

$$\frac{\text{Required exposure time}}{} = \text{meter exposure time} \times (1 + M)^2$$

eg. meter indicates $1/30$ $f/11$ $M = 1/2$

$$\therefore \text{Required exposure time} = 1/30 \times (1 + 1/2)^2$$
$$= 1/30 \times 9/4$$
$$= 1/15 \text{ sec. (approx.)}$$

∴ Set camera for $1/15$ $f/11$

Formula B

Required exposure time =

$$\text{meter exposure time} \times \frac{(\text{bellows extension})^2}{(\text{lens focal length})^2}$$

eg. meter indicates $1/125$ $f/8$, bellows ext. 200 mm, camera lens 85 mm

$$\therefore \text{Required exposure time} = 1/125 \times \frac{(200)^2}{(85)^2}$$
$$= 1/23 \text{ sec.}$$

∴ Set camera for $1/15$. $f/11$-$f/8$ (halfway between $f/11$ and $f/8$)

Table C

M	Multiply meter exposure by	OR	Open lens aperture by
1/4	1.5		1/2 stop
1/2	2		1
1	4		2
2	9		3
4	25		4 1/2

Unusual films to create unusual photographs

The usual type of film used in black-and-white photography is *panchromatic*, which has equal sensitivity to all colours (wavelengths) of light (fig 3.4). This means that mid-red, mid-green and mid-yellow all reproduce as a mid-grey in the photograph. Most panchromatic films are of the *continuous tone* type and therefore have the ability to record a wide range of brightnesses reflected from the different parts of the subject. If correctly exposed and processed, and then correctly printed on to photographic paper, the continuous tone pan film records the original colour scene as a continuous tone print which realistically mirrors the brightnesses of the actual subject.

3.4 The spectral sensitivity of an emulsion can be plotted as a graph, this is called a spectrogram. The examples shown indicate the response of the main film types. For specific information on any film, consult the manufacturer's data sheet.

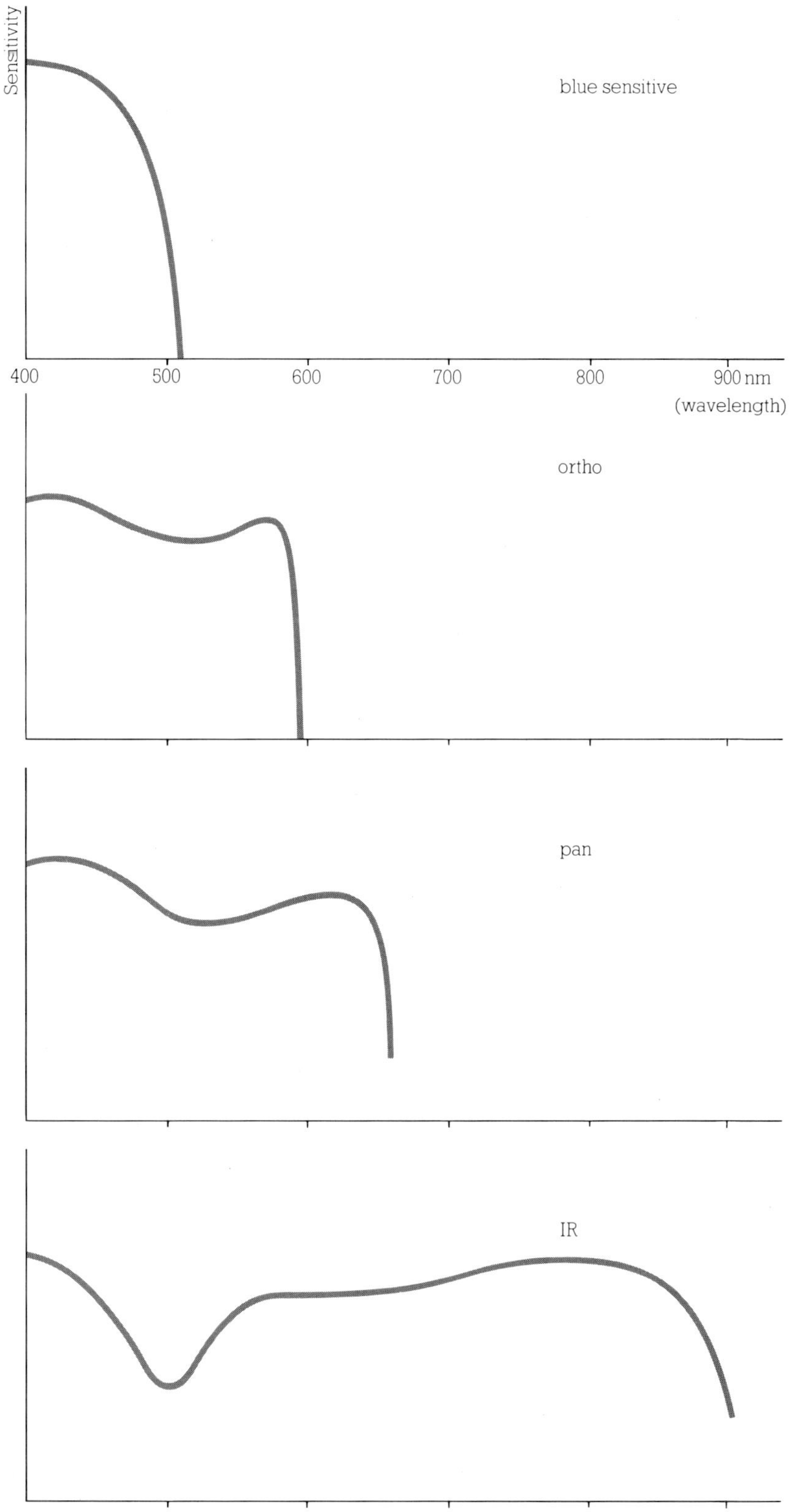

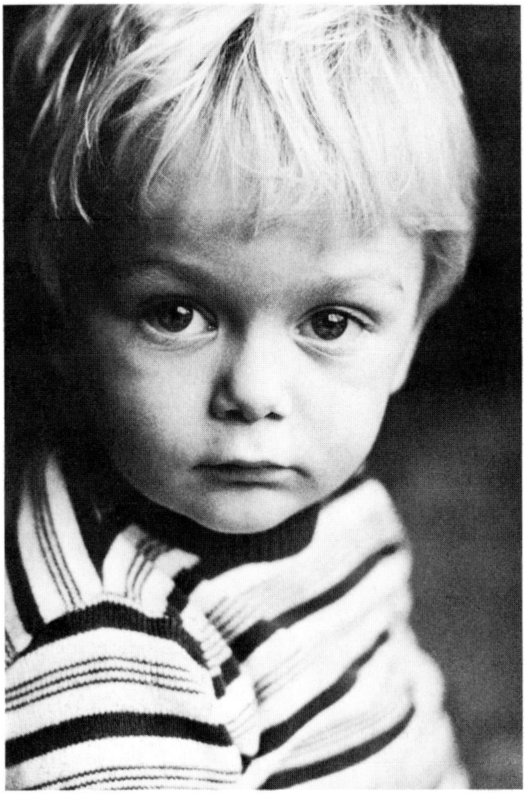

30-34 All these photographs were taken within twenty minutes of one another, so the child had no time to become bored. To get a variety of pictures it was necessary to crawl around the floor using a fast film (ASA 400), a fast lens (85mm f/2) and sometimes fairly slow shutter speeds ($^{1}/_{15}$–$^{1}/_{125}$ sec). A room with large windows, in this case patio doors, is ideal as it gives reasonable amounts of daylight and pleasant soft lighting. Be prepared to take at least 36 exposures so that you have a reasonable choice for enlarging.

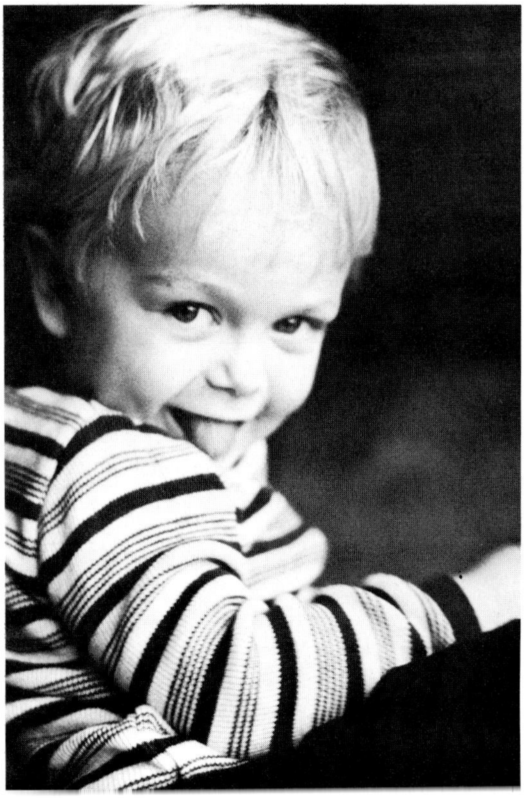

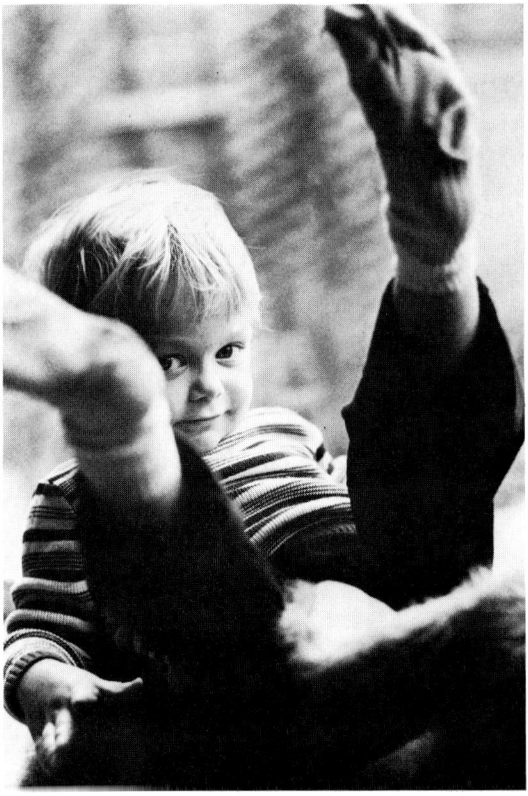

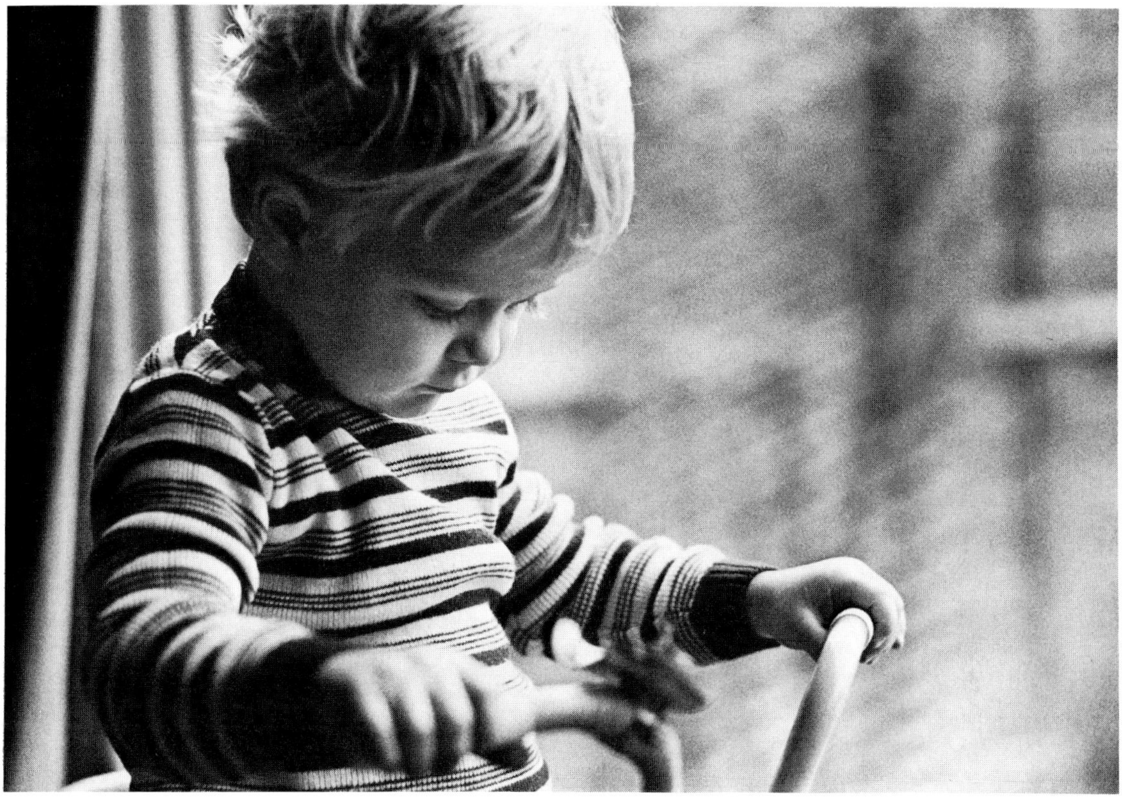

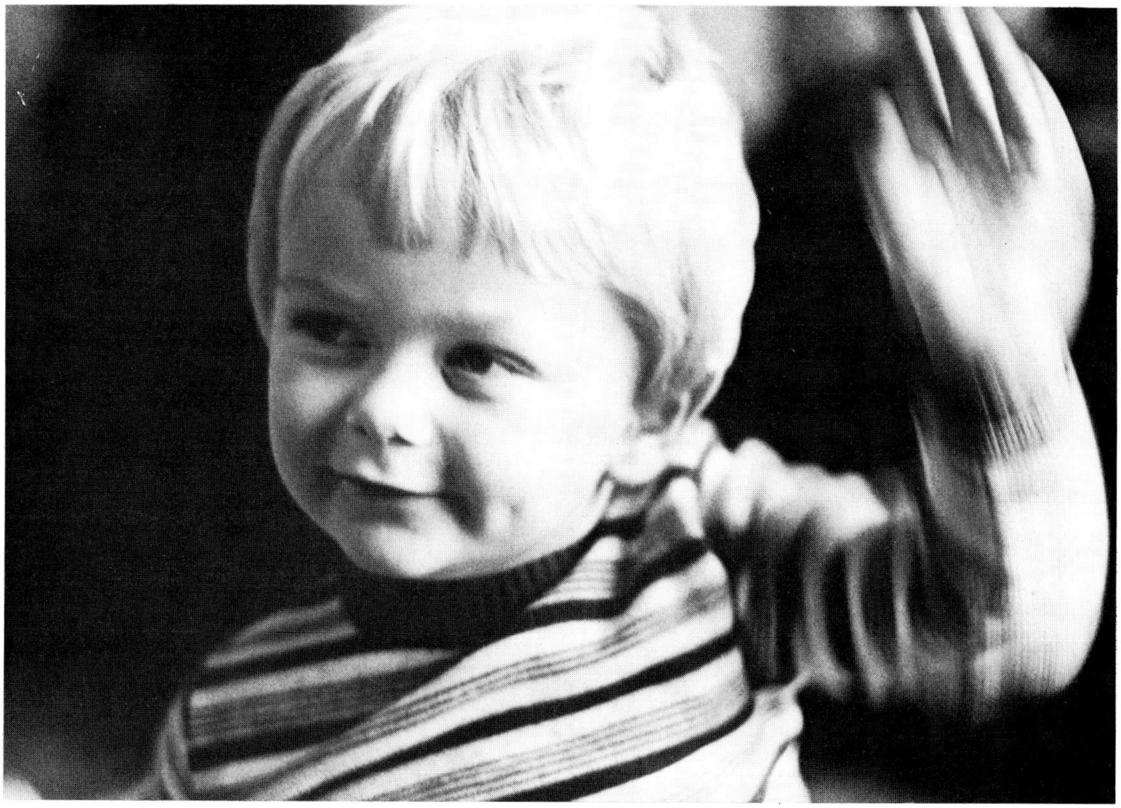

However, if you wish to depart from this conventional black-and-white reproduction, there are a number of films which can 'distort' the standard tonal reproduction, or alter the usual image characteristics (eg. grain, sharpness). The main varieties are non-panchromatic, high contrast, high speed, and infra-red film.

Blue sensitive and orthochromatic films

There are a few continuous tone films (eg. Kodak's blue-sensitive Gravure Positive, Ilford's ortho film) which do not have full colour sensitivity. They are designed primarily for copying black-and-white continuous tone images such as photographs or negatives and are intended to be handled mainly in darkrooms lit by yellow (for blue sensitive film) or red (orthochromatic film) safelight.

If used in the camera to photograph a colour scene, the ortho (blue and green sensitive) materials reproduce all reds as dark in the final print, and the blue sensitive films reproduce both greens and reds as dark. Unless such effects are specifically intended these non-panchromatic films have little value as camera films; also they are generally only available in sheet film form. However, they are very useful for darkroom manipulations (see Chapter 8).

High contrast films

Intended as a means to increase image contrast and remove mid-tones, high contrast films are mainly used in the darkroom for copying black-and-white negatives or positives. They can be loaded into a camera and employed to reduce the original scene to basically two tones, ie. black and white, although there are more convenient ways of achieving this result. It is better to photograph the original scene using a continuous tone film and thus record as much image information as possible. It is then a simple matter to *select* at leisure the tones you wish to reduce to black and those which are to be reproduced as white. This darkroom technique is explained fully in Chapter 8.

Most high contrast films have ortho sensitivity, and therefore can be used under red safelight. However, if you wish to reduce a colour film image to high contrast black and white and do not want the reds to be reproduced as dark in the final positive print, you must use a panchromatic high contrast film. As with all pan films, they must be handled in total darkness.

Consult the film manufacturer's data for details of how to develop each specific film. The very high contrast 'lith' films must be developed in lith developers which are made up (usually from two separate solutions) immediately prior to use and must be discarded after about two hours.

High speed films

The qualities of sharpness and graininess in the image are dictated mainly by the film emulsion. Faster films are less sharp and more grainy than slower ones, so if you need high resolution and a smooth texture in your prints, you should select the slowest film possible for the subject and lighting conditions.

If, on the other hand, you prefer a coarse 'gritty' image, you can either 'push process' the film to a higher ASA setting (see Chapter 5 for details) or use a high speed film. There are a number of fast films of about ASA 400/27 DIN (ISO = 400/27°) which can be uprated to ASA 800 or more and there are a few ultra fast films which, even without extended development, give a 'peppery' image quality due to the large grain size.

One popular ultra fast film is Kodak Recording film type 2745, which is rated at about ASA 1250, and is ideal when lighting levels are very low or when high shutter speeds are necessary, such as at indoor sports meetings. The grain pattern of this film is quite distinctive, appearing very like a texture screen. If you want to use the film in normal daylight conditions, you may need to place neutral density (ND) filters in front of the camera lens to avoid overexposure and consequent loss of detail in the subject's highlights.

Infra-red black-and-white films

There are only a few infra-red sensitive (IR) black-and-white films available and you normally need to obtain them from a specialist supplier or directly from the manufacturer. To get the best results the film should be stored in a freezer until about two hours before it is loaded into the camera. This is because of the relatively unstable IR sensitivity of the film. The film cassette must never be exposed to light, so it must be removed and replaced in its protective container in total darkness.

Conventional light meters are designed to respond to all visible light and are not suitable for measuring infra-red wavelengths. However, light meters can be used to give an educated 'guesstimate' of exposure for IR films. The manufacturer gives an approximate ASA setting for the meter, depending on the filter used in front of the camera lens. For example, Kodak recommend a setting of 50 ASA when using High Speed IR film and a Wratten 25 (red) filter.

Because of the difficulty of assessing exposure for IR films, it is essential to bracket exposures to ensure acceptable results. The author has found the three exposure, two stops under (−2), normal (N), and two stops over (+2), to be suitable for Kodak High Speed IR film.

The results you get from using IR film depend on the subject, the time of day, the time of year, and the filter used. For example, you can certainly get some dramatic pictures in the autumn, when the dying leaves have differing absorptions of IR, depending on the amount of chlorophyll still remaining in them. It would be well worthwhile buying several IR films of the same batch and running some tests before you embark on a serious day's photography.

One last point when using IR film: because most cameras are focused by looking through the viewfinder, they produce sharp images for visible light. Infra-red radiation does not come to focus at the same plane as visible light so it is necessary to adjust the lens focus when using IR film. The easiest way to do this is first to focus the lens visually, note the reading on the lens distance scale, and then rotate the lens until this reading appears opposite the IR mark (usually red) on the scale.

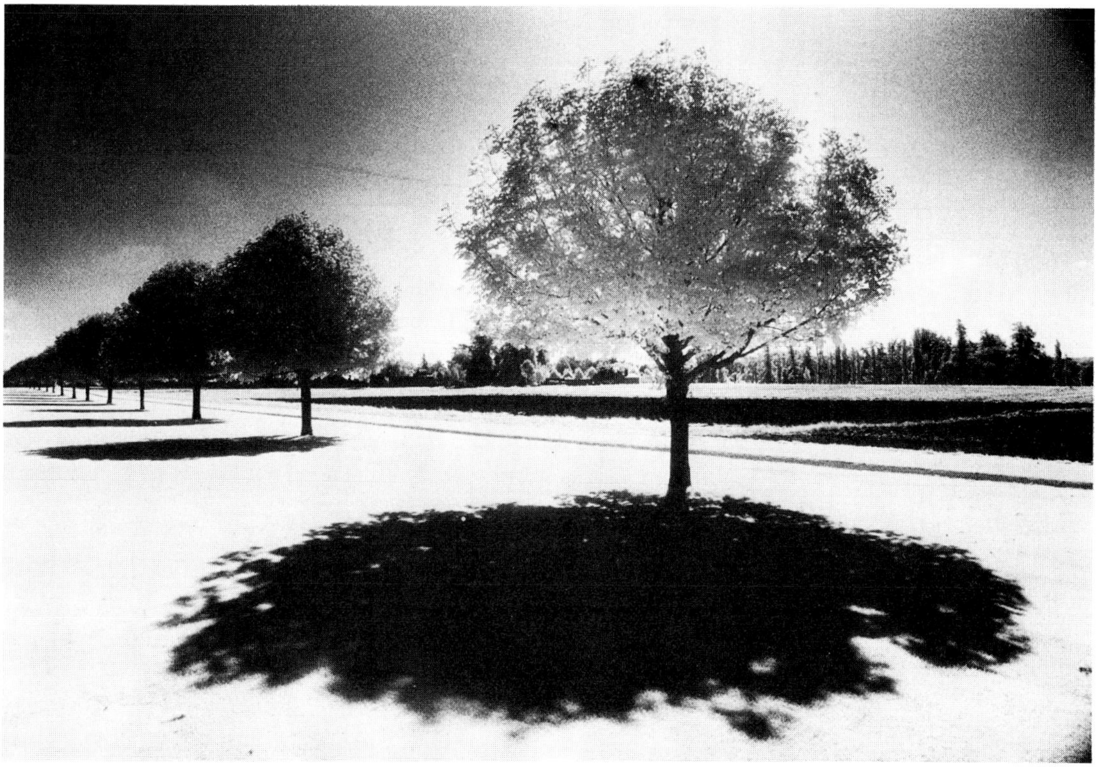

35 The combined effect of strong back lighting and infra-red film has produced this surrealistic graphic image. Because the amount of IR energy cannot be measured by a conventional light meter, it is essential to set the meter on the manufacturer's guide ASA and bracket exposures over a two stop range, ie. −2, normal, +2.

4 THE CORRECT EXPOSURE

It is often assumed that all a photographer has to do in order to obtain a correctly exposed piece of film is to point the lightmeter at the subject and set the camera shutter speed and aperture according to the lightmeter reading. And, in most situations, this method will prcduce acceptable results. However, if you want to get the best out of your equipment and materials you must have a greater knowledge of exposure, and learn how to cope with unusual subjects and lighting.

Exposure cannot be discussed as an isolated topic, but needs to be related to film development and print making. Therefore, the ground covered in this chapter is very closely linked to that in Chapter 5 (film development) and Chapter 6 (print making).

The meaning of correct exposure

In fact, there is no precisely correct exposure for any scene or lighting conditions; the exposure you give the film depends on how you want the final print to look. However, the ability to previsualise the final photograph and give the 'correct' exposure (and film development – see Chapter 5) is a difficult skill to acquire and one which will only be reached through experience.

One example of different 'correct' exposures producing quite different prints is that of a person lit mainly from behind, ie. backlit. If you decide to base your exposure on the bright light behind this person, your portrait will resemble a silhouette, with the main subject lacking detail and appearing dark, and the background showing detail in both highlights and shadows. If, on the other hand you calculate your camera exposure according to the light reading from the face, ignoring the bright background, your final print will show good tonal detail in the face but the background will be very light and 'burnt out'. In this example, you can of course reduce the brightness difference between the face and the background by using either fill-in flash to lighten the face, or a simple reflector to 'bounce' light into the subject.

The real meaning of correct exposure is only apparent when you know precisely what result you want to achieve.

How image light reaches the film

The subject in front of the camera is seen by it as a multitude of small areas reflecting different amounts of (coloured) light towards the lens which are then imaged at the appropriate subject position on the film. Most subjects consist of areas that reflect very little light (ie. shadows), reflect reasonable amounts of light (ie. mid-tones) and parts which reflect most of the light falling on them (ie. highlights).

For ease of understanding, it is often convenient to regard subjects as a grey scale, ie. with subject tones ranging from black, through greys to white which reflect light towards the lens and cause a range of brightness to reach the film. To record *all* the details of the subject, from shadows through to highlights, the processed film must be able to translate the different subject brightnesses into different darknesses (densities) in the film. The ability of a particular film to achieve this goal depends on the brightness range of the subject, the exposure given, and its degree of development.

Subject brightness range

The amount of light reflected towards the camera from a particular part of a scene depends on the nature of this area and the amount of light falling on it. The nature of the area determines how much light it absorbs and in which direction the light is reflected; for example, shiny black objects absorb a lot of light but reflect light along specific paths to give 'specular' highlights. Matt white objects reflect most of the light falling on them in all directions.

For any given scene, the brightness of the image at the film plane ranges between dark areas (shadows) through to light areas (highlights). For a seascape, this would range from the whites of surf to, say, the dark areas under the pier. On a bright sunny day the brightness range would be considerably greater than that for the

36 The meaning of correct exposure can only be related to how you want the final print to look. This 'mood' photograph is not how the photographer saw it, but as he wanted it to be viewed. For example, the pier is seen in silhouette although shadow detail was visible at the time of exposure, the sand was lighter in tone and the sun appeared relatively brighter. For this photograph, the camera exposure was biased towards the highlights (ie. 'underexposure'), film development was reduced to retain as much of the subject's wide brightness range as possible, and it was printed darker than 'normal' with the sky area burnt-in.

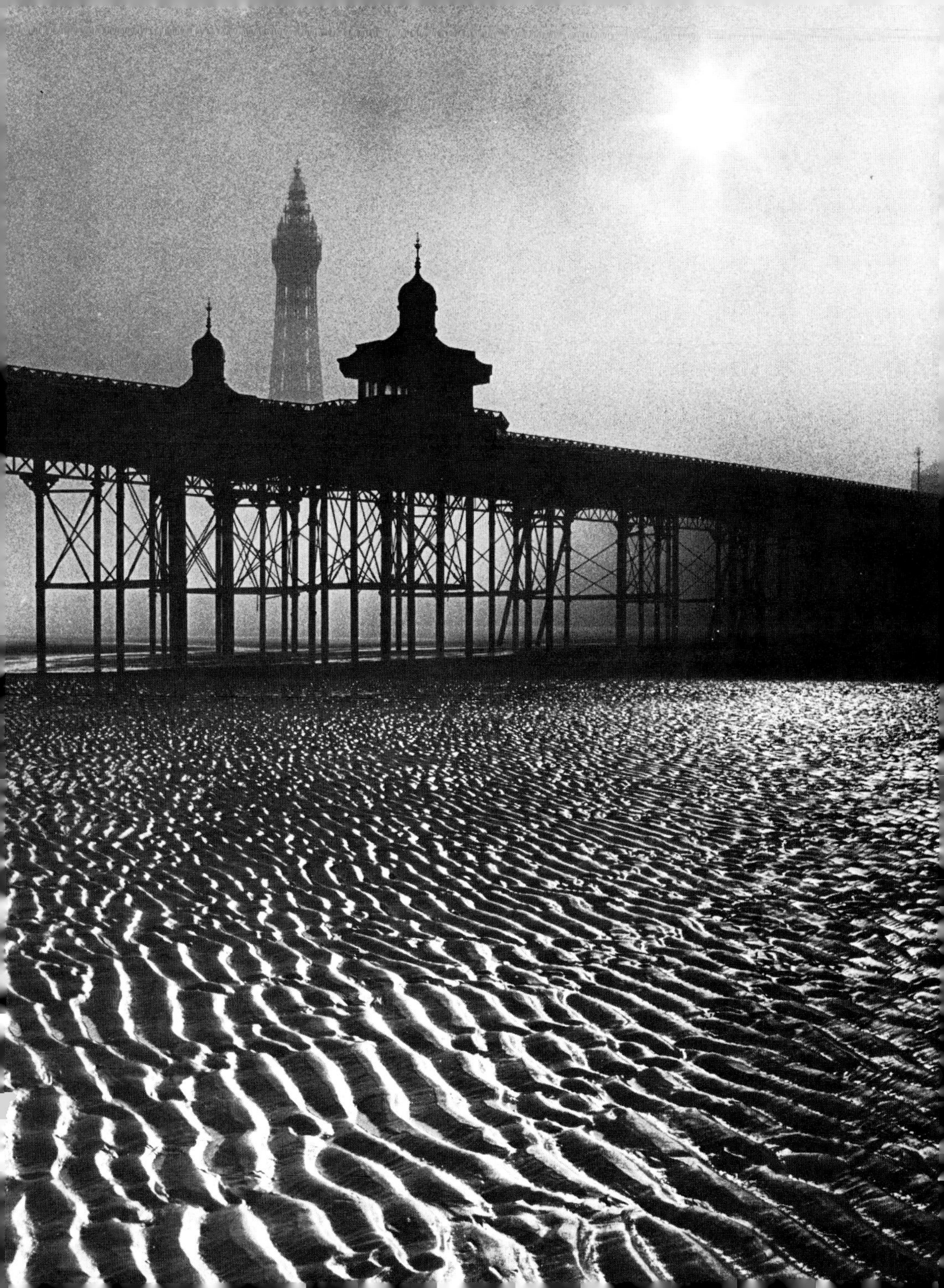

same scene photographed when the weather is overcast. Any film ideally should be able to cope with the different brightness ranges given by different subjects photographed under varying light conditions. It is a lot to ask of any one photographic material to have such wide flexibility, but if the photographer can recognise these subjects and lighting differences he can alter exposure and/or film development to get the most out of the situation. This topic is discussed in more detail in the next chapter (film development).

37 Subjects like this, which have an average brightness range, should be exposed as the meter indicates and developed for the recommended time. Although photographed on a moderately overcast day, the subject is slightly backlit. To avoid underexposure from a false reflected reading, it is best to take a close-up meter reading from the face.

Characteristic curves

Photographic manufacturers distribute technical information on their films and other materials, which inform the user precisely how they record image detail and how this response changes with different development. When comparing various manufacturers' products it is very helpful to consult these technical pamphlets.

Data sheets usually contain a characteristic curve or family of curves, which describes how the film responds to light and development. The characteristic curve for each film is a graph with Density as the vertical axis and Log Exposure as the horizontal axis; these graphs are sometimes referred to as D/Log E curves. Although these curves may appear complex at first, with a little patience you will learn to interpret them and obtain a lot of information from them. They are used in this book to explain how photographic materials respond, and thus help the photographer 'predict' the appearance of the print.

Exposure and D/Log E curves

To simplify this initial discussion on D/Log E curves and how they can be used in practical ways to obtain better quality results, it is assumed that each film is developed according to the manufacturer's 'normal' recommendations. Chapter 5 deals with variations in development.

As mentioned previously, each subject and lighting situation has its own brightness range. If all the subject details are to be recorded, the film must respond to the lowest amounts of light (shadows) reaching the film and also to the highest light levels (highlights). If *correctly exposed,* the average subject (any subject which has an average brightness range of about 1:128) is recorded in full detail on the film. The shadows are recorded on the 'toe' region of the curve, the midtones are recorded on the 'straight line' portion, and the highlights are recorded as higher densities towards the 'shoulder' of the curve (fig 4.1). If correctly printed, this 'perfect' black-and-white negative reproduces all the tonal differences of the original subject. This is why most 'average' subjects produce good black-and-white prints if the film exposure is correct–this is the case when using most modern TTL metering systems, whether completely automatic or of the semi-automatic ('match needle') type.

It should be pointed out at this stage that the tonal distribution of the print does not match the reflectances of the subject areas. The mid-tones of the subject are reproduced in the print in much the same proportion as they are seen, whereas

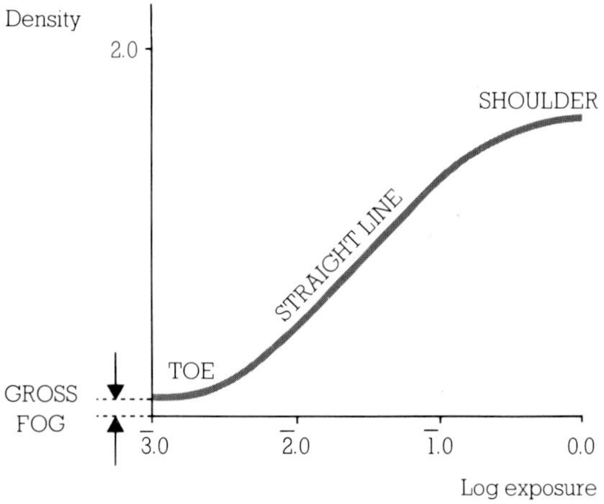

4.1 Representative characteristic curve of a negative black-and-white film processed in a general purpose developer. Film density (see fig **4.2**) is plotted against log exposure (for those not familiar with 'bar', or negative, logs, $\bar{2}.0$ means –2.0. Therefore $\bar{2}.0$ is larger than $\bar{3}.0$, ie. exposure increases as you go from left to right along the horizontal axis). A correctly exposed subject records its dark areas (shadows) on the *toe* region of the curve, and its light areas (highlights) on the *shoulder.* Intermediate tones register on the *straight line* portion. In this example, any subject tone causing an exposure of less than about $\bar{3}.0$ or greater than 0.0 does not image on the emulsion and will produce clear film (D min) or maximum density (D max) respectively.

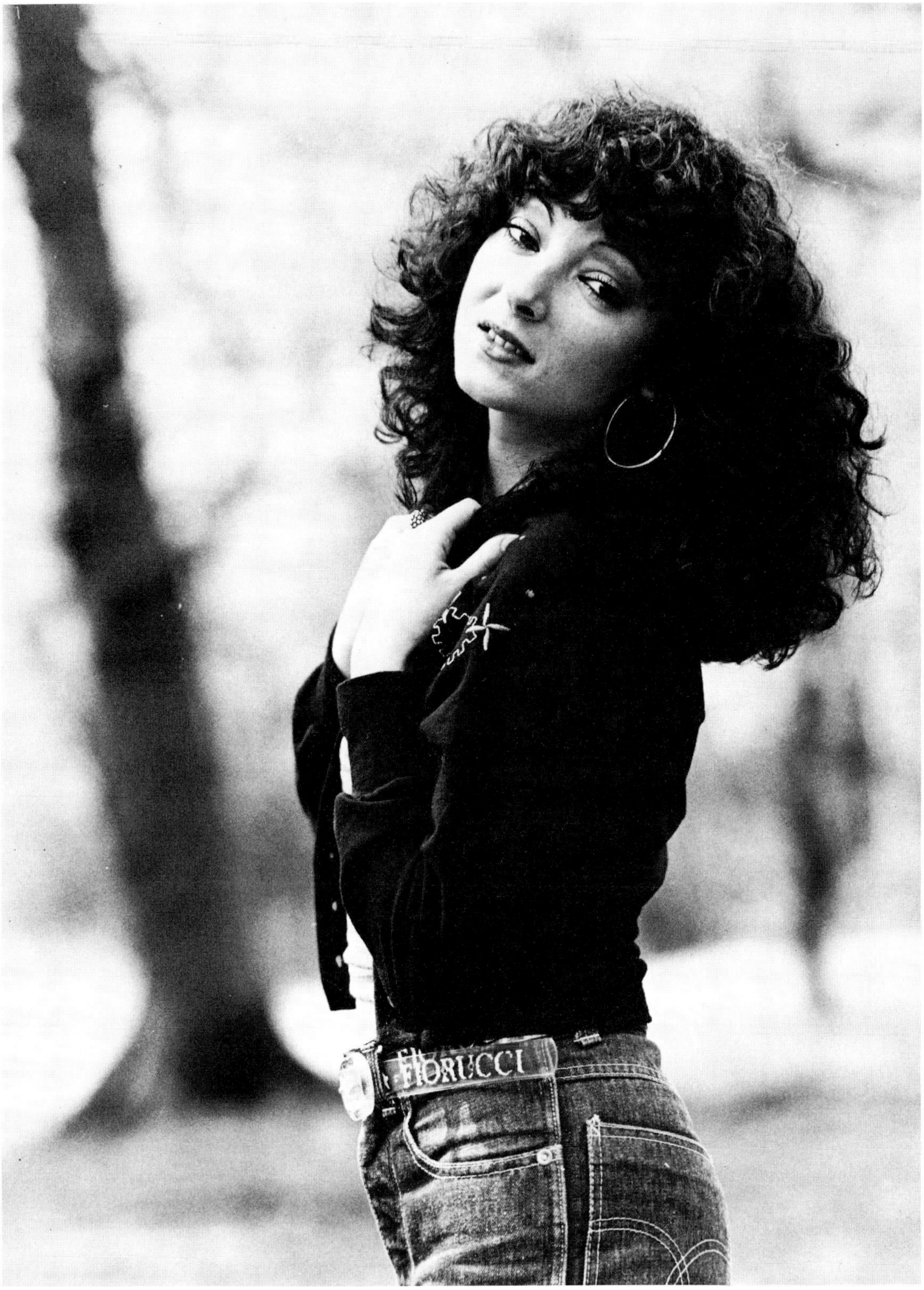
FIORUCCI

4.2

Transmission (T) (per cent)	Opacity (O = 1/T)	Density (log O)
100	1	0.00
90	1.11	0.05
80	1.25	0.10
50	2	0.30
25	4	0.60
12.5	8	0.90
10	10	1.00
5	20	1.30
1	100	2.00
0.1	1000	3.00
0.01	10000	4.00

4.2 Opacity is a measure of 'light stopping' ability and is defined as 1/T, eg. if T = 0.5 (ie. 50 per cent) then O = 1/0.5 = 2. Density is defined as log 0, eg. a transmission of 0.01 (1 per cent) means a density of log 1/0.01 = log 100 = 2. Notice how a halving of transmission causes an increase in density of 0.3, eg. transmission values of 1 (100 per cent), 0.5 (50 per cent), 0.25 and 0.125 give density values of 0.0, 0.3, 0.6, 0.9. This means any filter with a density of 0.3 must be compensated by a doubling of exposure (open up by one *f*-stop), 0.6 filter by opening up by two *f*-stops, 0.9 by three *f*-stops.

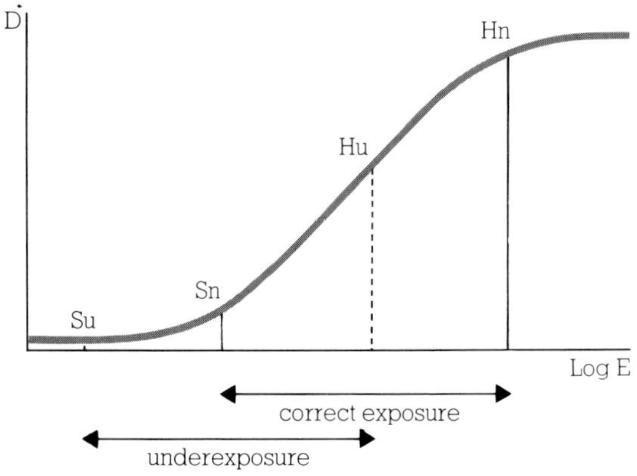

4.3 Normal correct exposure causes the shadows (Sn) of an average subject to be recorded on the toe of the curve, while the highlights (Hn) are placed on the curve's shoulder–all subject tones are fully recorded. However, underexposure causes the shadows (Su) to be placed on the flat part of the curve (D min) and thus are not visible. Underexposed highlights (Hu) do not lose detail but give a lower negative density. The net result of underexposure is loss of shadow detail.

both the highlight and shadow tonal differences are compressed due to the shape of the characteristic curves of the film and paper emulsions (fig 6.16).

Underexposure of the 'average' subject

A change of exposure to the film does not alter the characteristic curve, it simply alters the portion of the curve on which the subject brightness range is recorded. The shape of the curve can only be modified by development changes.

If you underexpose your 'average' scene, either by using too small an aperture (eg. *f*/16 instead of *f*/8) or by setting the shutter speed too high (eg. 1/500 sec. instead of 1/125 sec.), you will lose subject detail. The diagram (fig 4.3) explains why shadow detail is lost, while no loss occurs in either the mid-tones or highlights. In fact, the highlights are now less compressed and will show greater separation in the print.

For the average subject, it is possible to underexpose by about one stop from the correct exposure (eg. 1/125 sec. *f*/11 instead of 1/125 sec. *f*/8) and still produce a print which is visually very similar to the 'correct' print. The greater the degree of underexposure, the greater is the loss of shadow detail; and with gross underexposure (three stops or more) there is also loss of mid-tone detail – and it may be impossible to produce an acceptable print.

This heavy underexposure produces a negative of short density range which may not give a sufficiently wide printing exposure range to the paper to give both a clean white and a maximum black. More details of printing are given in Chapter 6.

As previously mentioned, the concept of correct exposure depends on the final image you have in mind. If you deliberately underexpose the subject, increase film development to increase contrast (see Chapter 5) and then print on to a high contrast grade of paper, the result may be very dramatic. The photograph will have both 'clean' whites and deep blacks, and will accentuate the highlights of the subject.

Overexposure of the 'average' subject

It is also possible to overexpose the average subject by about one stop (eg. 1/60 sec. *f*/4 instead of 1/60 sec. *f*/5.6) and obtain a print which is virtually indistinguishable from the correctly exposed negative. However, if you overexpose by more than one stop the photograph will show loss of highlight detail (see fig 4.4) – instead of appearing with a subtle difference of tone in the highlights, the area appears very white or 'burnt out'.

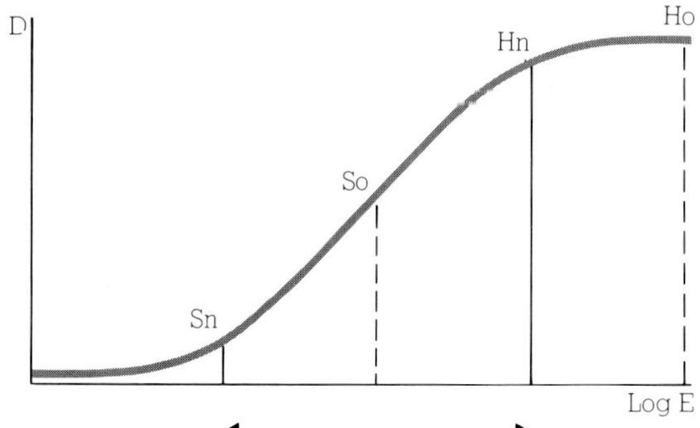

4.4 Compared to the correct exposure of the average subject (shadows and highlights as Sn and Hn), overexposure causes the negative density of the shadows (So) to increase and the highlight density (Ho) to fall on the flat D max. Thus, overexposure causes loss of highlight detail.

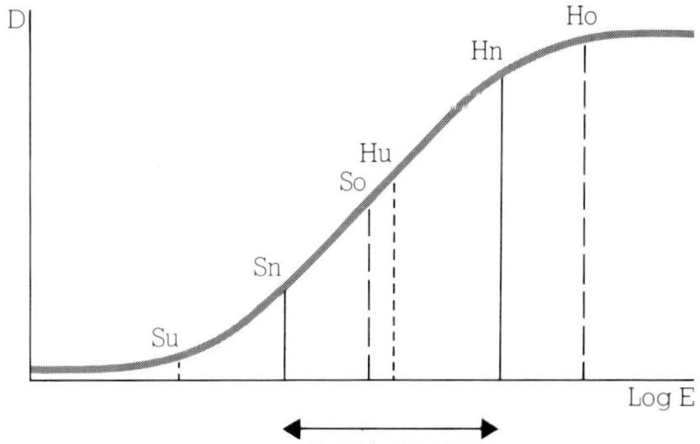

4.5 For subjects of short brightness range, moderate under- or overexposure causes no loss in either shadow or highlight detail; notice that Su (underexposed shadows) and Ho (overexposed highlights) are both placed on the characteristic curve. The reduced density range of the negative means that higher contrast papers (grades 3,4,5) must be used–see Chapter 6.

Unlike deliberate underexposure, which can produce dramatic photographs, deliberate overexposure rarely results in worthwhile images. This is because the highlights of the print are the most important, and attract the viewer's attention most. Burnt-out highlights frustrate the viewer because he is unable to find the image detail for which his brain is searching. Overexposure also causes loss of image sharpness due to optical spreading of the light as it enters the film emulsion (ie. irradiation). The speed (ASA or DIN) ratings of films are calculated on the *minimum* exposure required for an average subject.

Subjects of short brightness range

When the difference between the light reaching the film from the shadow and highlight areas of the subject is relatively small (say, a ratio of 1:32), as often occurs on overcast days, the film can easily handle this short brightness range. The camera exposure latitude is fairly wide and it may be possible to depart from the correct setting by as much as two stops in either direction and still obtain prints which are very similar. It requires gross under- or overexposure of the film for shadow and highlight detail to be lost (see fig 4.5).

Unfortunately, subjects with a short brightness range produce negatives of short density range which are therefore difficult to print. An ideal negative has a density range of about 1.0 because this 'matches' perfectly most manufacturers' normal paper grade and gives a full-toned print with clean whites and maximum black. The negative of short density range (less than 0.8) must be printed on 'hard' paper (grades 3, 4, 5) and requires careful control of printing exposure. In some cases the ('flat') negative may have such a low density range that the print still lacks sparkle even if printed on grade 5 paper.

To compensate for very low subject brightness range, it is necessary to increase the resulting density range of the negative by increasing film development (see page 68). It is then possible to print a low contrast subject (short brightness range) on to, say, grade 2 or 3 paper. This technique is often used when photographing on dull, overcast, winter days.

Subjects with wide brightness range

Occasionally you will encounter subjects with an extremely wide brightness range, such as on cloudless days at the seaside, or bright sunny days on the ski slopes. The film cannot cope with these situations; even correct exposure may cause loss of shadow and/or highlight detail–the subject brightness range simply cannot fit within the D/Log E curve (see fig 4.6).

There are four possible solutions to this problem. You must either:

1 Accept some loss of shadow and highlight detail, or

2 Adjust the exposure so that you retain all highlight information but lose shadow detail (ie. 'underexpose'), or

3 'Overexpose' to record shadow detail but sacrifice highlight detail, or

4 Change the shape of the D/Log E curve by variation of development so that the brightness range just fits within the new curve.

The best choice is solution 4, and this is explained in the next chapter. Solution 3 and, to a lesser extent, solution 1 will only have limited suitability because, as previously mentioned, highlights are generally considered to be the most important visual elements of the photograph.

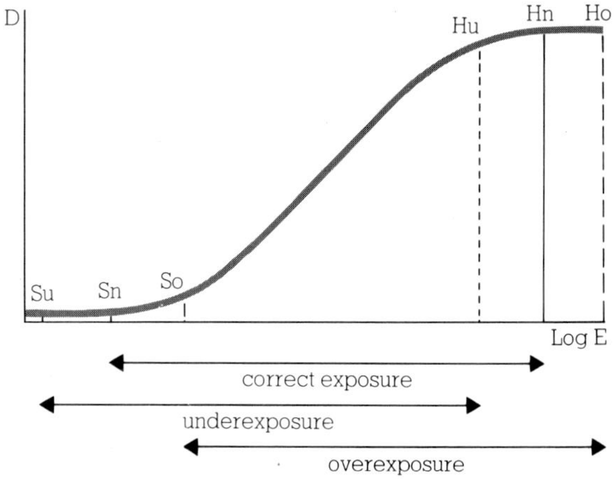

4.6 Even if correctly exposed, subjects of wide brightness range may cause a loss of shadow and highlight detail (Sn and Hn). Underexposure places the subject's highlights (Hu) on the shoulder of the curve, giving excellent highlight detail but causing greater loss of shadow detail (Su). Overexposure gives the best curve placement for shadows (So) but causes severe loss of highlight detail (Ho).

Estimating exposure

The discussions so far will have been wasted if the photographer is unable to determine the correct exposure accurately. There is a wide range of exposure meters on the market, all of which claim to be extremely accurate. As with most sensitive instruments, the true worth is not in the meter itself but in how it is employed and the user's ability to interpret readings.

Rather than discussing the merits of the various types of exposure meter, we will concentrate here on the different ways of using meters. The main methods of exposure determination are by readings taken from reflected light, incident light, grey card, spot measurement, and highlight or shadow areas.

Reflected light readings

This is the most popular method of estimating exposure because it is the simplest – you just set the ASA film speed on the dial, point the meter at the subject and then select one combination of aperture and shutter speed from the many possibilities indicated. Your choice of aperture/shutter speed depends on factors such as depth of field, subject movement, camera shake, etc. (These topics were discussed in detail in Chapter 2.).

All cameras with through-the-lens (TTL) metering measure the light reflected from the subject. They either set the aperture and/or shutter speed automatically, or require the photographer to rotate either the aperture scale or shutter dial until needles or LEDs are correctly aligned. The simplicity of TTL metering sometimes hides the fact, as previously mentioned, that the reading is only as good as the user's ability to understand each specific situation. Before discussing other methods of obtaining readings we should look at what the readings obtained actually represent.

How are exposure meters calibrated?

Most meters work on the principle of an average scene reflecting 18 per cent of the light falling on it. So, the calculator dial or direct readout gives the correct exposure for this average scene. For outside use, most manufacturers recommend that the meter be pointed slightly downwards to avoid too much influence from the sky. Many cameras with built-in meters have a sophisticated sensitivity pattern which automatically compensates

38 A beach scene on a sunny day usually has a very great brightness range, so you may have to 'underdevelop' the film in order to reduce the density range of the negative. In this example, the brightness range is wide but is moderated by the cloudy, but bright conditions.

39 This reflection in an ice covered pond on an overcast day is an example of a subject with short brightness range. To partially compensate for this, the film was developed for slightly longer than normal and then printed on to grade 2 paper. The gentle mood of the picture has been retained by avoiding excessive build-up of contrast.

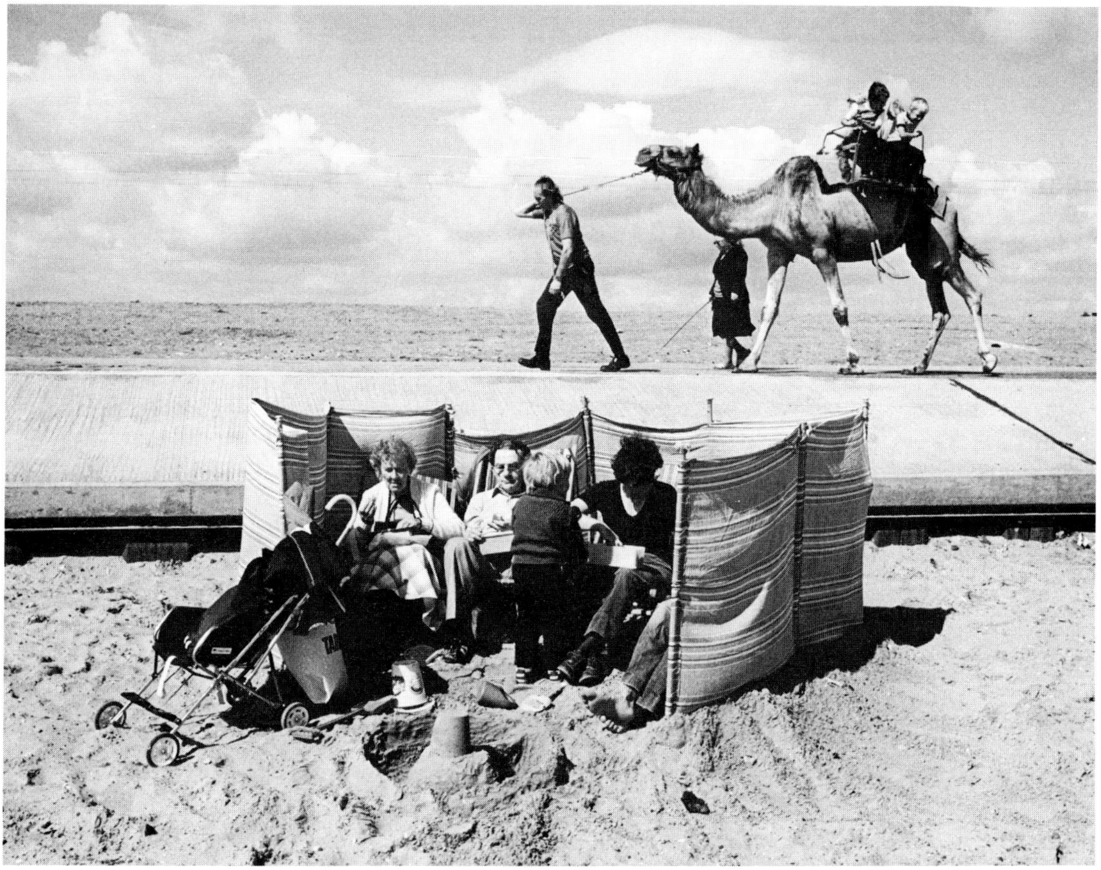

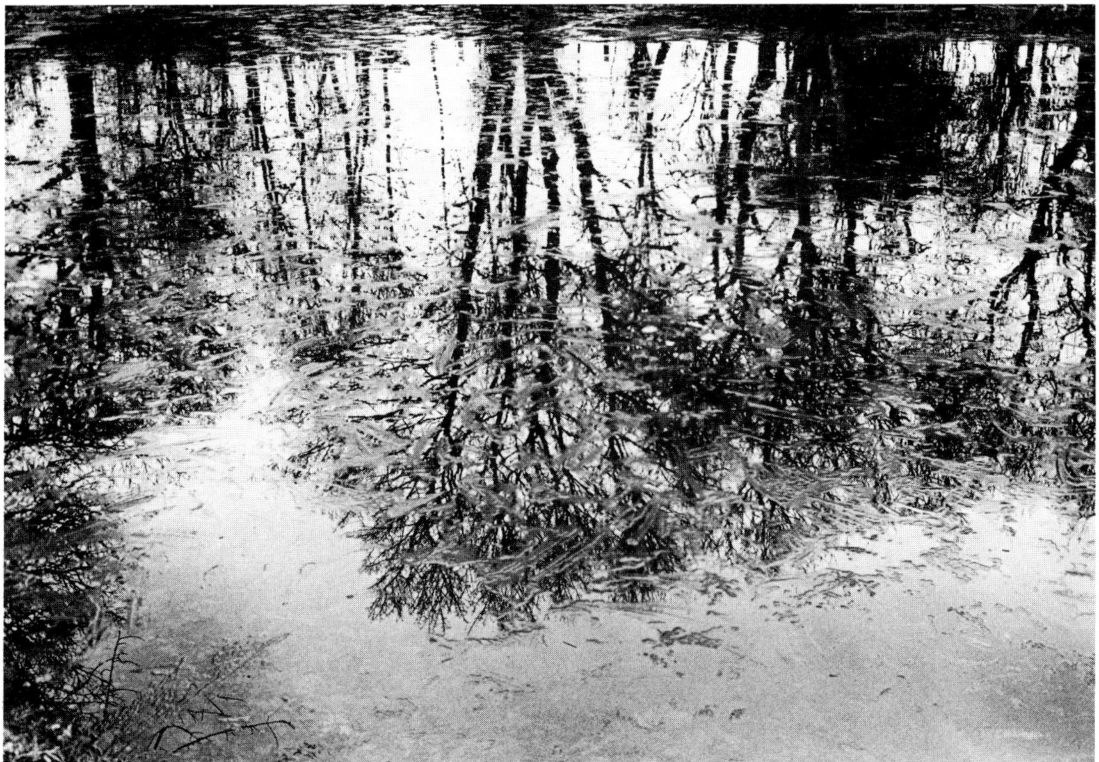

for too much 'weighting' from the sky.

Surprising though it may seem, most photographic subjects are sufficiently within the 18 per cent reflectivity zone to give excellent results with this simple method. However, it is essential that you learn to recognise subjects and lighting conditions outside the 18 per cent norm, or your film will be incorrectly exposed and you will not be able to produce high quality black-and-white prints.

Non-average subjects

When photographing a subject which consists mainly of light tones ('high-key' subject), such as a beach scene, the reflected reading obtained by the meter is higher than that for an average subject (18 per cent reflectivity) in the same lighting conditions. For correct exposure both scenes should have the same range of possible aperture/shutter speed settings. However, the high reading of the high-key subject leads to underexposure of the film and consequent loss of shadow detail.

40 Because of the use of a long lens (300mm on a 35mm camera) in this case it was only practical to work from the reflected light reading given by the camera's TTL meter. However, in these circumstances it is important to point the lens so that it reads from an area of mid-grey (say, the face and hat) and then frame the subject as you want.

41 This snow scene is a high key subject which gives a false reflected reading (ie, too high) and causes the film to be underexposed. Use one of the other metering techniques instead, such as highlight reading, incident or grey card (see text). In this example, it was decided to reproduce the snow without texture, thus emphasising the 'keep out' sign.

42 Low key subjects like this contain predominantly dark tones and are likely to give false reflected readings (ie. too low) causing the film to be overexposed. If you are taking a reflected reading (eg. TTL), then meter off a mid-grey area (say, head and box in this picture) if you can.

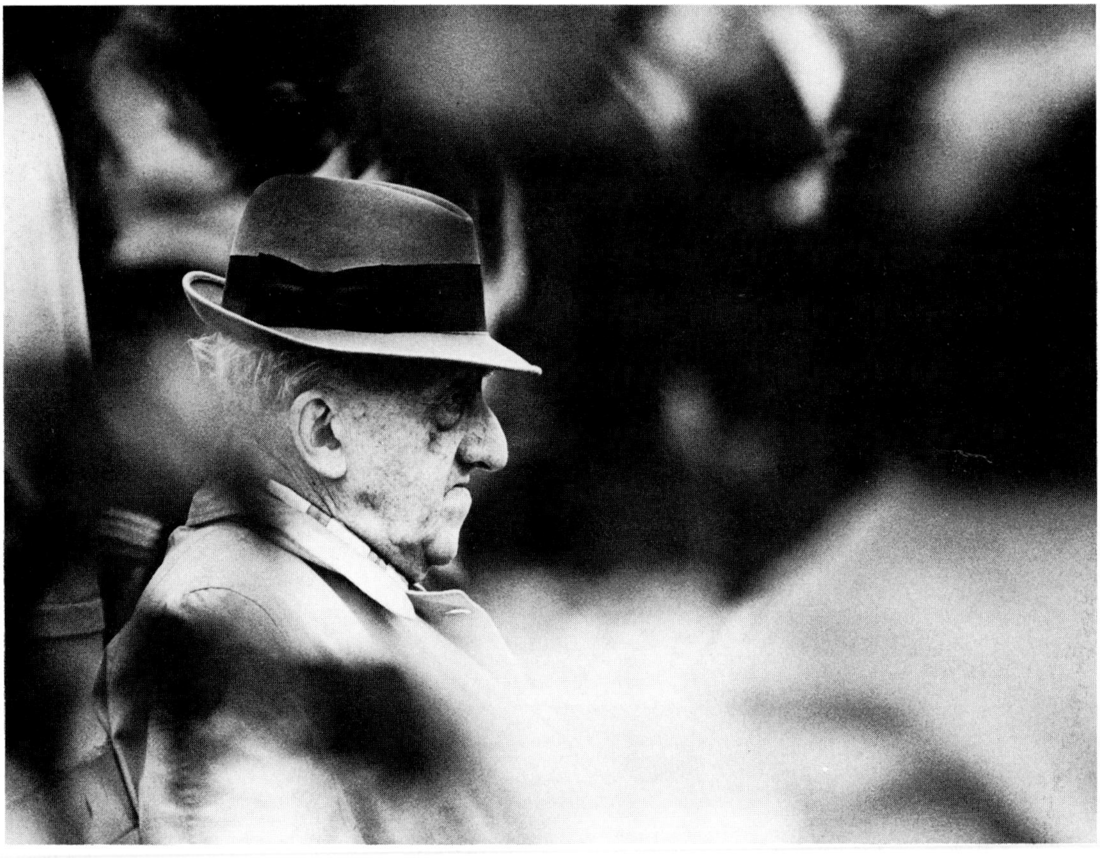

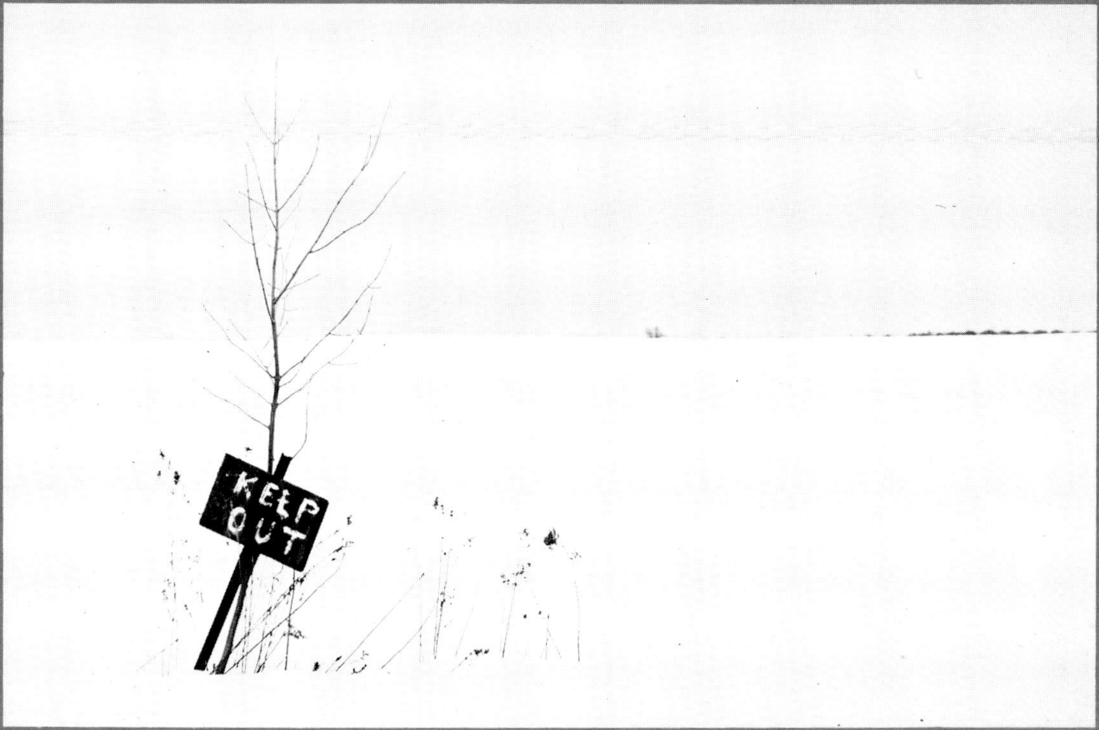
KEEP
OUT

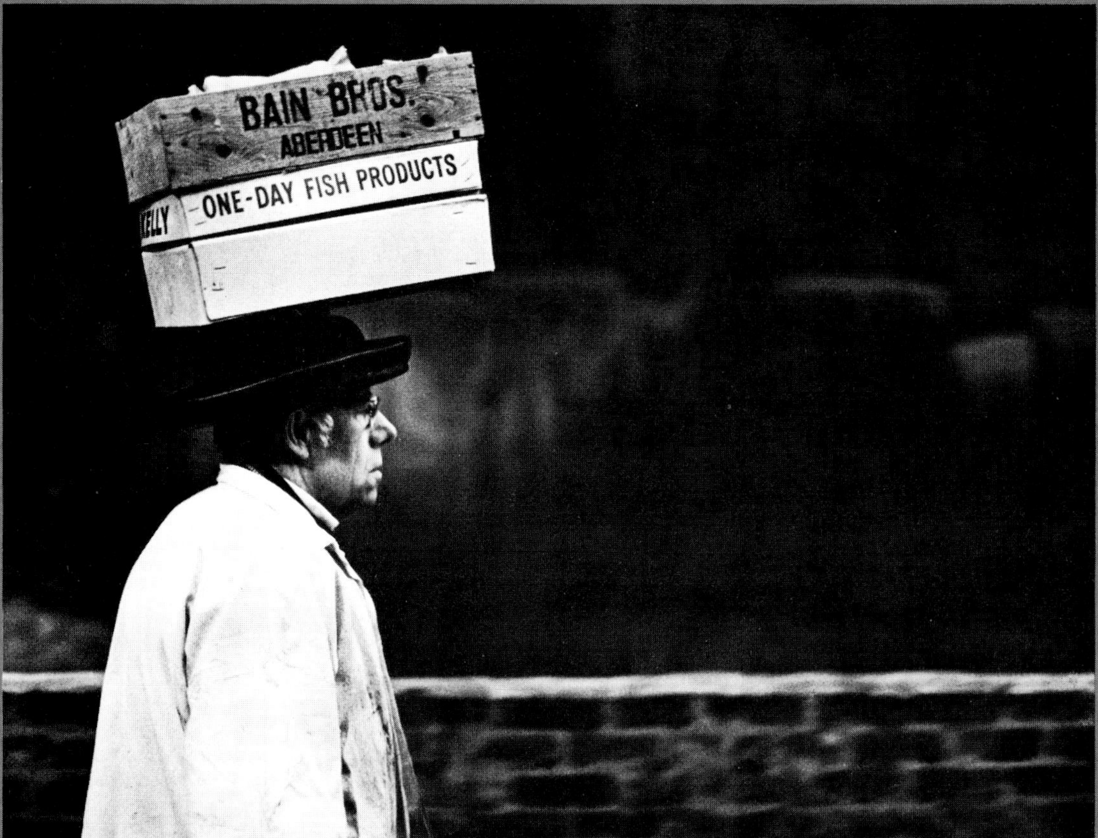
BAIN BROS.
ABERDEEN
ONE-DAY FISH PRODUCTS

A subject consisting mainly of dark tones ('low-key' subject) has a low reflectivity and gives lower meter readings than our 18 per cent norm. If this reading is used to determine the exposure, the film will be overexposed and the resulting print will show some loss of highlight detail; this would happen if, for example, you have to photograph a person against a dark background.

When photographing non-average subjects, you can use one or more of the following methods to ensure correct exposure:

1 Use your experience of a similar situation and adjust the exposure accordingly. For example, you might decide to give a high-key subject two more stops exposure than the meter indicates (say 1/60 sec. *f*/8 rather than 1/250 sec. *f*/8). For low-key subjects, try reducing exposure by two stops from the settings indicated by the meter.
2 Make more than one exposure of the subject so that you have a choice of negatives from which to make the print. 'Bracket' the exposure with one-stop intervals on either side of the reading indicated by the meter, say over the range −2 to +2.
3 Move in close to the subject and take your meter reading from an average part of the scene; use this close-up reading for exposure estimation. Many automatic cameras have a memory facility which 'holds' a particular light reading or aperture/shutter speed combination.
4 Use one of the methods of exposure estimation described below, which is independent of the subject photographed.

Incident readings

Most separate hand meters are able to take reflected readings or can measure the light incident on the subject (fig 4.7). An incident reading is achieved by placing a special plastic dome or screen over the meter window and so collecting the light falling on to the subject. The meter is placed close to the subject and pointed at the camera. The dome placed over the sensitive cell is designed to transmit 18 per cent of the light incident upon it.

The main advantage of the incident light reading method is that readings are independent of the subject and are determined only by the lighting conditions. Thus, if an average, low-key, or high-key subject is placed in the same lighting situation, they all give the same possible camera settings, and thus ensure that shadows, mid-tones and highlights are correctly recorded by the film, irrespective of the subject itself.

Incident readings are only practical when you can take a meter reading close to the subject or, at least, in a similar lighting situation as the subject. The latter applies if, for example, you are taking a landscape which is perhaps several kilometres from the camera – you would simply point the meter from the camera position in the direction of the lighting.

Grey card reading

Manufacturers sell grey cards which have an 18 per cent reflectance and can be actually placed in a scene for the purpose of taking light readings. The grey card is a substitute for an average subject and it is a simple matter to take a reflected reading from the card to ensure correct camera settings.

The grey card method is ideal for any meter, such as TTL systems, which can only take reflected readings. As with integrated readings, it may be impossible to place the card close to the subject but, again, you can instead position the card in similar lighting conditions to the inaccessible subject.

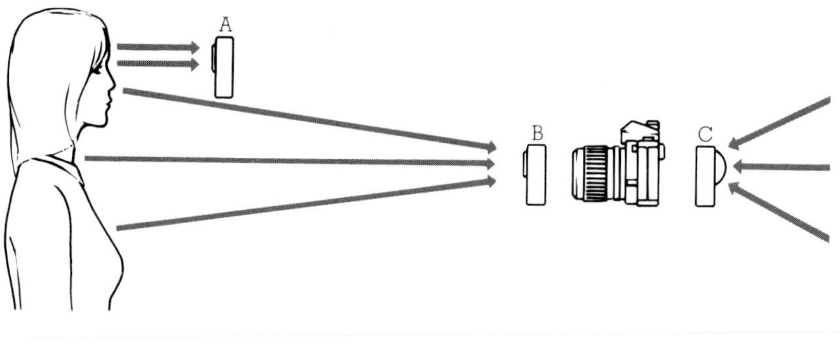

4.7 When photographing a subject surrounded by a large amount of background, such as a waist-length portrait, light meter readings vary according to the technique used and the reflecting of the background. Taking a reflected reading from the camera position (B) will cause the meter to measure both the subject and background; a light background will give a 'too high' reading resulting in underexposure of the film, and a dark background a 'too low' reading, with the film overexposed. To remedy this, either take a close-up reflected reading off the subject's face (A) or an incident reading from the camera position (C).

Spot lightmeters

Most meters receive light from an angle of about 50° (similar to the angle of view of a standard lens) and average (integrate) all the light falling on the meter; they are ideal for most general work.

There are a few, often expensive, meters which receive light from a narrow angle (about 1°) and can be sighted at a specific part of the scene. These so-called 'spot meters' usually have a standard viewfinder with a small circle marked near the centre of the field indicating the precise area which is metered. To operate the meter, you point the gun-like barrel at the subject and select the small area to be metered. The readout is either in direct form in the viewfinder or has to be transferred to the normal dial calculator.

These meters are extremely accurate and enable the photographer to measure the reflectance from various parts of the scene, from shadows, through mid-tones, to highlights. It is therefore possible to measure not only the light from an 18 per cent reflectance area of the scene, but also to measure the subject brightness range. This sensitive instrument is ideal for use with the Zone System of exposure determination.

The spot meter must be used with great caution, and is only really an asset when used by an experienced photographer who is very aware of tonal distribution within the subject. To begin with, it is also worthwhile carrying an ordinary meter, and comparing its readings with those from the spot meter. More information on the application of a spot meter is given in Chapter 7 which is largely concerned with the Zone System.

Highlight and shadow readings

A number of meters have a mark on either side of the normal large index which can be used for highlight and shadow readings, for example, the 'O' and 'U' marks on a Weston meter. To base your camera settings on the subject's highlights, you should measure the reflected reading from the brightest part of the scene in which you wish to record subtle detail and then place the highlight mark of the calculator dial against this reading (see fig 4.8).

The highlight method ensures that the highlights are correctly recorded on the shoulder region of the D/Log E curve and all other tones will fall into position on the lower parts of the curve. If the subject's highlights are difficult to measure, a piece of white paper can be placed within the scene as a substitute for metering purposes. In

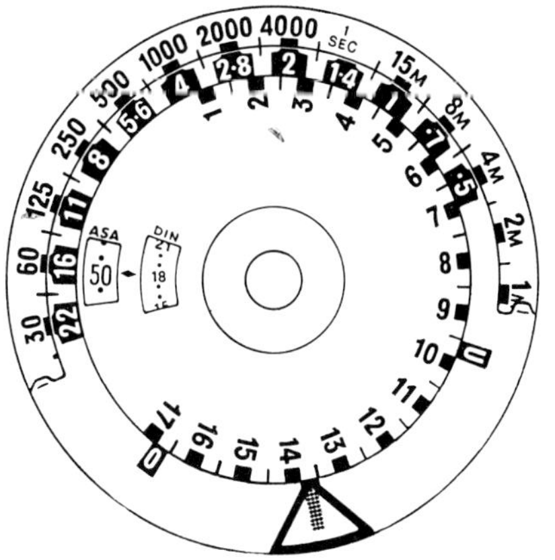

4.8 Metering of highlights and use of the '0' setting on the meter calculator dial ensure accurate recording of highlight detail, and are also very useful in low levels of illumination. If shadow detail is very important, set the 'U' mark of the dial against the reading obtained from the darkest subject tones that you want to record. For full technique see text.

fact, when photographing in low levels of lighting which are too dim for the meter to read easily, this white paper technique enables it to give a reasonable reading.

If the shadows of the scene are very important and need to be recorded accurately, you should base your exposure on a shadow reading. This involves getting close to the darkest area of the subject that you wish to record and placing the resulting meter reading against the 'shadow' mark on the calculator dial (see fig 4.8). This method is only applicable within the useful sensitivity range of the meter and for selenium meters (eg. Westons) that usually means fairly brightly lit daylight scenes. The more sensitive meters, such as CdS and GPD, have a more practical range for the shadow-reading technique.

Zone System

The basis of the Zone System of exposure estimation and film development is the precise matching of the subject's brightness range (or, in reality, the brightness range the photographer wishes to record) to fit the film's characteristic curve perfectly. When correctly applied, as in the photographs of Ansel Adams and his contemporaries, the final prints have a tonal quality and clarity that is breathtaking.

The Zone System enthusiast is a perfectionist when it comes to photographic technique–he takes meticulous care with exposure measurements and controls film development precisely.

The system can strictly only be applied to sheet film, but can work in a modified form for the roll film user (see Chapter 7).

Determining exposure without a meter

The early photographers were able to judge camera settings very accurately by using their experience and knowledge of lighting conditions. Nowadays, this skill is rarely needed because lightmeters are so accurate and reliable. However, there are times when a limited ability to 'guess' exposures is extremely useful.

In the unlikely event that your meter has broken down, perhaps because you have forgotten to replace the battery (which should usually be done about once a year), you can apply a simple exposure guide system (fig 4.9) which follows the same principle as that recommended by the leaflet enclosed in the film box. This 'judge the weather' method of setting exposure obviously relies on the photographer's ability to accurately gauge lighting conditions and it is therefore worthwhile to occasionally 'guess' the exposure before you use your meter, simply to keep this skill in practice. This guessing 'game' sharpens your skills of observation and ensures that you are not at a loss to find the exposure when your meter fails.

Shutter speed 1/ASA

Bright or hazy sun on light sand or snow	Bright or hazy sun (distinct) shadows)	Cloudy bright (no shadows)	Heavy overcast or open shade
f/22	*f*/16	*f*/8	*f*/5.6

4.9 Should your meter be faulty, making it necessary for you to guess exposure, this table is a useful guide. For example, ASA 400 film in bright sun requires 1/500 sec *f*/16 or its equivalent.

If you customarily use automatic or semi-automatic cameras, it is easy to become blasé and accept whatever camera settings the technology provides. For 99 per cent of the time the built-in camera exposure system performs very well, and provided you are able to recognise non-average subjects, you will obtain excellent results. But every once in a while (usually because of some mechanical or electrical malfunction) the meter generates nonsensical readings, which may, in fact, only be recognised by the astute photographer who has some idea of what the correct exposure should be. The 'auto control' can then be overriden and the exposure set manually. No true photographer wants to be completely at the mercy of automation.

Finally, if all else fails and you have a subject which 'must' be photographed, you should guess the exposure and, if possible, bracket it widely into both under- and overexposure, say −3 to +3 stops.

Choice of film

Most camera work requires the use of panchromatic films, only occasionally employing specialist materials such as ultra high speed, high contrast (lith), and infra-red (IR) film. Pan films can be sub-divided into three broad categories designated by their sensitivity, ie. slow, medium and fast films.

The general rule to apply when choosing a film is to load the slowest film possible for the subject, lighting conditions, and the image you want; this takes into account decisions on shutter speed (hand-held, tripod, subject movement, etc.) and aperture (depth of field, optical quality, etc.). Whatever the resulting image quality (definition and graininess) differences between using, say, a medium speed film (eg. FP4, Plus-X, Agfapan 100) and a fast film (eg. HP5, Tri-X, Agfapan 400) are far less than most people imagine. If you are careful to give the film correct exposure and controlled development, fast films are capable of yielding excellent results, even on 35mm. It is very illuminating to make a test of the three film types (eg. Pan F, FP4, HP5) by photographing a static subject which has a large amount of fine detail.

For versatility, it is difficult to fault the high speed films of around ASA 400/27 DIN (ISO = 400/27°)–they permit photography at low light levels (even hand-held) and are still practical to use on bright days. Many of the photographs in this book have been taken on ASA 400 film.

If you require the ultimate in definition and fine grain, try using the slow films of around ASA 50/18 DIN (ISO = 50/18°). But remember, these slow films are inherently more contrasty than faster films and can produce over-contrasty negatives especially as they are used mainly on bright days when lighting contrast is normally high; you should avoid overdevelopment (see page 68).

Chromogenic black-and-white films

Before settling on a film and developer combination to suit your general photography, it is worth trying chromogenic black-and-white films (eg. Ilford XP1, Agfapan Vario-XL). These products

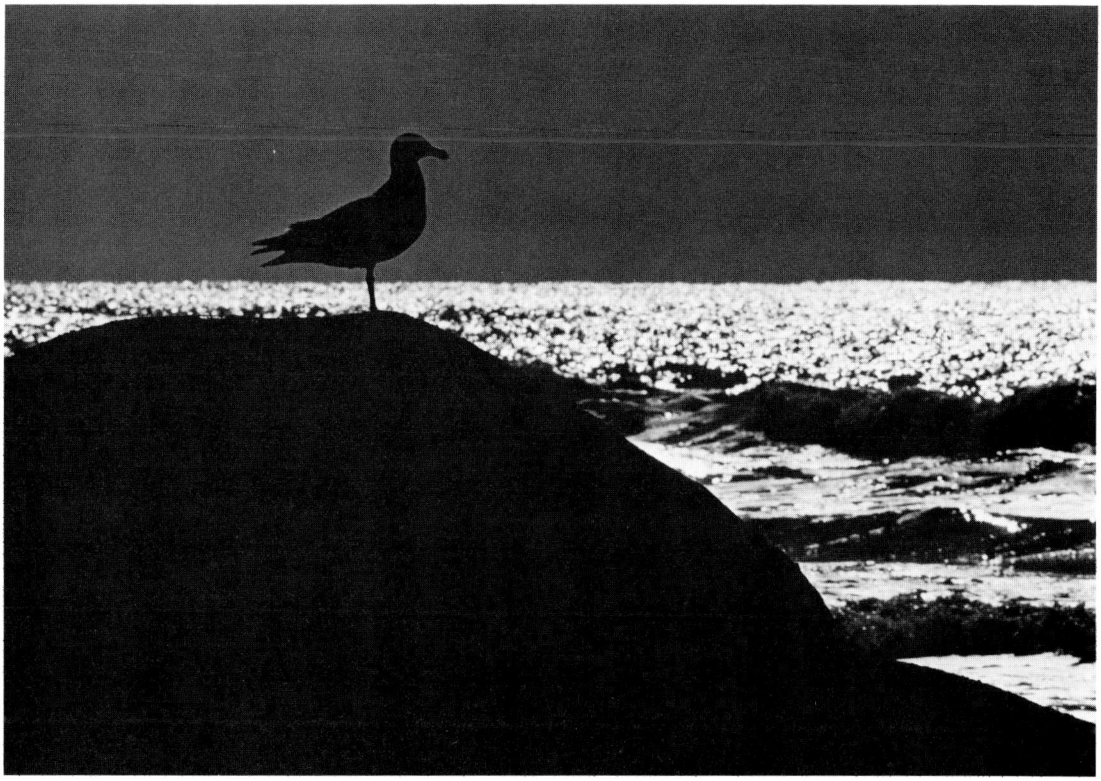

43 For difficult lighting conditions, such as those present with this back-lit subject, a spot lightmeter is ideal because it allows you to determine precise readings on which you can base your camera settings. In this case the exposure was set to ensure that there was no detail in the shadows (ie. silhouette), a mid-grey for the sky and moderate retention of highlights.

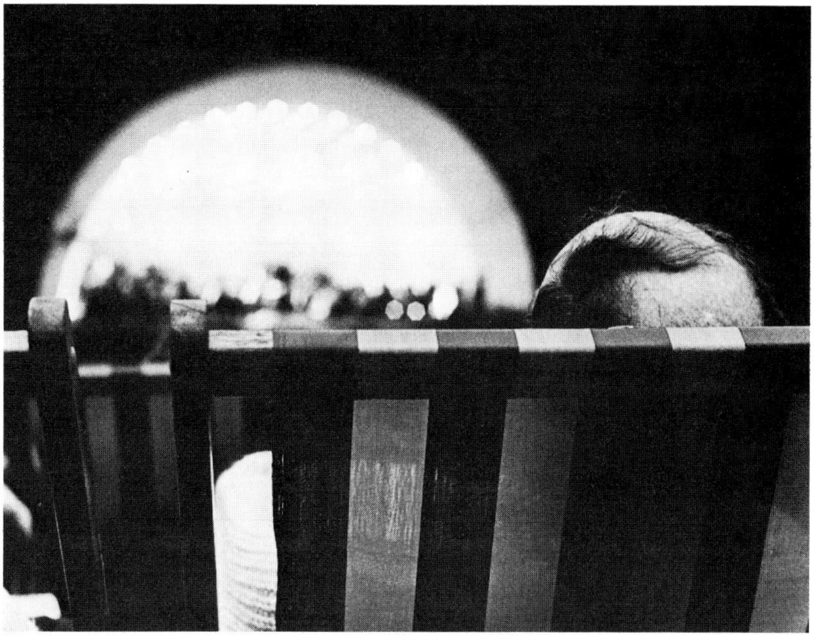

44 This photograph was taken at an evening open-air concert just as the light was fading. The highlight reading method was used to base exposure on the reading given by the roof of the concert bowl, where slight detail was required.

offer variable film speed setting within the same roll of film. For example, you can expose one frame at ASA 125/22 DIN (ISO = 125/22°) and the next at ASA 1600/33 DIN (ISO = 1600/33°). Development is made easy by being able to use the readily available C41 colour negative process. The image quality of these films is excellent especially where graininess is concerned; they can give the granularity of ASA 125 conventional silver film even when used at speed settings of ASA 400.

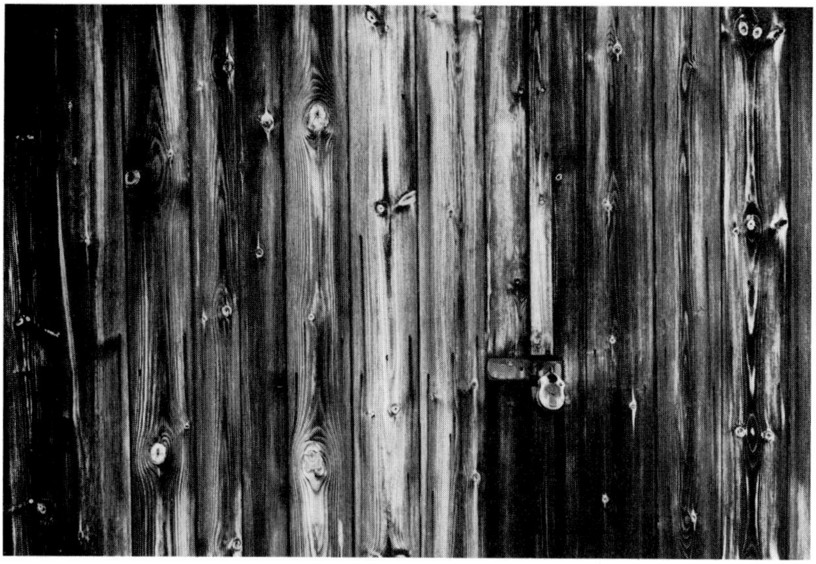

45 The fine graininess produced by the use of XP1 film suits the full tonal range of this subject. Notice how the composition obeys the 'law of thirds' (Chapter 2) by placing the padlock at one of the intersections of the thirds.

The only technical disadvantages of chromogenic films compared with the conventional black-and-white type are the more critical development control (only of concern if you process at home), the longer printing exposures, and the fading of the dye images. The dye fading depends on the keeping conditions and, if the negatives are kept in low humidity, low temperature, and in dark storage they should be usable for decades. The main archival difference between other colour materials and chromogenic black-and-white films is the fact that once printed on to black-and-white papers (see archival processing page 94) the photograph can be made stable for centuries, whereas colour photographs are far less permanent.

The development of chromogenic films is discussed on page 79.

Buying and storing film

Black-and-white film varies slightly from batch to batch and is best bought in reasonable quantities, especially if you plan to practise the Zone System. To keep film in good condition it should be stored in a cool, dry place; a freezer is ideal but remove the film from the unit at least two hours before opening to avoid the risk of condensation marks which may be visible after processing.

For economy, it may be worth buying 35mm film in bulk lengths (eg. 17m, 30m) and loading it into reusable cassettes. However, you must take great care to keep cassettes very clean as the smallest piece of grit caught in the felt of the light trap can cause black 'tramlines' to be cut in the film emulsion and so to appear on the final print. Also, avoid buying cheap out-of-date film as it is likely to be slower in speed than indicated, more grainy, and have a higher base fog level. The last fault causes the loss of shadow contrast and detail. If you are likely to spend much time on photography, it is sensible to buy only 'fresh' film; do shop around for the best prices, especially as many stores offer attractive discounts for bulk purchasing.

Film exposure, development and printing

The two chapters that follow deal with film development (Chapter 5) and printing (Chapter 6) – topics closely linked to film exposure. In fact, all three stages of print production are closely interconnected and it is not possible to change one stage without this having an effect on one or both of the others.

The discussions so far on film exposure have assumed that standard film development and printing are to be used. However, as more variations in development and printing are introduced, so greater flexibility becomes available for camera exposure. In the following two chapters, therefore, we see how camera exposure is influenced by processing and printing.

5 FILM DEVELOPMENT

Many photographers consider film development to be a mechanical process–they simply measure the temperature of the developer, look up the development time in the manufacturer's data sheets and process the film accordingly. Unfortunately, in doing this they have also lost the opportunity to control the development in such a way that they could extract the highest quality from the film, and ultimately produce finer prints.

This chapter shows how film development can be modified to compensate for different exposure conditions and to produce the 'best' negative for the photograph you want.

Standard development

The development time specified by the manufacturer as the 'correct' time for a particular film/developer combination is based on an average subject receiving correct film exposure. For many situations, this standard development produces ideal negatives. However, if your subject is a non-average one or you do not require a standard print of your subject, then you will need to alter either the degree of development or the type of developer.

Ultimately, you will refine your film processing so that you obtain negatives suited to your equipment and style of working. Indeed, so many steps are necessary to produce the final print that it is inevitable that each photographer must 'tune' his system as he wants. The variables of printing (enlarger, lens, paper, development) are dealt with separately in Chapter 6.

Which processing steps can be changed?

The only stage of film processing which should be varied is the development, and the steps following should always be carried out to completion. This means that you should not shorten the times for which the film is treated in the stop bath, fixer or wash. These post-development stages have no influence on the printing qualities of the negative, but are crucial to ensure that it will not deteriorate with storage.

The best way to understand how development changes affect the film is to refer to D/Log E curves.

With a little practice you will be able to interpret the curves and select the best development conditions for your exposed film.

Changing development times

The shape of the film's characteristic curve is changed by the degree of development and, to a lesser extent, by use of a different developer. Extending the development time (or increasing temperature and/or agitation) causes the S-shaped curve to 'stand up', whereas reduction of time in the developer causes a 'flattening' of the curve. Film manufacturers publish families of curves which indicate precisely how each specific film/developer combination responds to development changes (fig 5.1).

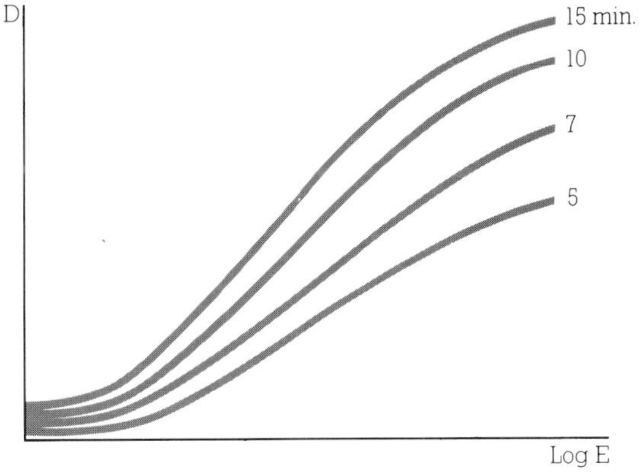

5.1 Representative family of curves which indicates how different development times affect the shape of the D/Log E curve. Note how the longer times give a steeper curve gradient and also a slight increase in D min due to increased fog level. The change in curve shape becomes gradually less as the developed time grows–compare the 5, 10 and 15 minute curves.

The standard development time is designed to produce a negative from the average subject which has a density range of 1.0 (the difference between the density of highlights and shadows). This negative should then print easily on normal (grade 2) paper when a diffuser enlarger is used. If you increase development time, the average subject will produce a negative density range greater than 1.0 which will have to be printed on to a soft paper (grade 0 or 1); reduction of development time produces a negative of density range less than 1.0 – this 'flat' negative needs to be printed on to a hard paper (grades 3, 4 or 5). Fig 5.2 shows how the negative's density range can be found from a D/Log E curve.

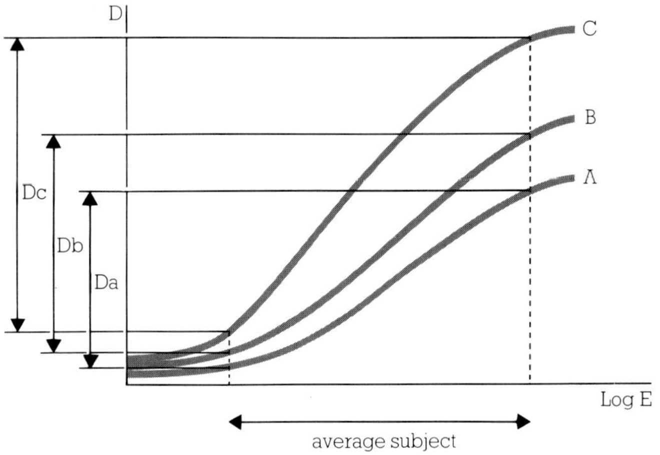

5.2 The curve B represents 'normal' development time which, for the average subject, will produce a negative density range (Db) of about 1.0 which should print well on grade 2 paper. If less than normal development is given (curve A) the density range of the negative (Da) will be less than 1.0, while a longer development time (curve C) gives a higher negative density range (Dc).

Subjects of short brightness range

When photographing on dull overcast days the brightness range of the subject is low (say 1:32 ie. 5 stops) and if standard development is given to the film, a negative density range of less than 1.0 is produced, thus necessitating printing on hard grades of paper. Because of their high contrast, hard grades of paper are difficult to work with and the slightest error in printing exposure causes a relatively large shift in image tone. In extreme cases where lighting is very flat (say 1:8 ie. 3 stops), the negative may produce unacceptable prints which lack a good deep black and clean whites, even if printed on grade 5 paper.

The film development time should be increased to compensate for the low contrast lighting. This simple technique increases the density range of the negative so that printing is easier and a high quality print can be obtained (fig 5.3).

The amount of extra development obviously depends on the subject's brightness range and the film/developer combination, but as a guide try increasing the standard development by 25 per cent for slightly overcast days, 50 per cent for heavily overcast days, and when lighting is very flat, such as in heavy rain or fog, try doubling the development. As previously mentioned, it is not possible to give precise recommendations as each photographer has his own set of equipment and his own ideas of what constitutes a good print. Experiment with different times and developers to suit your own needs. The technique of *push processing* is discussed on page 79.

Subjects with wide brightness range

For subjects which have a wider range of brightness than average there are two approaches to film development. The easy option is to use the standard development time and then print the resulting negative which has a density range greater than 1.0 on to a low contrast paper (grades 0 or 1). This technique works if the subject brightness range is not too great and it is able to fit on to the D/Log E curve (see fig 4.6); however, camera exposure latitude is minimal and you must either bracket your original exposure for 'insurance' or determine the exposure very precisely by metering several areas of the subject as is done in the Zone System (Chapter 7).

The preferred approach for subjects of large brightness range is to reduce the development time to obtain a negative density range of about 1.0 (fig 5.4). This second technique not only gives you a negative which is easier to print but also increases camera exposure latitude. There is not so much leeway with underdevelopment of a film as there is with overdevelopment because below a certain length of development the solution has insufficient time to establish itself within the emulsion and its chemicals cannot perform their particular functions. Very short times may also give uneven development.

As a guide, for subjects of moderately wide brightness range (say 1:256 ie. 8 stops) try decreasing development by 10 per cent, and for more extreme lighting conditions try a 25 per cent reduction of development. Slower films are prone to produce negatives of wide density range and it is therefore preferable to err towards 'underdevelopment' of these films.

Development times of roll films

Ideally, each subject should be photographed and then developed separately, in accordance with the factors discussed on page 96. This technique forms the basis of the Zone System

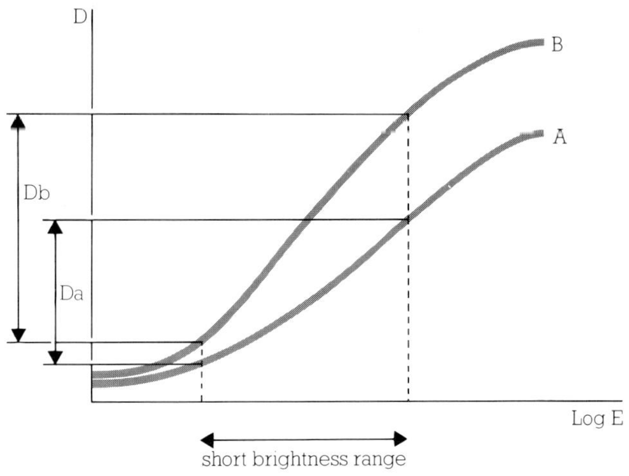

5.3 When developed for the normal time (curve A), a subject of short brightness range gives a negative density range (Da) which is too low to print successfully on grade 2 paper. An increased development time (curve B) produces a larger density range (Db) which is more suitable for printing.

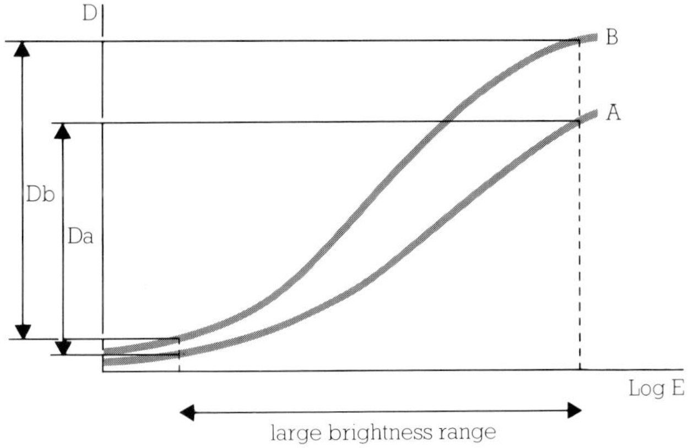

5.4 The negative density range (Db) produced when a large brightness range subject is developed normally (curve B) is greater than 1.0 and is not suitable for grade 2 paper. To remedy this, a reduced development (curve A) gives a density range (Da) which is more easily printed.

(Chapter 7) but can, strictly, only be applied to sheet film. The 35mm and 120 film user cannot develop each exposure so that it perfectly matches the D/Log E curve.

Fortunately, the overall idea of development control can be applied to roll film provided that you are prepared to accept a few compromises. During a single photographic session there may be similar lighting conditions throughout, or a gradual change from one to another (eg. bright sunshine to overcast skies).

It is a simple matter for you to number your rolls of film as you finish them and then make notes of the lighting conditions. When processing, select the appropriate development time for each film, and then combine films with similar subject brightness ranges. If you use small tanks it is possible to combine several rolls requiring different development times in the same tank. For example, if you are processing three films with developing times of 10, 8 and 7 min, you should adopt the following method:

1 With the room lights on, measure the correct amount of developer for the three films (at the correct temperature) into the small tank. Do not put the lid on the tank.
2 In complete darkness, load all three films on to spirals, making sure you know which is which.
3 Drop the ten-minute film into the tank, start the clock, and put the lid on the tank. With normal agitation, process the film in accordance with your usual technique but *keep the lights off.*
4 Just before two minutes of development has elapsed, lift the lid off the tank. Place the eight-minute film in the tank after precisely two minutes of development. Replace the lid and continue processing in darkness until nearly three minutes has elapsed.
5 Remove the lid once more and place the seven-minute film in the tank after precisely three minutes of development. Replace the lid, turn on the lights, and develop all three films until ten minutes has elapsed on the clock.

6 Complete processing as normal ie. stop bath, fixer, wash, wetting agent, dry.

Because there are relatively few exposures on one roll, it is easier for the 120 film user to give each roll the 'best' development time; however, the 35mm enthusiast should be prepared to sacrifice some film. One approach is to wind off the 35mm film and remove it from the camera if lighting conditions change drastically, and reload with another cassette. Each film can then be developed according to the prevailing conditions. If your 35mm film is about half exposed at the end of a photographic session, it is best to take the camera into the darkroom, waste a few frames, open the camera back in complete darkness and cut the film. The cut length can be loaded straight into the spiral for processing, while the rest of the roll can be exposed at another time. If you load your own cassettes from bulk lengths of film then it is a simple matter to use short lengths and thereby have more flexibility in development times.

Measuring the degree of development

Photographic manufacturers have devised a number system to help gauge a film's response to development. The basic principle involves measuring the gradient (γ ie 'gamma') of the film's characteristic curve (fig 5.5).

Unfortunately, each manufacturer uses his own system to generate these numbers and it is therefore not possible to interrelate them easily. However, the numbers are roughly similar and also serve the same purpose. Agfa measures its film gradients in γ (gamma) units, Ilford uses $\overline{G}$ ('G bar'), and Kodak prefers CI (contrast index). The best method is to use γ when dealing with Agfa films, $\overline{G}$ when discussing Ilford's films, and CI for Kodak products.

Gamma measurements

The simplest measure of film contrast is gamma,

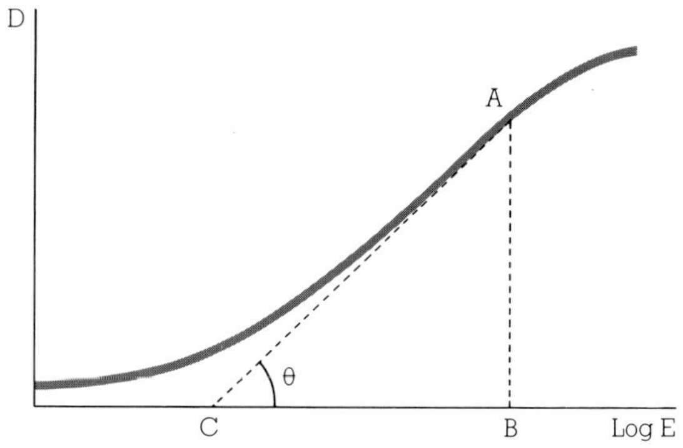

5.5 Gamma is the slope of the tangent (AC) to the characteristic curve, and is given by tan $\theta = AB/CB$. It is customary to select the steepest part of the curve when determining gamma. For most camera films, gamma has a value of 0.5 – 1.0.

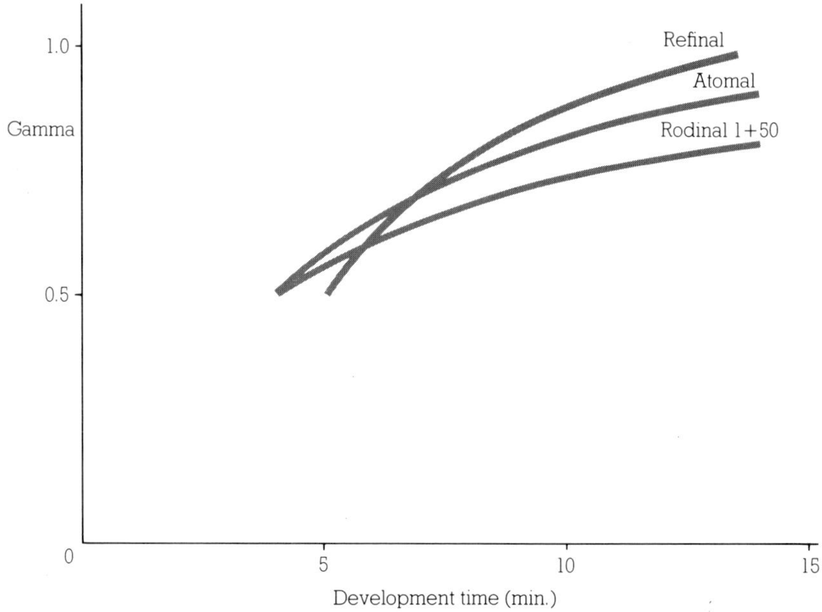

5.6 Typical gamma/time curves for one film processed in three different developers. If your selected gamma value is 0.75, the required development times obtained from this graph are 8 min (Refinal), 8½ min (Atomal) and 10½ min (Rodinal 1 + 50).

ie. the slope of the tangent to the D/Log E curve (fig 5.5). As previously mentioned, the slope of the characteristic curve increases as the development time increases and the slope decreases with reduced development. Consequently, the value of gamma increases with development time.

From a family of curves (fig 5.1) which plot how the densities of a film change with the amount of development, it is possible to determine the gamma for each development time. These various gamma values can then be plotted against development time to give gamma/time curves (fig 5.6).

Agfa recommend that their films should be

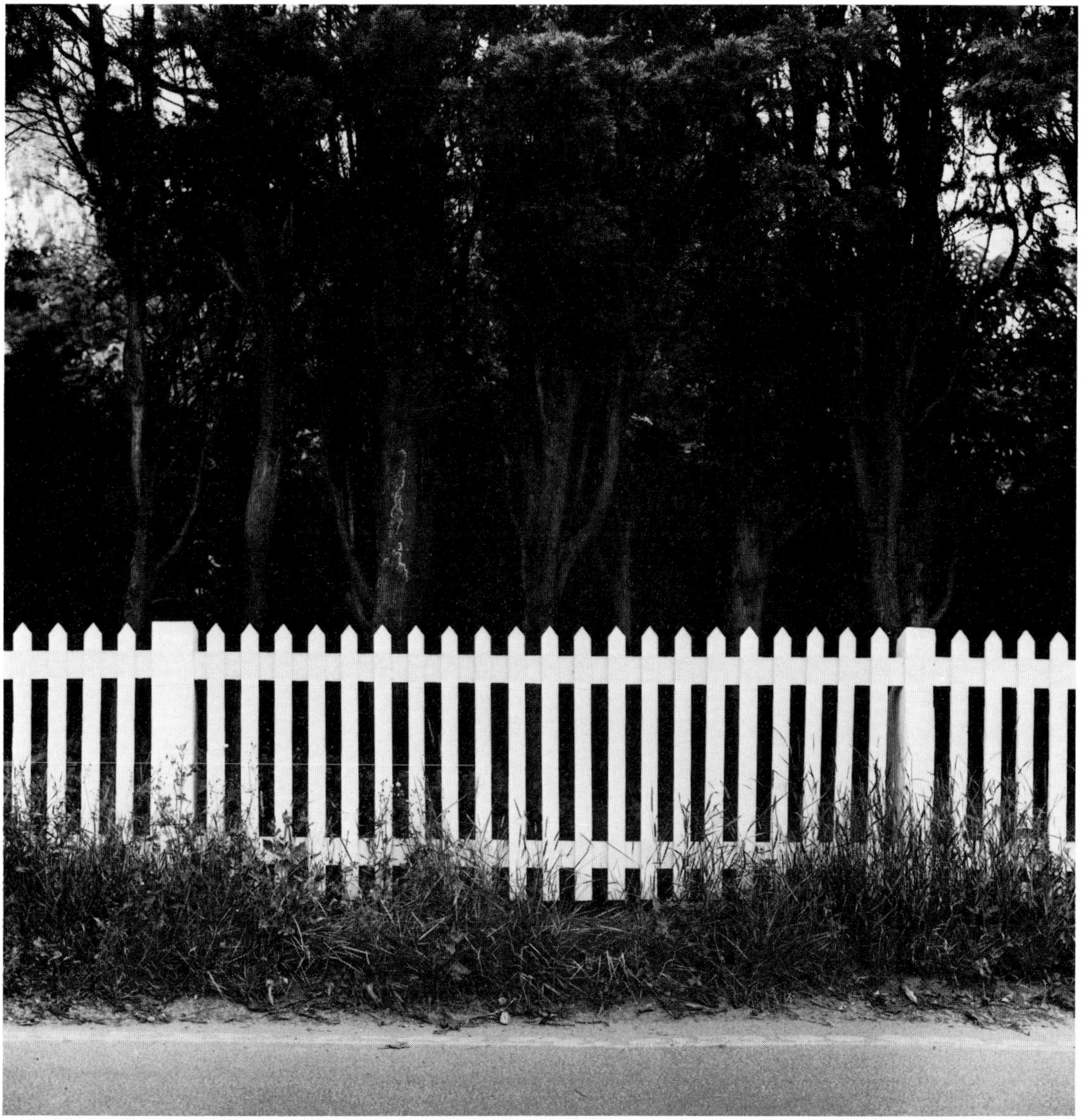

46 Although taken when the daylight was 'flat' (overcast) this scene has a normal subject brightness range, so the film was developed as recommended by the manufacturers. The white fence should not be overexposed as this would lose detail, but sufficient exposure is needed to record the important shadow detail within the trees. Development times depend not only on lighting conditions but also on the range of subject reflectivity.

developed to a gamma of 0.7 for a subject of average brightness range. Most of the resulting negatives should then print on normal (grade 2) paper. After some experience you will be able to determine which gamma values best suit your method of working and specific subject/lighting conditions; it is then a simple matter to determine the correct development time from the appropriate gamma/time curve.

Other measurements of film contrast

Most camera films have a long 'toe' region which gradually becomes the straight line portion of the characteristic curve. Consequently, a reasonable portion of the subject's exposure is recorded on this long sweeping toe, and the simpler gamma measurement is considered by some film manufacturers to be insufficient for use and so another measurement is needed.

Ilford supply a general guide to film contrast which they consider to give a better indication of final print tonal range than gamma values. In practice, if two different films are used to record the same subject, and they are developed to the same contrast value (eg. N+) then the two resulting negatives should print on the same grade of paper to give similar prints (apart from possible graininess/sharpness differences).

In a similar manner to gamma/time curves, you can use contrast/time curves (fig 5.7) to determine the development time for your chosen contrast value.

Contrast values take into account the long sweeping toes of D/Log E curves, and are largely derived from practical and not sensitometric tests, so they are an extremely useful guide to precise film development.

The *contrast index* (CI) system was invented by Kodak as its method of taking account of the sweeping toes of most black-and-white films. If two films are developed to the same CI value, then the two films' negatives (of the same subject) should produce identical prints on the same paper grade. In practice, this means that the same CI has produced negatives with the same density range (fig 5.8).

Contrast index is a more complex measurement than gamma and is best found by placing a CI meter over the D/Log E curve. For an average subject Kodak recommends developing its films to a CI value of 0.56, assuming use of a diffuser enlarger for printing. Like other manufacturers, Kodak publish CI/time curves (fig 5.9) for film/developer combinations, and once you have settled on a suitable CI value for your equipment you can use these graphs to determine development times.

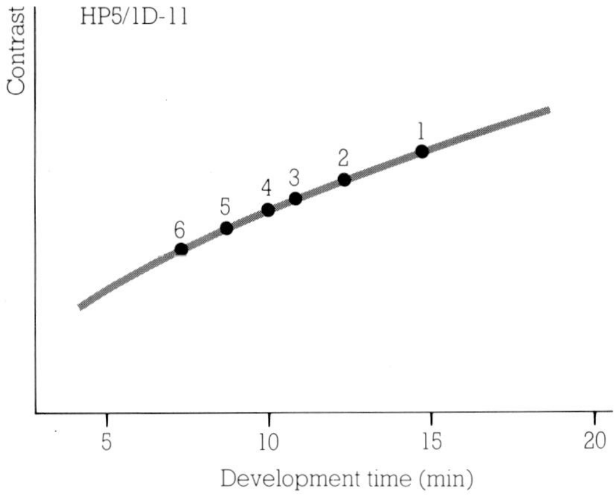

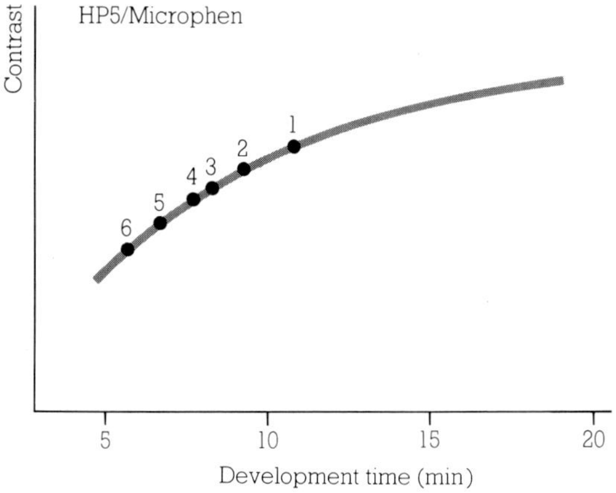

5.7 Ilford contrast curves for HP5 in ID-11 and Microphen. The numbers refer to contrasts of H+(1), High (2), H−(3), N+(4), Normal (5), N−(6). If you use a condenser enlarger (see Chapter 6) you will probably standardise your development on Normal (5) while a diffuser enlarger usually requires High (2). When the subject's brightness range is wider than normal, use the H−(3) and N−(6) values, while short brightness range subjects require development times given by contrast values of H+(1) and N+(4). Precise control values can only be found by experiment, eg. if a 10 min development time of HP5 in ID-11 is found to give 'perfect' negatives for average subjects (corresponding to point 4), the corresponding time needed for Microphen is found from point 4 on the curve, 7½ min.

The best film developer

The history of black-and-white photography is filled with inventors and their 'magic brews', with

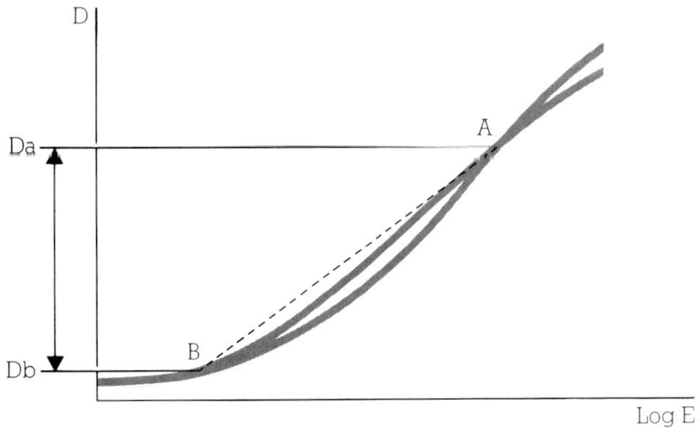

5.8 Two films developed to the same contrast index which therefore have the same negative density range (Da-Db). The prints from these two negatives will be virtually identical, but because of slightly different curve shapes there will be some subtle differences in tonal distribution.

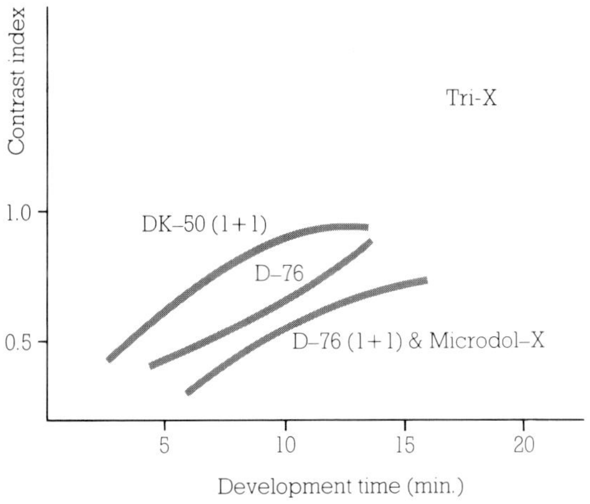

5.9 CI/time curves for Tri-X film in three different developers. Note that DK-50 is the choice if you require maximum contrast or shorter development times.

each solution able to extract maximum sharpness, low graininess and superb tonal rendition out of even the fastest films! Unfortunately, most of these whiz-kids were more interested in photographic image structure than photography.

By all means, you should try several different film/developer combinations and discover the one (or two) which suit(s) your needs. But once you have made your choice it is best to stay with it and spend your time learning how to get the best out of this combination.

It is therefore worth examining the pros and cons of the different types of black-and-white films and their developers.

Choice of film

The first decision you should make is the speed of the film. This, of course, depends mainly on the lighting conditions and the type of photographs you want to produce. When you require small apertures and/or fast shutter speeds you need a fast film, whereas static subjects and cameras on tripods usually suggest slow films.

If possible, select the right film for the job and avoid uprating or downrating a slower or faster film. Manufacturers have produced the best film they can for a given film speed–the results of using, say, an ASA 50/18 DIN (ISO = 50/18°) film and uprating it to ASA 125/22 DIN (ISO = 125/22°) are inferior to those from a genuine ASA 125 film which has been developed normally. If the results from the pushed film were superior to those of the normally developed faster film, then the manufacturers would not need to make faster films. A full explanation of the effects of changing film speed and development is given later on.

The development process

A basic understanding of what goes on during development is helpful in selecting the appropriate developer for your needs; remember, each film/developer pair has its applications and there is no one combination which is suitable for all uses and users.

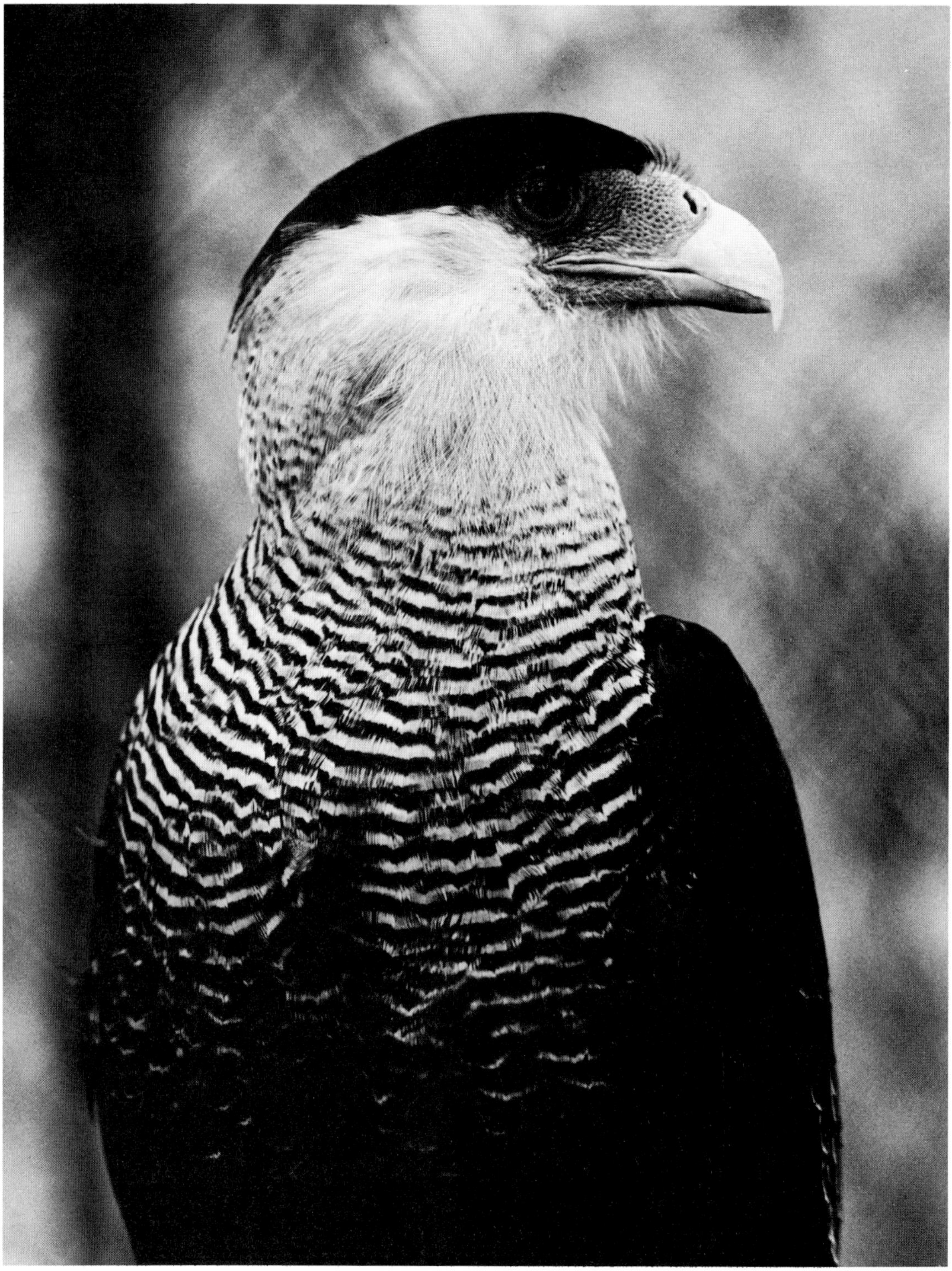

47 Because the overall lighting was very diffuse ('flat') on this overcast day, the ASA 400 film was rated at ASA 800 and developed for 50% longer than normal. Despite this push-processing, the negative needed to be printed on grade 4 paper. The increase in graininess caused by longer development times is not apparent because of the moderate degree of enlargement needed for 120 roll film.

48 The success of this photograph depends on its soft gentle mood, so the film was developed normally even though the lighting was flat. The extra quality obtained by using 120 roll film is most noticeable on delicate subjects such as this.

49 Taken from a roll of 35mm medium speed (ASA 125) film containing similar subjects with wide brightness range; it was decided to reduce development by 25 per cent from the normal time so that the full tonal range (deep shadow to delicate highlights) was recorded. To compensate for this pull-processing, the film was slightly overexposed by setting the exposure meter for ASA 80, thereby ensuring adequate shadow exposure–note the detail within the shadows of the leaf.

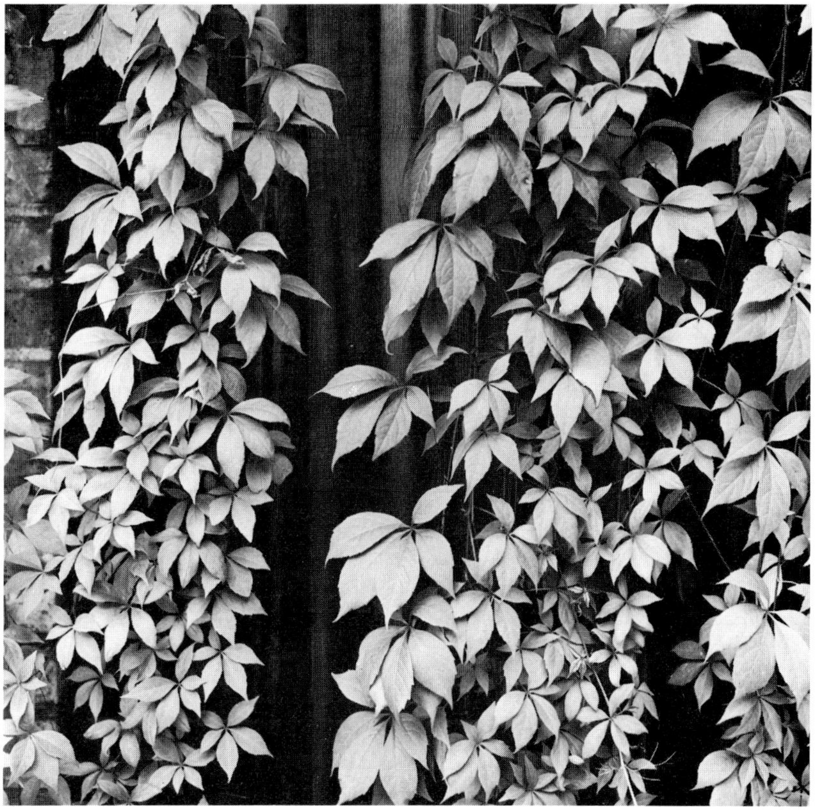

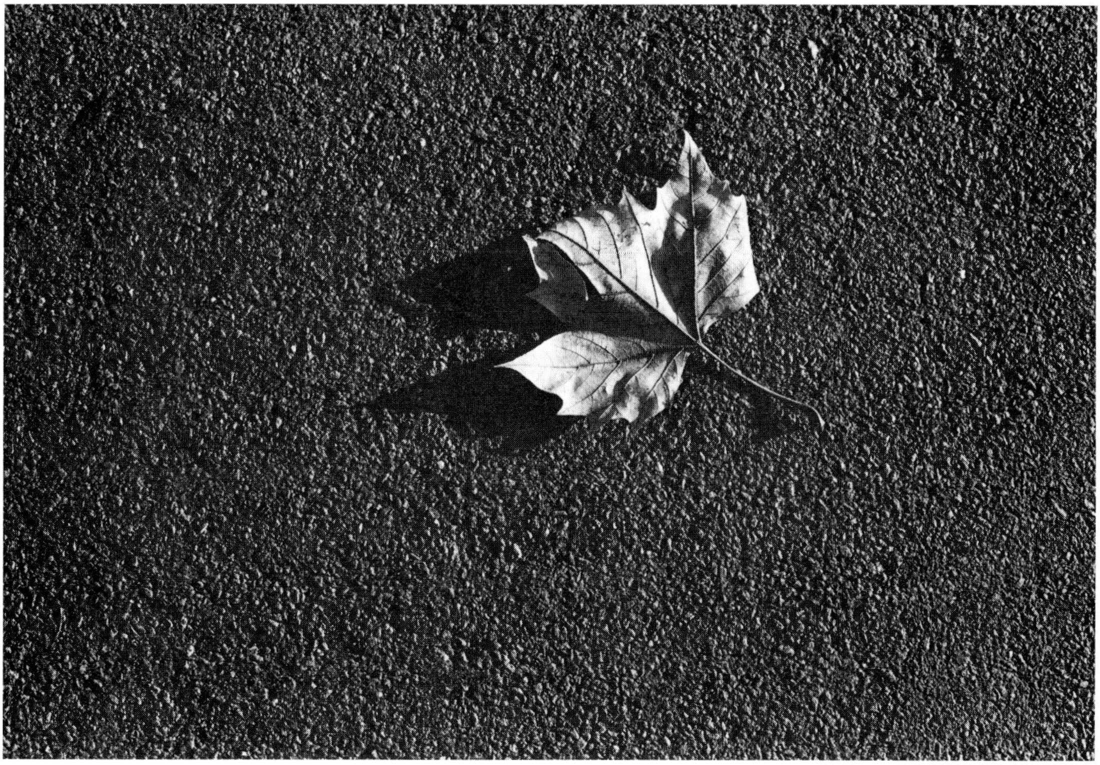

Photographic film consists of a suspension of extremely small silver halide (silver bromide and silver iodide) crystals in gelatin which is coated on to a plastic base. When the image produced by the camera lens is briefly (in most cases) allowed to strike the film 'emulsion' the number of grains exposed in each small area of the film will depend on the brightness of the scene in that image area. The subject's highlights expose most of the grains, the mid-tones cause about 50 per cent to be exposed, and the shadow areas of the image cause only a relatively few grains to be exposed. The film now has an invisible 'latent image' which is made visible by the developer.

The developer solution searches out those grains in the emulsion which have been exposed and converts them to black metallic silver. The number of developed grains is related to the amount of exposure in any given area of the film. Shadow areas of the subject appear as light parts of the negative (a few black grains surrounded by larger clear areas), mid-tones as fairly dense areas, and highlights as dark *negative* tones. Following the developer step, the stop bath simply halts the action of the developer, the fixer dissolves away all the remaining (undeveloped) silver halide crystals which, if left in the film, would go dark on exposure to light, and the final wash removes all processing chemicals to ensure a permanent stain-free negative.

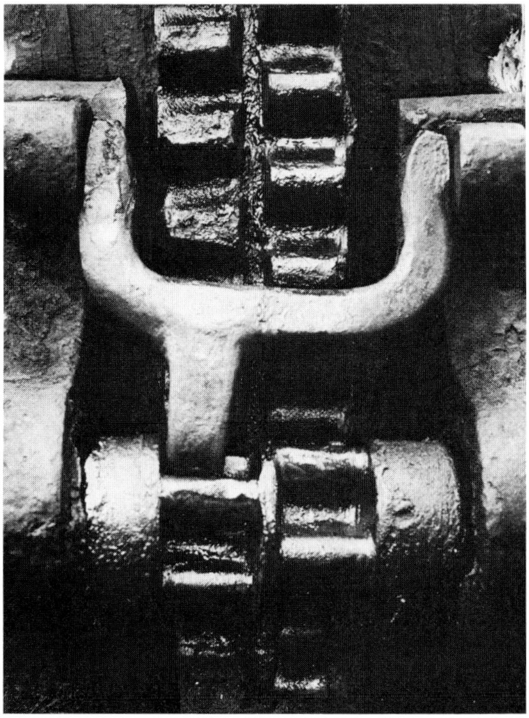

50 For most types of subject photographed in average lighting conditions, like this piece of a lock gate, general purpose developers are ideal. GP developers give fine grain coupled with full emulsion speed.

Constituents of a developer

Most black-and-white developers contain the following basic ingredients:

1 *Developing agent(s).* This chemical seeks out the exposed silver halide grains and converts them to silver. There have been many developing agents used over the years but most readily available developers now contain hydroquinone (quinol) together with metol (ie. an 'MQ') or Phenidone ('PQ').
2 *Preservative.* Substances such as sodium sulphite and potassium metabisulphite reduce the rate at which oxygen from the air attacks the developing agent, and thereby maintains the concentration (activity) of the developing agent. These chemicals are also silver halide solvents and affect the character of the developed image.
3 *Alkali (accelerator).* Most developing agents only function in an alkaline environment; the stronger the alkalinity the more active is the developer. A convenient measure of alkali strength is pH, where 14 is very alkaline and 8 is a mild alkali. The alkali is normally used in combination with a weak acid as a 'buffer' solution which keeps the pH and therefore the activity of the developer stable. The most common developer buffers are borax/boric acid (pH 8–9), sodium carbonate/sodium hydroxide (pH 10.5–12).
4 *Restrainer (antifoggant).* An ideal developing agent only converts exposed grains to silver. However, in practice all developing agents also attack some unexposed grains. To minimise this 'fogging' of the emulsion (an analogy is the 'noise' of an amplifier), chemicals such as potassium bromide or benzotriazole are used as restrainers.
5 *Solvent.* This is always water, and in most situations the use of tap water rather than distilled water does not affect the developer's performance. Some developers contain a chemical, such as Calgon (sodium hexametaphosphate), to prevent the formation of scum on the film surface.

General purpose developers

The majority of film developers are called

'general purpose' developers and they allow you to rate the film at full emulsion speed, ie. the ASA speed stated on the box. The GP developers produce negatives of fine grain and excellent sharpness and can be used on slow, medium or fast films. Many of the GP formulations have been on the market for decades and have been well proven. Examples of general purpose developers are Kodak's D–76, Ilford's ID–11, and Agfa's Refinal.

For small format (35mm, 120) films it is better to employ these developers as 'one-shot' chemicals which are used once and then discarded. The advantage of this technique is that development, and the condition of the developer, can be exactly reproduced each time.

Most GP film developers are of the MQ or PQ type and relatively low in pH, usually employing a borax/boric acid buffer (pH about 9). These 'soft working' developers minimise clumping of silver grains (ie. lower graininess) by containing a silver halide solvent (such as sodium sulphite or sodium thiocyanate) which has the effect of 'smoothing' the grains. A slight loss of very fine detail is caused by these silver halide solvents.

If you need very low graininess and are prepared to sacrifice about ½ stop loss in film speed, then it is worth considering ultra fine-grain developers such as Kodak's Microdol-X, and Ilford's Perceptol.

High definition developers

High energy developers, such as Kodak's HC–110 and Ilford's Microphen, offer improved edge contrast (acutance – see fig 5.10) and a small gain in film speed (about ½ stop) at the expense of increased graininess. This apparent increase in definition is caused by the use of low concentrations of developing agents coupled with a relatively high pH and a small amount or absence of silver halide solvents. When a high exposure area (ie. highlight) borders a low exposure area (shadow), the fresh developer from the shadow area increases the rate of development at the adjacent highlight and produces a higher density than the rest of the highlight; also the by-products (especially bromide) from the rapidly developing highlight diffuse across the boundary to the shadow area where they inhibit development and cause a consequent drop in negative density. The net result is an apparent sharpening of edge detail.

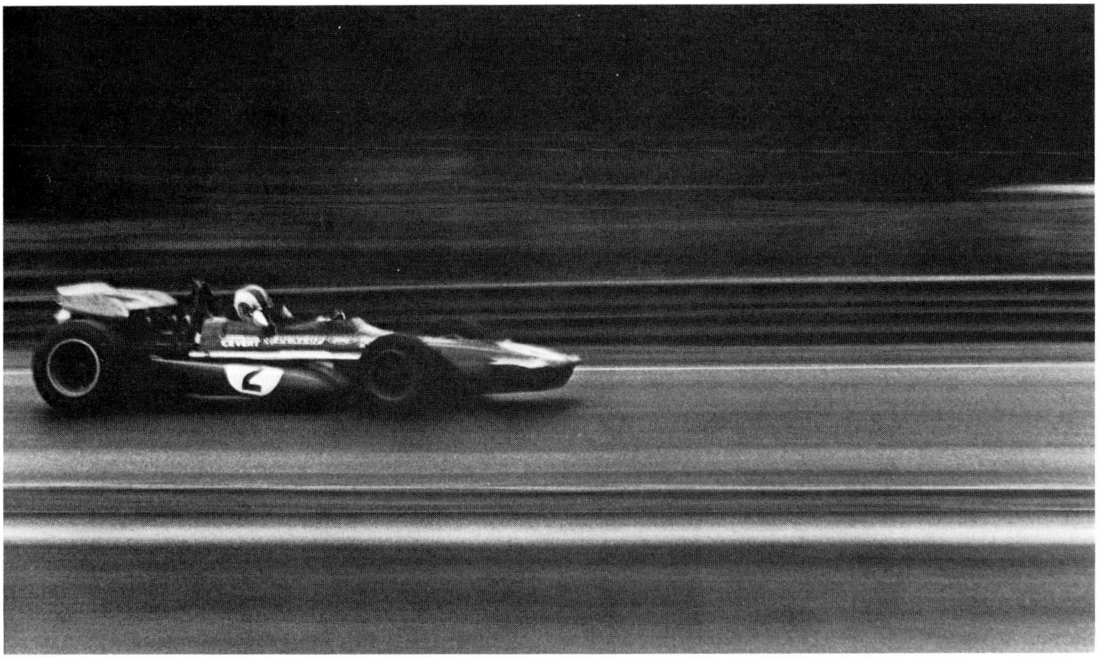

51 At this Grand Prix motor race, the use of an acutance (high definition) developer gave a useful slight increase in film speed (ASA 400 film was rated at ASA 650) without disturbing the tonal reproduction (compare push processing). The increase in graininess produced by this type of developer is only slight and does not detract from the total impact.

The amount of agitation during development can affect apparent image sharpness, as too much causes both a rapid removal of inhibiting development by-products and a fresh supply of developer to the whole of the highlight area; this will minimise any 'adjacency' effects. On the other hand, too little agitation causes uneven development of a more general kind which, in extreme cases, may cause 'bromide streaks'. This is the effect where 'streamers' of lower density are caused when the heavy 'inhibiting' bromide molecules are allowed to fall across the undisturbed film on their way to the bottom of the tank. Obviously, a compromise in agitation is needed to obtain both even development with the absence of bromide streaks and maximum acutance. For small tank processing, this usually means an agitation cycle of two inversions of the tank at one-minute intervals.

If GP fine-grain developers, such as D–76, are used diluted with water (eg. 1 + 1, 1 + 4, developer + water) there is an increase in acutance and an improvement in tonal scale. Extension of the development time is needed to counteract the lower activity of the diluted developer. The slight improvement in tonal scale is due to the 'compensating effect' whereby excessive highlight density is avoided by the use of diluted (therefore less active) developer while allowing longer time for the separating of shadow detail.

It is worthwhile experimenting with different developers and dilutions, but you should remember that the main influence on image quality rests with your choice of film. Also, the 'correct' exposure should be given to the film to obtain maximum print quality, and you should especially avoid overexposure as this causes both an in-

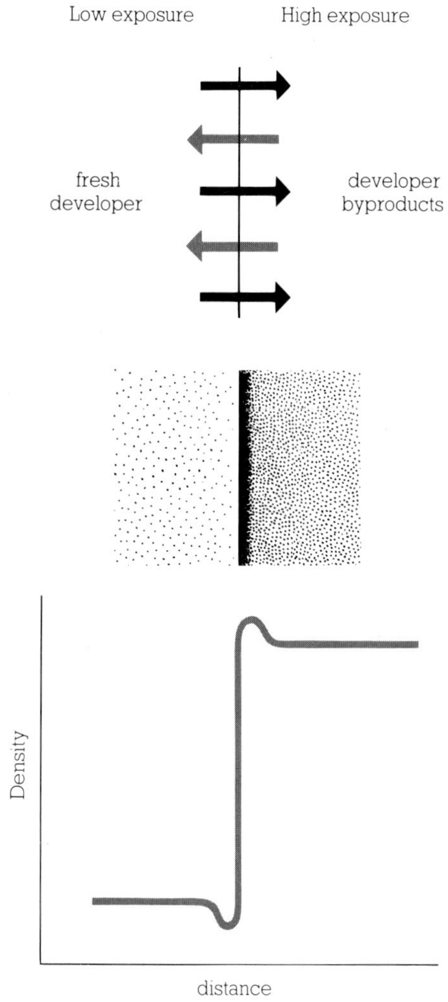

5.10 Acutance effect to increase apparent image sharpness. The flow of fresh developer from left to right across the boundary causes an increase in density at the edge, while the flow of inhibiting by-products from right to left gives a reduction in density at the other side of the boundary. The microdensitometer trace (bottom) shows the two 'ears' which give edge detail extra contrast and apparent sharpness.

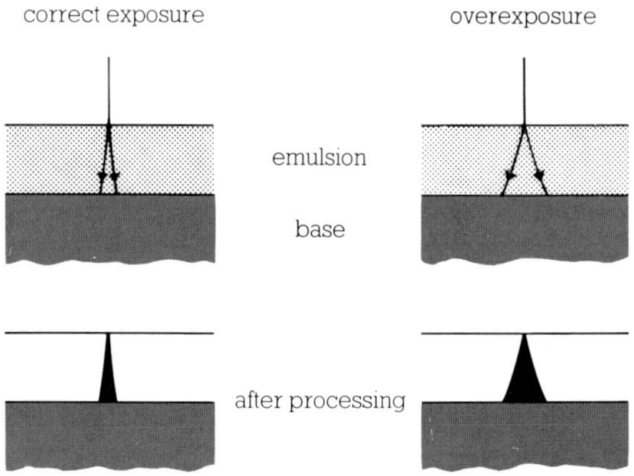

5.11 These film cross-sections show how larger amounts of light passing through an emulsion widen the spread of exposure. Consequently, overexposure causes greater spreading of light (irradiation), producing a less well-defined image.

crease in graininess and a loss of sharpness due to *irradiation*–the spreading of the image as it penetrates the emulsion (fig 5.11).

Chromogenic development

Colour film technology is used in the manufacture and processing of some black-and-white films. During processing the silver within these films is completely removed to leave an image made up entirely of dyes. Films such as Ilford XP1 and Agfa Vario-XL are basically colour negative materials and as such can be processed in standard colour negative chemicals (C41), see fig 5.12.

Ilford's XP1 gives slightly sharper results if it is processed in Ilford's XP1 chemicals (fig 5.13) rather than C41. This is due mainly to the loss of edge definition (acutance) caused by the continuous agitation of the standard C41 process and because the XP1 developer is formulated for optimum results for only the one film. For small tank processing, both Agfa Vario-XL (fig 5.14) and XP1 can be processed at any temperature between 30°C and 38°C; the lower temperatures offer much easier control and reproducibility for home processing.

If you have been using conventional black-and-white materials which develop to give a black silver image, the dye negatives at first appear very strange to print. If you intend to try these chromogenic black-and-white films, do give them a fair trial and do not be tempted to abandon them after only one film. As with any new material you must allow yourself time to 'tune' the system.

Increasing film speed by processing

When lighting levels are very low or if you wish to use high shutter speeds to 'stop' the action (for example, at indoor sporting events) you may need to increase the ASA speed of your film. In these situations you can either use a special developer, which brings out the maximum speed of a film, or you can *'push process'*.

As we have already discovered, there are a few developers which produce a slightly improved emulsion speed at the expense of graininess. Each developer's gain in speed is about half a stop, for example, HP5 film ASA 400/27 DIN (ISO = 400/27°) becomes ASA 650/29 DIN ISO = 650/29°) when developed in Microphen. If you need such a marginal speed increase, these special developers are your best choice because they do give a true increase in film speed (cf. push processing) as shown by an increase in shadow densities of the negative.

Restating what was said about choice of film (page 64), there is no advantage in using slow or medium-speed films and uprating them, because

5.12 Process C-41

	38°C
Developer	3 min 15 sec
Bleach	6 min 30 sec
Wash	3 min 15 sec
Fixer	6 min 30 sec
Wash	3 min 15 sec
Stabiliser	1 min 30 sec

5.13 Process XP1

(Times in min.)	30°C	33°C	35°C	38°C
Developer	9	7	6	5
Bleach fix	9	7	6	5
Wash	5	5	4	3
*Final rinse	1	1	1	1

* Normal wetting agent eg. Ilfotol (1 + 400)
Agitation of four tank inversions/min.

5.14 Agfacolor Process F
(Small tanks)

Times (min.)	30°C	33°C	35°C	38°C
Developer	7½	6	5	3¼
Bleach fix	11	10	9	8
Wash	4	3½	3½	3
Final bath	1	1	¾	¾

Agitation is continuous for the first min; then two inversions per 30 sec.

better results are obtained by use of faster films in normal developers. The only time when push processing of a slow film makes sense is in an emergency situation, for example, when you need a film of ASA 400/27 DIN (ISO = 400/27°) but you are only carrying ASA 125/22 DIN (ISO = 125/22°) film.

Push processing

There are many half-truths concerning the technique of push processing; the main one is that you can achieve almost any speed from a film simply by developing it for longer and longer times. This is simply not true. However, push processing is a useful *emergency* procedure which can help to produce photographs in what otherwise might be considered hopeless situations.

In fact, the technicalities of push processing have already been described in this chapter during our examination of what happens to an overdeveloped film. If you refer to fig 5.1, you will notice that the slope of the D/Log E curve increases with longer development and there is also a *slight* increase in threshold speed. This means that as development times lengthen there is, at most, a half stop gain in emulsion speed, ie. ASA 400 becomes ASA 600. This small gain is clearly not sufficient to deal with many situations.

Underexposure and overdevelopment

Film speeds are calculated on the *minimum* exposure needed to record a complete range of image tones. If exposure is reduced below this minimum, the details in the shadow areas of the subject start to 'disappear', as they are not recorded by the film. The greater the degree of underexposure, the greater the loss of shadow detail (fig 5.15), and extreme underexposure (say, three stops) will also cause loss of mid-tone detail.

Underexposing the subject by two stops is equivalent to using a film speed setting of ASA 1600/33 DIN (ISO = 1600/33°) for a normally ASA 400/27 DIN (ISO = 400/27°) film. If these ASA 1600 exposures are processed normally, the negatives will lack shadow detail and almost certainly have a very low density range. Even if they are printed on grade 5 paper, the photographs are likely to look flat and grey. However, overdevelopment (push processing) of the underexposed film will increase the negative's density range (fig 5.15), and this means that good prints (minus shadow detail) can be obtained by printing on intermediate paper grades. In effect, you are recording the subject's mid-tones and highlights further down the characteristic curve and then 'stretching' them to ensure that you have a negative of sufficient density range for printing. Overdevelopment also produces an increase in graininess.

To sum up, push processing means a loss of shadow detail and increased graininess but allows you to take photographs in virtually impossible lighting conditions.

When to push process?

Push processing of film is suitable when the subject brightness range is average or low, because the longer development times increase contrast, or when the subject's highlights are the main element of the picture. But if shadow detail is important, push processing is highly unsuitable and you are advised to use ultra-fast films such as Kodak's recording film 2475 (35mm) or Royal-X pan (120 size and sheet) which can be rated between ASA 1000/31 DIN (ISO = 1000/31°) and ASA 3000/36 DIN (ISO = 3000/36°).

When photographing high contrast subjects, such as musicians at work under spotlights, it is best to avoid push processing because the contrast then increases to unprintable levels. Your final prints will probably resemble line images, containing only blacks and whites with no mid-tones. Again, the best solution is to use ultra-fast films.

Pull processing

The technique of overexposing film (ie. downrating the film speed) and then compensating by reducing development time is known as 'pull processing'. The principles of pull processing have already been explained on page 68 where subjects of wide brightness range are discussed.

As we have already seen, the only occasions on which pull processing should be applied are to ensure that the film records the subject's complete tonal scale when considerable differences

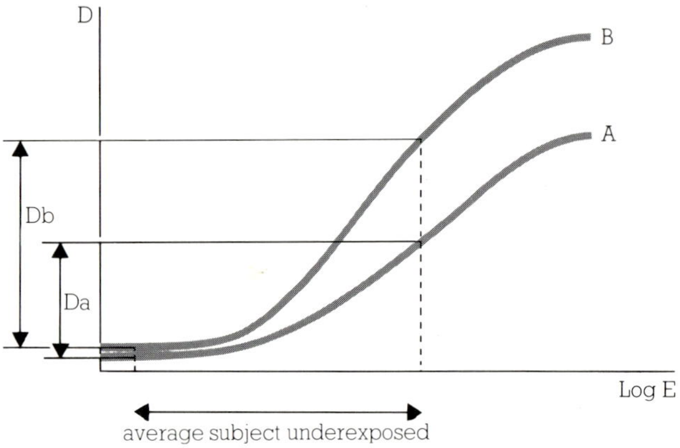

5.15 Underexposure and normal development (curve 4) gives loss of shadow detail and a short negative density range (Da), likely to produce very inferior prints. As curve B shows, increasing development ('push processing') of the same underexposed subject gives a density range (Db) which is very printable, but does not regain any lost shadow detail.

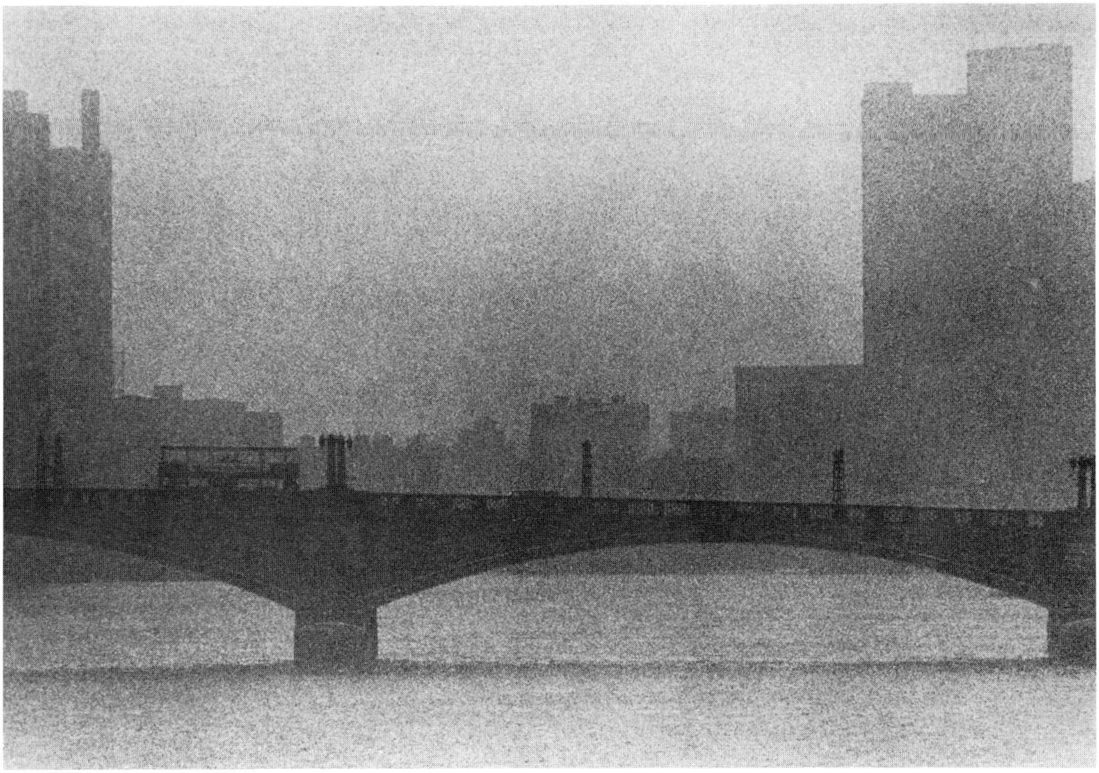

52 The combination of fast film, extended film development to increase negative contrast, a high degree of enlargement, and printing on grade 4 paper produced this grainy photograph heightening the mood of this city bridge shrouded in fog.

in brightness exist between shadows and highlights (eg. brightly lit snowscenes) and as an emergency procedure when a too-low ASA setting has been used. However, even in the latter situation, provided that overexposure is by no more than two stops, it is still probably preferable to give standard film development to subjects of average brightness range–the exposure latitude of the film should be able to accommodate two stops of overexposure.

Push processing XP1

The standard development time for XP1 film is designed to give a black-and-white negative of a subject of average brightness range (about 1:128) which prints satisfactorily on grade 2 paper. In contrast to conventional silver negatives, where diffuse-source enlargers require about one grade of paper harder to print a negative than if printed on a condenser enlarger, the dye image of XP1 can be printed on both types of enlarger using the same grade of paper.

When photographing subjects of short brightness range or when a higher speed index than ASA 400/27 DIN (ISO = 400/27°) is required the development time using XP1 chemicals should be increased to 6½ min. for ASA 800/30 DIN (ISO = 800/30°) or 7½ min. for ASA 1600/33 DIN (ISO = 1600/33°) at the process temperature of 38°C; the bleach-fix time should not be altered. The corresponding times for C41 push processing at 38°C are 4¼ min. (ASA 800), 5 min. (ASA 1600). As with all push processing there is some sacrifice of shadow detail.

Processing for long keeping

It is important to process films very carefully if they are to survive for a long time, as it is always possible to make new prints provided that the original negatives are in good order and have not faded or stained. Fortunately, the procedures for archival processing of film are quite straightforward.

An important precaution is to ensure that all your processing chemicals are fresh or, at least, well-kept. Developers should be bought in quantities sufficient to last for no more than six months and should be stored in dark, filled bottles. Stop baths and fixers should be discarded well before they are exhausted; it is a false economy to overwork solutions.

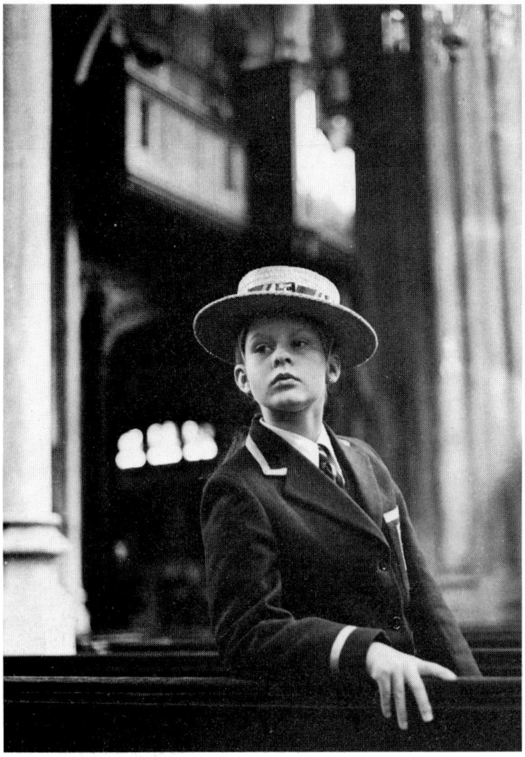

53 Although the low levels of light found in this cathedral might at first suggest rating the film at higher speed than normal, this would increase negative contrast, destroying the mood. Instead, the film has been exposed and developed normally and a wide aperture has been used to ensure adequate exposure.

54 The slow shutter speed (about 1/8 sec) combined with a panning camera to dramatise these commuters, reduces the overall contrast of the subject–light areas 'wipe' across dark areas and vice versa. To restore normal negative contrast the film was overdeveloped by 50 per cent.

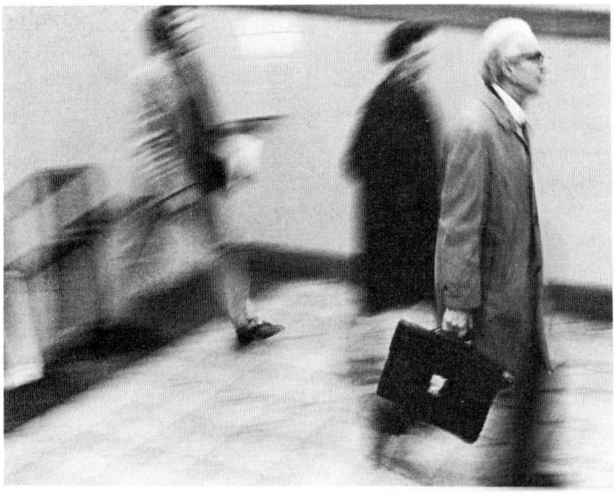

A quick check on the activity of the fixer is to take a small piece of unexposed film and, in the light, 'dunk' it in the solution. Time how long it takes for the film to 'clear' ie. lose its milkiness. If this is longer than half the manufacturer's recommended total fixing time then discard the fixer. As a guide, most rapid fixers should clear the film in about two minutes, while standard fixers should take about four minutes. A more precise method of testing for fixer exhaustion is to use silver estimating test papers which are dunked in the solution and their colour is compared to a standard measuring scale. These papers are available from some film manufacturers or from specialist suppliers.

If your films are not fully clear and appear slightly milky, even after they have been stored in negative files for a while, simply re-fix them in a fresh solution of fixer and wash normally. In most cases, the negatives will become clearer and at the least will now be prevented from deteriorating further.

The permanence of black-and-white negatives is mainly determined by the efficiency of, and time spent in, the final wash. For most purposes, it is recommended that films should be washed in running water (18–24°C) for at least 30 minutes. For archival permanence you should use a hypo clearing agent, followed by a 15 minute wash.

Storage and care of negatives

After washing, negatives should be soaked in a wetting agent for about one minute and then hung up to dry in a dust-free atmosphere. If possible, it is better to allow the films to dry slowly overnight than to subject them to the hazards of heated cabinets with blower fans, as there is always a chance that the films will be overheated, causing blistering of the emulsion, and that dust may be blown on to the damp emulsion surface.

Once dry, negatives can be stored in loose-leaf negative files and kept in a dry, cool and dust-free area. For convenience, it is best to cut 35mm films into strips of six frames, and 120 film into strips of about three or four frames each.

If you do not take care of your negatives the resulting prints will show blemishes such as white marks caused by dust or fingerprints, or black or white lines due to scratching. If your negatives are not clean, carefully rewash them and then, very gently wipe both sides of the film before hanging them up to dry. (One method of doing this is to run

55 Negatives and prints that are likely to be sought by fine art collectors must be processed to archival standards. This superb picture has been purchased for several collections.

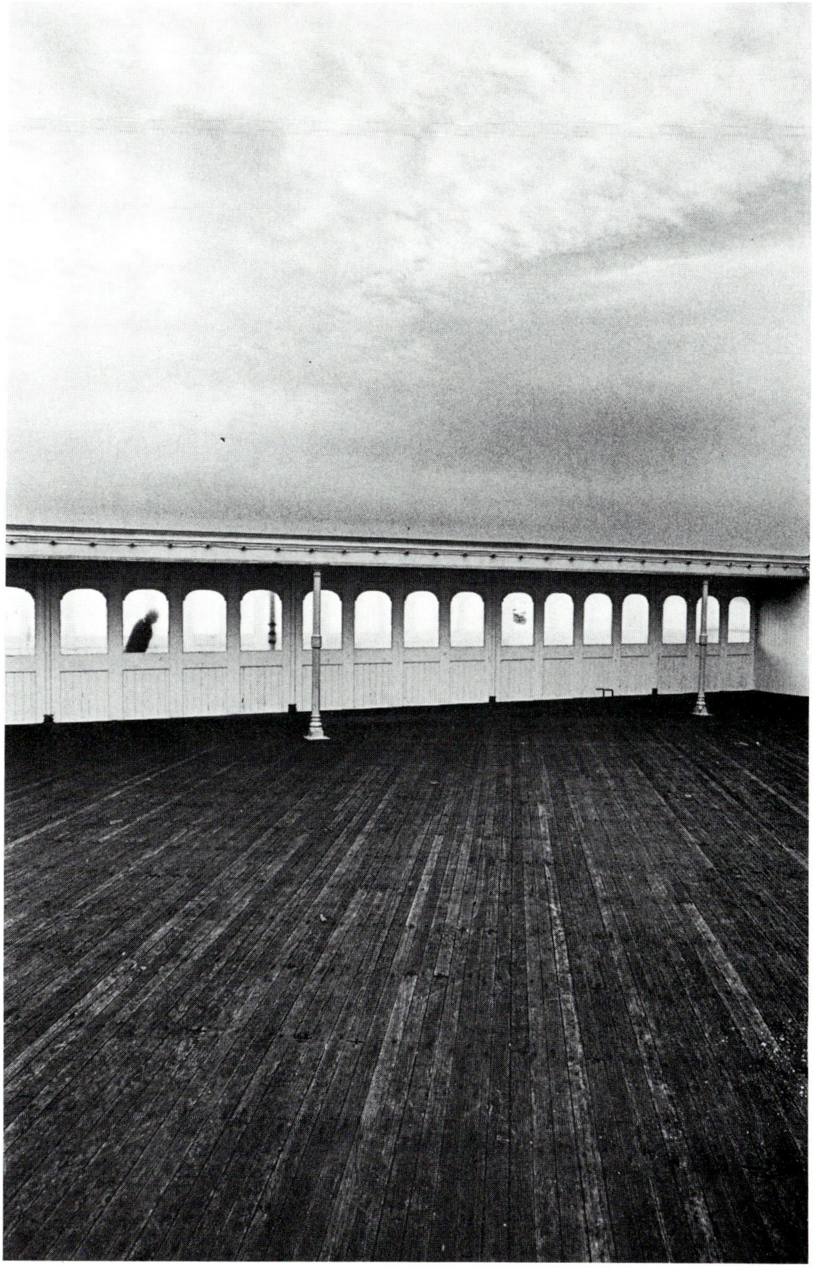

the film gently through the fleshy parts of two *clean* fingers.) Rubber squeegees, tongs, or chamois leathers are not recommended because of the danger of collected grit which would, of course, scratch the film. For stubborn marks, you can soak the negatives in a dilute solution (about 5 per cent) of sodium carbonate for about 10 min. before the running wash. Very badly scratched negatives should be printed using a diffuse enlarger which will minimise marks on the print. As a last resort, you can buy special oils to coat on to the negative before printing (motion picture laboratories which print old movies are probably the best source of such viscous liquids). As you have no doubt gathered, prevention is better than cure!

You should number all your negatives and cross reference them to contact prints, so that retrieval is quick and easy. It is also worthwhile writing your negative identification number in soft pencil on the back of the photographic paper before it is exposed and processed.

6 MAKING THE FINE PRINT

Printing is the final photographic stage, in which all your hard work should come to fruition. The success or failure of your photograph rests largely on your ability to produce a fine print which brings out all the qualities of the original subject and your visualisation of it.

When working in the darkroom, there is often a great temptation to print as many negatives as possible in one session, but this should be avoided at all costs. Instead, try to make each print as near perfect as you can, and do not accept second best.

This chapter concentrates on the production of high quality 'straight' prints, while Chapter 8 will deal with darkroom methods of manipulating the image.

The darkroom

Although it is not the intention of this book to cover basic techniques, it is nevertheless worthwhile discussing aspects of the darkroom which are important to the more advanced photographer. It is important to make your darkroom a pleasant and relaxing place in which to work.

The ideal darkroom is purpose-built, with facilities such as separate wet and dry benches, a large sink with hot and cold water, ample power points, pull-cord operated safelights and roomlights, good ventilation, a light trap entrance, handy storage for chemicals and equipment, etc. If you are fortunate enough to possess such facilities, you should consult the photographic manufacturers' literature on the design of a professional darkroom; a few hours reading could save you some headaches and help you to build the best darkroom given your available space.

At all costs, try to avoid using a bathroom as a makeshift darkroom. Not only is it unsafe for electrical equipment but it is also extremely inconvenient for the rest of the family. It is far better to use part of a bedroom where you can leave your equipment set up and carry the necessary solutions to the room each time before you start. If you design an efficient, quickly installed blackout system, you could be ready for printing within about twenty minutes.

Enlargers

There are many excellent enlargers on the market and you should buy the best you can afford. Although many refinements have been added, the basic design of enlargers has not changed for years. So a good enlarger should last you for decades and prove a wise investment. The main points to consider when you buy your enlarger are that it should be of solid stable construction, with easily operated controls (eg. baseboard controls for print size and focus are a superb facility, if available), a well-designed film carrier with options for glass and glassless operation, a reasonable-sized baseboard, and the ability to produce, for example, a 40 x 30cm. (16 x 12in.) print from the whole negative without having to reverse the head. It is often worthwhile searching the classified advertisements of professional and amateur photographic magazines for a bargain second-hand enlarger.

The basic types of enlarger illumination are condenser ('point source') and diffuse; fig 6.1 illustrates the optics of the two systems. The *con-*

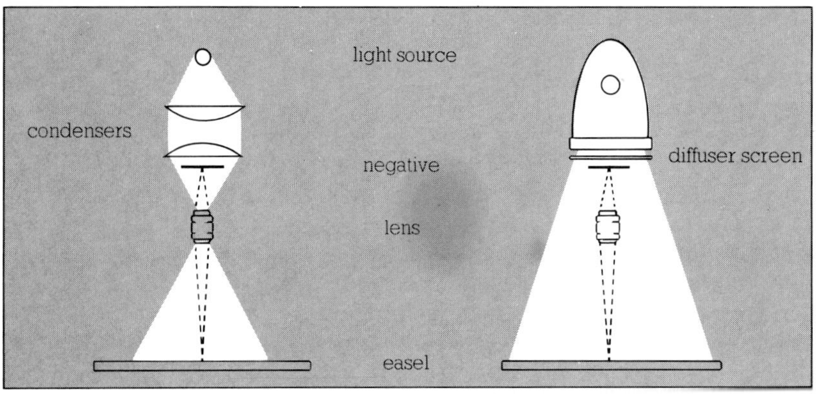

6.1 The two basic types of enlarger. The condenser enlarger (left) has a compact light source which is focused by condensers on to the enlarging lens; the system must be kept scrupulously clean to avoid white dust marks appearing on the print. The diffuser enlarger (right) consists basically of a diffuse light source to illuminate the negative and is much more tolerant of dust, etc. In practice, most enlargers are part condenser and part diffuser (see fig 6.2).

denser enlarger consists basically of one or more lenses (condensers) which control the light from the lamp so that its rays are directed towards the enlarger lens–there is a beam of light aimed through the negative which comes to 'focus' within the enlarger lens. Compared with the diffuse type, the condenser enlarger gives maximum contrast and slightly greater tone separation, especially in the highlights but shows up any marks or scratches on the negative. The true 'point source' enlarger, which has a clear lamp with a small well defined filament, is fiddly to use because the position of the light source has to be re-adjusted for every enlargement of a different size.

Diffuse enlargers, which include most colour enlargers, consist simply of a light source which is well diffused, either by having a diffusing screen just above the negative or by using a broad light source such as a cathode tube. They produce a lower contrast image and make less efficient use of enlarger illumination than condenser types and are ideal if the negative is scratched or if any re-touching has been done on the film. Because of their less efficient use of light they are more suitable for lower degrees of magnification, and are therefore best suited to large formats such as 5 x 4in. sheet film.

In practice, many enlargers use a mix of both systems with a pair of condenser lenses and an opal light bulb as the light source (fig 6.2). This compromise gives reasonably efficient use of light, moderate contrast, no need to adjust the position of the light source once it is set up, and some tolerance to marked negatives.

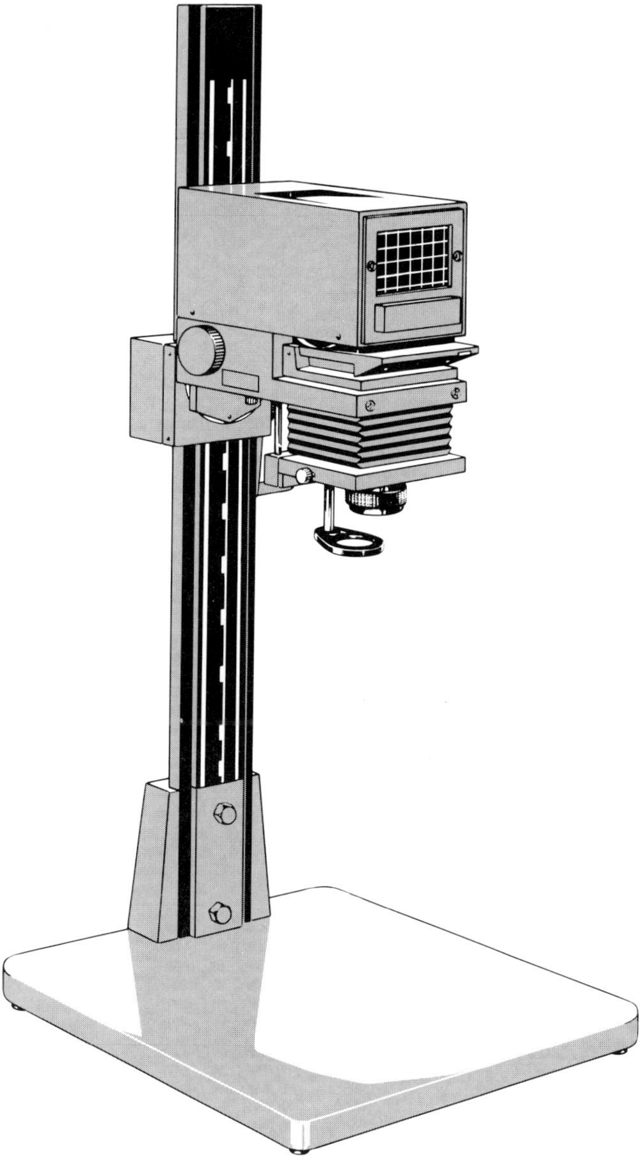

6.2 An example of a modern diffuser-condenser enlarger. This particular design uses an opal (diffuse) bulb and a 45° mirror to reflect the light through a sealed double condenser. This 'folded' light path helps to make the enlarger more compact.

Colour enlargers for black-and-white

Most colour enlargers have a diffuse illumination system which produces excellent results with the dye images of colour films; most colour papers are, in fact, designed for use with low-contrast enlarger light sources. Therefore, if you use a colour enlarger for black-and-white work, it is important to develop your negatives to a fairly high contrast (CI = 0.56, gamma = 0.70) to compensate for the diffuse light source.

Chromogenic black-and-white films when processed in a standard commercial C-41 solution are developed to standard non-variable contrast which is ideal for printing the average subject on grade 2 paper. Very low contrast subjects may print unsatisfactorily, even on grade 5 paper. The best solution is to ask the laboratory to push process your film (if they will) or to do your own processing and control the negative contrast precisely as you want (see page 81).

The colour heads of many enlargers can be removed and replaced with a condenser type black-and-white head and for most monochrome photography, especially for 35mm and 120 users, this is the best approach. Colour heads can be used with the variable contrast papers (eg. Multigrade, Polycontrast), see page 90.

Enlarger lenses

To spend a large sum of money on good quality camera equipment and lenses and then to economise by purchasing a cheap enlarging lens, does not make sense. To extract all the tonal quality and definition from your negatives you should only fit the best lenses to your enlarger; even the most costly enlarging lenses are relatively cheap. High quality lenses really show their worth when they are used near, or at, full aperture, as often happens when large scale enlargements are made.

A top quality enlarging lens produces a sharp image across the entire negative area and is virtually free of harmful faults such as chromatic aberration (different colours focusing in different planes), and does not distort the image (eg. with pincushion or barrel distortion). They are also free of lens flare and therefore do not soften image contrast, which would be most noticeable as a flattening of shadow detail in the print.

Keep dust away from your enlarger when it is not being used; a simple plastic bag over the enlarger will suffice. At the same time, you should remove the lens from the enlarger and store it in the dust free container in which it is usually supplied.

Enlarging aids

A few extra accessories are very worthwhile. Top of this list must be an enlarger timer, which ensures that you get accurate, repeatable exposures. It is also useful when printing times are short (less than 10 sec.). The timer should have an operating range of 1–60 sec, and give a clearly visible indication of the time that has elapsed or remains as the exposure takes place (this is particularly important when burning in or dodging). A useful extra accessory for your timer is a foot control, which allows you to start the exposure while keeping your hands free for shading. And, at least one company (Paterson) makes a 'bleeper' which gives either a bleep at every second or flashes a small red light; this is very convenient if you prefer to count the exposure, and it means that you can concentrate on the baseboard image throughout the exposure, making it easier to carry out dodging or burning in.

A simple but almost essential extra is a focusing aid, which is especially helpful for making large scale enlargements or when negatives are dense, as might be the case with a sabattier image (page 134). It not only only ensures accurate focusing but takes away some of the eye strain associated with concentrating on a projected image.

At this point, it is worth mentioning enlarging easels. It really is good sense to buy the best easel you can afford because in time it will probably repay the extra cost by avoiding wasted sheets of paper and frustration caused by easel movement or misaligned insertion of paper. Another advantage of using a good easel is its ability to produce wide print borders (up to about 7cm.). For maximum use of paper area, however, you might consider buying an easel which gives borderless prints.

Choice of papers

Over the years, the range of readily-available photographic papers has been depleted, due to manufacturers' 'rationalisation'. But to be fair, some manufacturers have gone to great lengths to ensure that a few 'fine' papers remain.

The two main types of black-and-white paper now on the market are the conventional fibre-based type and RC (resin coated) papers. The conventional papers (fig 6.3) consist of a paper fibre base overcoated with a thin gelatin layer containing baryta (barium sulphate) on to which the photographic emulsion is coated. The baryta serves both to prepare a flat bed for the emulsion to sit on and to improve the reflectivity (whiteness) of the print; most papers also incorporate chemicals (fluorescers) in this layer to give extra whiteness by converting UV energy into visible light (usually blue). RC papers, or PE as used by some manufacturers, have both sides of the paper base coated with polyethylene which makes the base waterproof; the emulsion is coated on the polyethylene. Both types of paper are supercoated with a thin gelatin layer for protection against physical damage (scuffs, etc.) to the print surface.

Over the years there has been many a heated debate on the relative merits of RC and conventional fibre-based papers but, unfortunately, much of the argument has been based on emotional 'feelings' rather than practical facts. The main differences between the two types of paper are:

1 RC papers are quicker to process because they are 'waterproof' and the processing chemicals do not penetrate the paper fibres. The main saving of time is in washing (about 4 min. compared with the 60min needed for double-weight fibre-based papers, although the use of washing aids does reduce this time to about 20 min.)

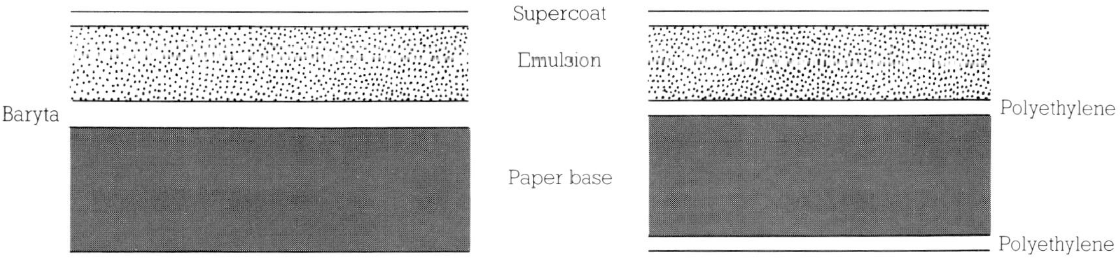

6.3 Cross-sections of conventional fibre-based (left) and resin-coated papers. The polyethylene layers act as a waterproof barrier and prevent chemicals from soaking the paper base, considerably reducing washing times. Many RC papers also incorporate developing agents in their emulsion layer to promote rapid development.

2 The degree of development is more easily controlled with fibre-based papers because the development rate is slower (on average, two minutes compared with one minute for RC papers). RC papers are principally designed for machine processing and their emulsions incorporate developing agents to facilitate rapid development.
3 RC papers can be dried rapidly, either with a hair dryer or a specially designed dryer which blows hot air across both sides of the paper. When dry they remain perfectly flat. For archival purposes, fibre-based papers need to be dried on racks or by sandwiching between special photographic blotters. Once dry, they are difficult to keep flat unless they are mounted on card. For non-archival purposes, fibre-based prints can be dried on heated flat bed or rotary dryers.
4 The tonal quality obtainable with fibre-based papers, especially in shadow gradation, is considered by some to be better than reproduction with RC papers but this is a matter of opinion. Manufacturers state that any density above 1.8 (some papers give a D max of about 2.2) is not readily detected unless the print is specially lit by spotlight–this is usually the situation with exhibitions. Do not listen to other people's opinions about what print quality is obtainable from different papers. Instead, try them out for yourself using your best negatives.
5 If exhibited for long periods of time in moderate daylight, the surface of RC prints may start to crack. This is due to the breakdown of the polyethlene layers when exposed to UV, highish temperatures, and relative high humidity. The most recent RC papers are designed to withstand these conditions to a much greater degree. However, where archival permanence is required, conventional fibre-based papers are the only possible choice at present.
6 Conventional fibre-based papers are easier to retouch than RC prints, although if your negative is kept in first class condition the need for retouching should be minimal.

From these facts, it is easy to see that if you require the ultimate in quality and archival permanence, and are prepared to put up with the many processing and drying inconveniences associated with conventional fibre-based papers, then they are the best choice. On the other hand, if you need rapid processing and drying, and flat prints without the trouble of mounting on card, RC prints are the answer. If you intend to mount an exhibition, to sell your photographs to 'print collectors', or leave them to posterity, you must select conventional papers. When photographs are to be kept for relatively short periods (say several years), such as with photographs to be reproduced in magazines, newspapers and books, RC prints have all the advantages.

Availability of papers

Photographic papers are usually classified according to the following:
Emulsion type. This label indicates the overall characteristics (tonal reproduction, image colour) of the paper. Some examples are Ilfobrom Galerie, Ilfospeed, Kodak Polycontrast (page 90), Kodabrome, Agfa Brovira-Speed, Agfa Portriga-Rapid.
Contrast grade. Numbers run from 0 to 5, which indicates the contrast of the paper (5 is max).
Paper weight. This signifies the thickness of the paper base. Conventional papers are usually available as single weight (SW) or the thicker double weight (DW); RC papers are only available as medium weight, ie. a thickness intermediate between SW and DW.
Paper surface. This describes the surface texture of the finished print. Some examples are glossy,

pearl and matt. The available maximum black (D max) of a print is largely determined by the paper surface (fig 6.4), with glossy surfaces yielding the highest densities and therefore the widest possible tonal range and matt surfaces giving the shortest tonal scale.

The number of permutations of these variables is enormous and it is hardly surprising that manufacturers are unable to offer all possible combinations. You must consult each manufacturer's current catalogue to discover which papers are offered in which variations of grade, weight, surface and size. Also, availability may differ from one country to the next, and this is particularly the case with Kodak papers.

Variable contrast papers

There are a few photographic papers which have variable contrast, ie. with which it is possible to use the same sheet of paper at different contrast grades. The different paper grades are obtained by changing the colour of the enlarger's light source, either by the use of filters or by fitting a special head to the enlarger. It is best to place the filters in the filter drawer, where they are outside the enlarger's optical system. However, if they are placed below the enlarging lens the filters must be kept very clean; any dirt or flaws could cause image deterioration.

The sets of filters designed for paper made by different manufacturers are not interchangeable (see below).

Papers such as Ilford's Multigrade and Kodak's Polycontrast (available in the USA) offer all the advantages of RC papers and the extra convenience and cost saving of only one box of paper to store for all your negatives. It is also possible to use half grades of paper, eg. grade 2½, and to print a negative using different printing grades in different parts of the image (page 102). Their main disadvantage is that they often need long exposure times when the higher number (grade) filters are used because of the great light absorption of these filters.

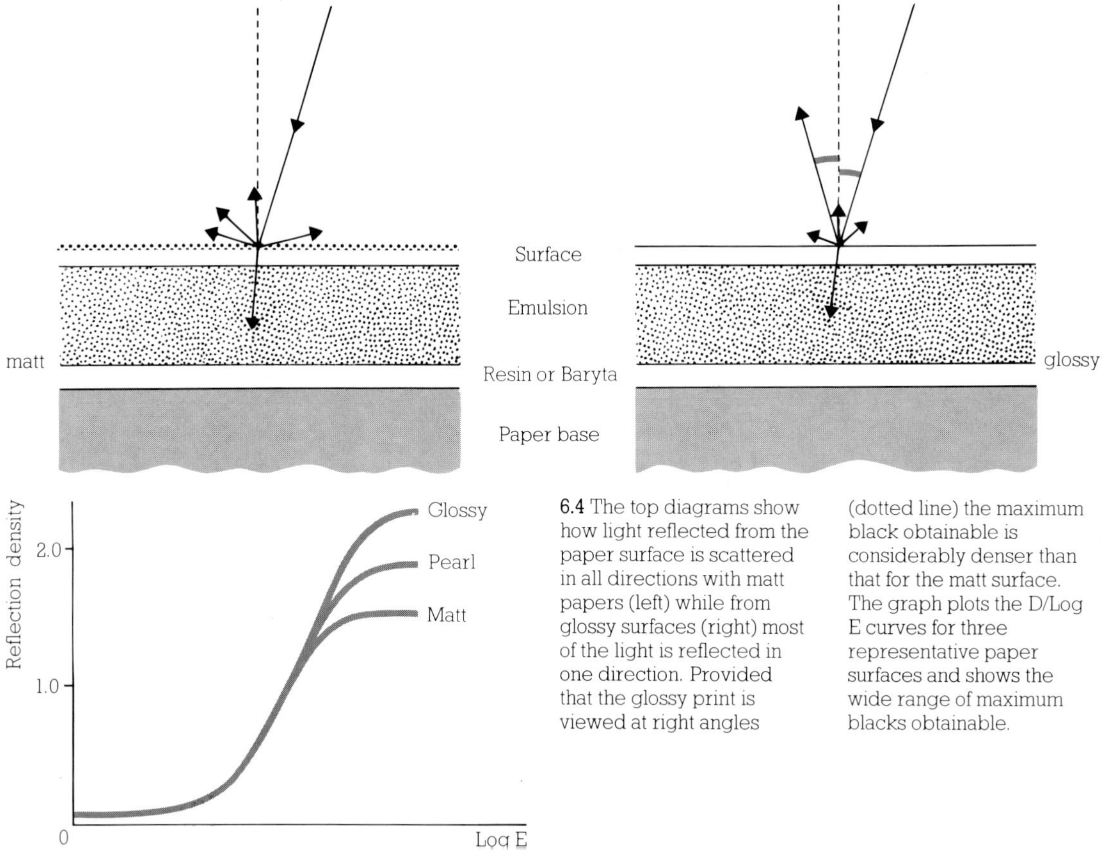

6.4 The top diagrams show how light reflected from the paper surface is scattered in all directions with matt papers (left) while from glossy surfaces (right) most of the light is reflected in one direction. Provided that the glossy print is viewed at right angles (dotted line) the maximum black obtainable is considerably denser than that for the matt surface. The graph plots the D/Log E curves for three representative paper surfaces and shows the wide range of maximum blacks obtainable.

56 This photograph was extremely difficult to print and required many areas to be dodged or burnt in; in particular, a face has been blacked-out from the bottom left corner, using a small penlight torch! Making your darkroom a pleasant and convenient place to work in may not sound like a top priority, but it is, and especially when you are working on a difficult print like this, if you are to be able to concentrate fully on what you are doing.

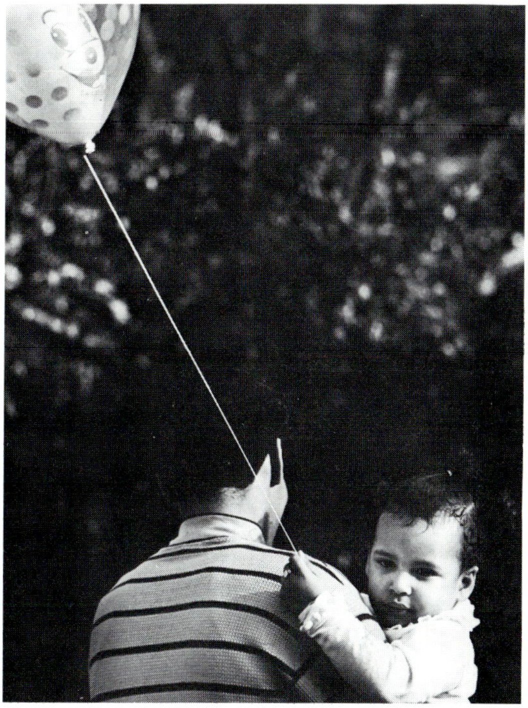

Ilford Multigrade paper

Multigrade is an RC paper available in glossy and pearl surfaces. It is used with a set of eleven filters to give a paper grade range of 0–5 with filter 0 producing the softest image and filter 5 the hardest (fig 6.5). Using no filter gives contrast equivalent to a slightly soft grade 2 paper.

The paper is a mixture of two emulsions, a higher contrast blue-sensitive emulsion and a lower contrast green (+ blue)-sensitive one. Therefore, if only green light is allowed to strike the paper, a low contrast image is obtained and, in practice, this is achieved by the use of a series of

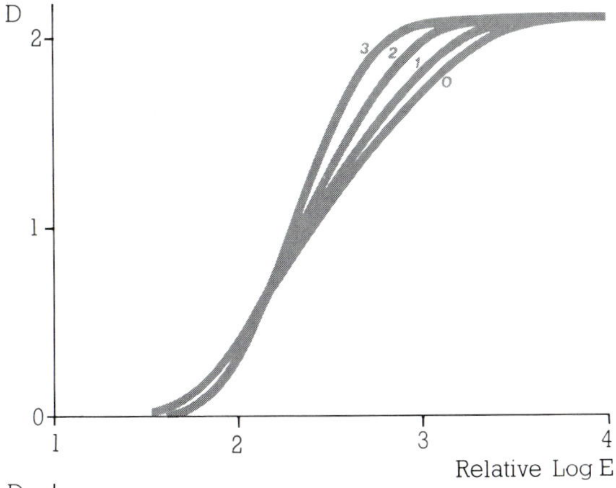

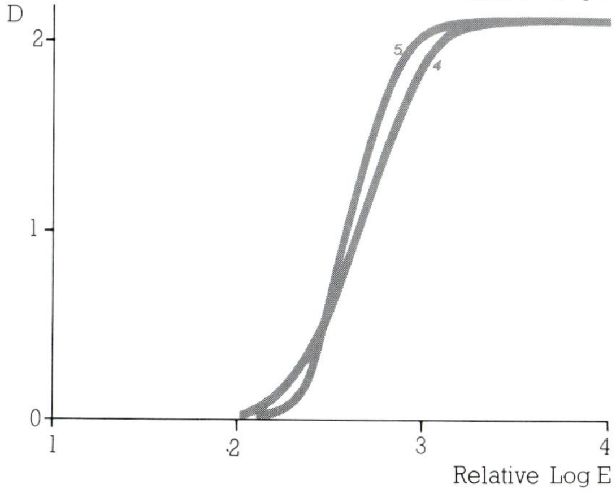

6.5 Characteristic curves for Multigrade II paper. The graph, top, shows the contrasts obtained when using filters 0–3 (for clarity, the intermediate half-grades have been omitted). Notice how the curves overlap at a density of about 0.6, this being a suitable value to judge paper speed. Thus, the filters 0–3½ produce the same effective film speed, and the same printing exposure time therefore gives 'matching' prints (except for contrast). The graph, bottom, indicates that filters 4–5 give a constant paper speed which is one stop (0.3 Log E to the right) slower than 0–3½. They require double the exposure time of the lower contrast filters.

6.6 Suggested colour head settings when using Multigrade paper

	Durst colour heads		DeVere colour heads	
Paper grade	Filter	Exposure factor	Filter	Exposure factor
0	110Y	1.8	170Y	2.3
½	90Y	1.6	150Y	2.1
1	70Y	1.5	115Y	1.8
1½	30Y	1.3	85Y	1.5
2	0	1	0	1
2½	30M	1.3	20M	1.1
3	45M	1.4	70M	1.4
3½	55M	1.5	90M	1.7
4	95M	2.0	120M	2.0
4½	130M	2.3	200M	2.8

Grade 5 is unobtainable with most colour heads

yellow filters to absorb blue light. Filter 0 is strongly yellow, filter 1 slightly less yellow and so on. At the other end of the scale the higher numbered filters are magenta (filter 5 being the most magenta) which absorb green light and therefore only allow exposure to reach the high contrast blue emulsion. The intermediate filters allow varying degree of exposure to the two emulsions.

In use, the step by step procedure for using Multigrade paper is:

1 Place the negative in the enlarger in the normal manner and estimate the required filter, say filter 4. Because the filters are made to a high optical standard, you can focus the image without the filter in place, and then insert the filter without affecting the image. This is particularly valuable when using the denser filters (4–5) which, inevitably, project relatively dim images.
2 Make a test strip in the normal manner and follow this up with a full-sized print.
3 If you judge your print to be slightly too contrasty then change your filter to the next one or two lower (eg. filter 3 to 2½ or 2). For over-soft print, increase the filter number by (eg. filter 3 to 3½ or 4). When changing between filters 0–3½ you can use the same exposure time, as the effective paper speed remains constant throughout this range. Filters 4–5 require double the printing exposure of that needed for the lower numbered filters.
4 Finally, make slight adjustments to exposure and contrast to suit your interpretation of the subject.

57 A versatile enlarger allows you to change the original scene first recorded by the camera into quite a different final photograph. The building was deliberately tipped on to its side while being enlarged and was printed much darker than it appeared in reality. To direct attention to the reflection of the sun and the top of the lampstand, the bottom of the print has been lightened by 'dodging' and the top darkened by 'burning-in'.

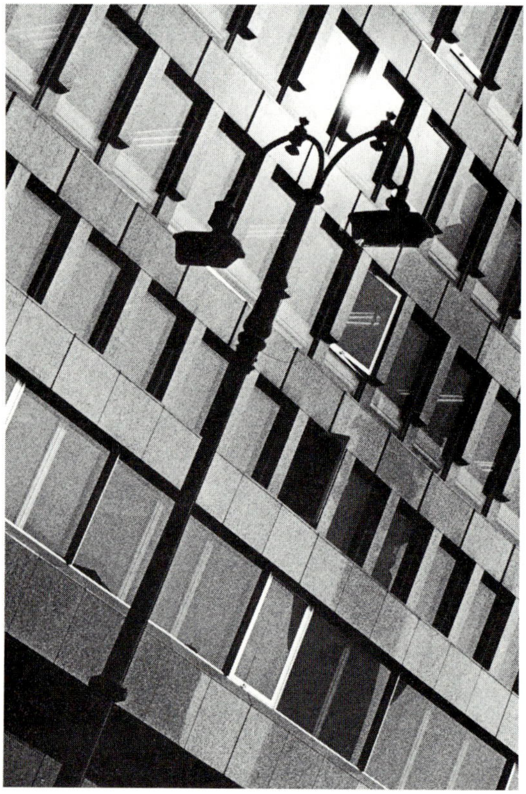

If you own an enlarger with a dial-in colour head you can use the yellow and magenta filters of this to achieve the various contrast grades. It is necessary to run some tests to determine the best settings but as a guide you could try the settings suggested in fig 6.6 on page 89. The higher contrasts may be difficult to obtain with a colour head because the Multigrade filters are more strongly coloured (ie. narrow cutting in their absorption) than those used for colour printing.

Ilford also manufacture a Multigrade enlarger head which couples with a special control unit and gives automatically timed exposures when switching from one filter number to another. Unfortunately, they are very expensive and are really only justifiable for the photographer who produces a large number of prints.

One last point concerning Multigrade–it is essential to use the Multigrade developer to obtain maximum contrast or, at least, thoroughly test alternative developers. Most general paper developers give rather flat results with Multigrade paper.

Kodak Polycontrast paper

There are three types of Polycontrast paper and these are available mainly in the USA. Polycontrast and Polycontrast Rapid, the more sensitive of the two, are conventional fibre-based papers, while Polycontrast Rapid RC is a paper primarily designed for machine processing.

As with Ilford's Multigrade paper, a series of colour filters is used to give a range of paper grades between 1 and 4. The lower grade filters (designated PC1, PC1½, etc.) are yellow and

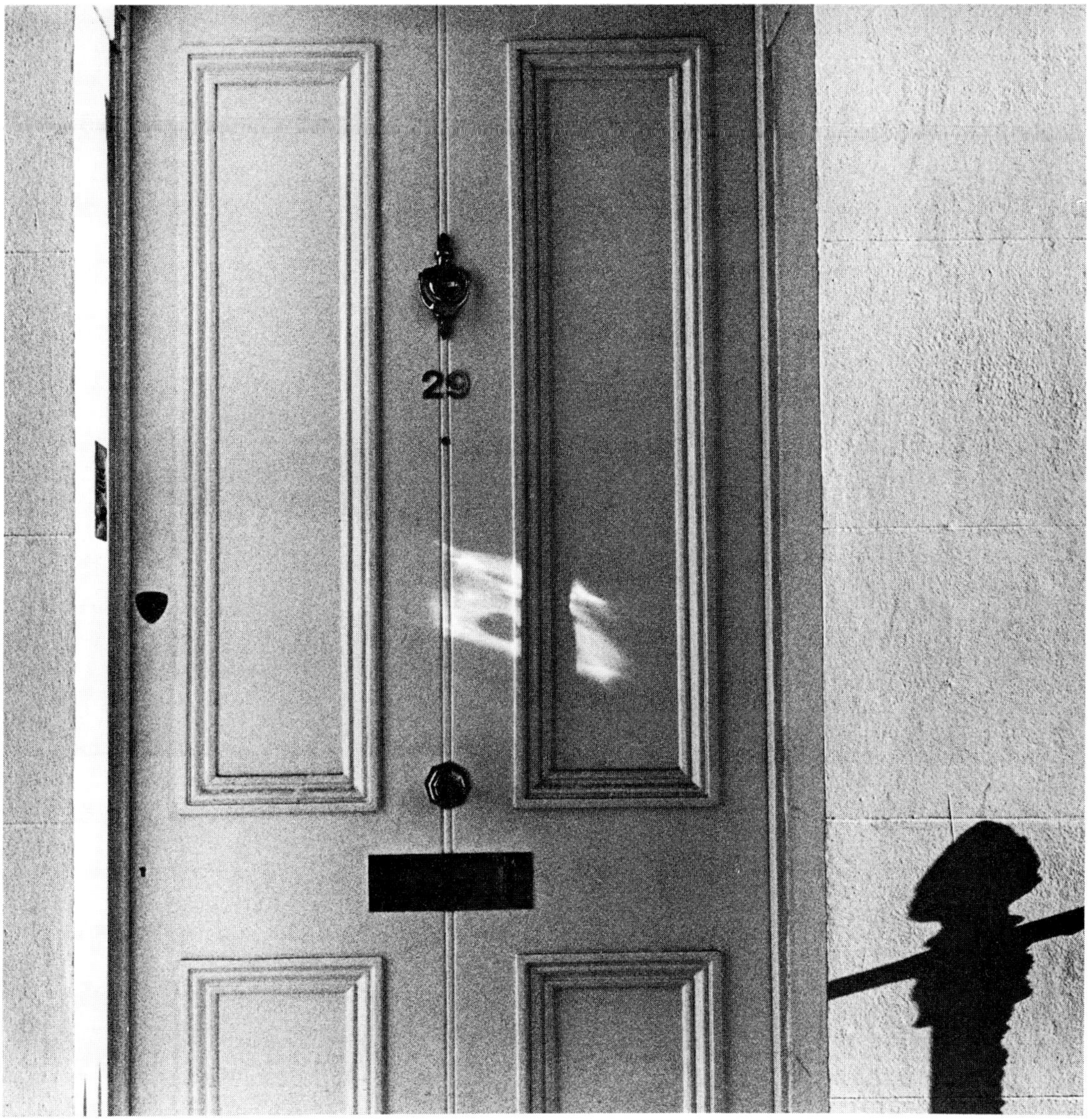

58 Photographs of this type, in which crisp detail is important in all parts of the subject, need the edge-to-edge definition obtainable only by use of a high quality enlarging lens. Notice also the overall even tonality of the print, produced by correct alignment of enlarger optics and precise positioning of the light source to give even illumination.

allow mainly green light to expose the lower contrast emulsion, while the higher grade filters (PC4, PC3½, etc.) are magenta and transmit mainly blue light to expose the higher contrast emulsion. The filter numbers are equivalent to 'one-grade' paper contrasts; for example, the use of PC3 filter gives a grade 3 paper, and PC 3½ is mid-way between grades 3 and 4.

Polycontrast filters are sold as a set, mounted in plastic holders, with a support so that they can be suspended just below the lens. They are available as gelatin filters to be cut and used in the image beam, or as acetate filters for placing in filter drawers. The acetate filters are optically inferior to the gelatin types and must not be used below the enlarging lens.

For those printers using colour heads, Kodak suggest the following filtration as *approximate* equivalents to PC filters. You can use these as a starting point for your own tests: 30Y (PC1), 20M (PC2), 100M (PC3), maximum M (PC3½). Most colour heads have insufficient magenta filtration to reach the equivalent of PC4.

The method for using Polycontrast papers is

identical to that just described for Multigrade, with the exception that the Kodak calculator uses ANSI (American National Standards Institute) paper speeds rather than filter numbers because of the different sensitivities of the various Polycontrast papers.

Developers for processing paper

The effect of a developer on a particular paper can only be discovered by experiment (see below). Each paper/developer combination exhibits three basic characteristics:

1 The rate at which the image develops can vary– some combinations give full print quality in 60 sec. or less, whereas others may take up to 2½ min.
2 The contrast of a particular paper can change slightly with the developer used.
3 The image colour can vary from warm (brownish) image tones to cold (bluish) blacks.

The paper has the major influence on these characteristics.

For greater control of print quality it is best for an image to reach full development in about 1½–2 minutes, as any shorter time than this may be difficult to control. Longer times are just too time consuming and inconvenient. Some paper/developer combinations develop the image very quickly and for the remaining development time the image changes very little, while others have a more even, gradual development (fig 6.7). It is largely a matter of preference which you use, but the middle course, ie. moderately rapid initial development with some image change with further time, is probably the most suitable for most printers.

The slight variation of image contrast produced by different developers can be adjusted by selecting a different paper grade. Also, slightly different tonal characteristics may be exhibited by one developer compared with another for one particular paper.

Choice of image 'colour' largely depends on the photographer's own preference and also on the subject matter. For example, portraits tend to be more pleasing when produced as warm image tones, but on colder papers the subject may appear more dramatic and less 'relaxed'. Photojournalists often prefer colder papers (eg. bromide emulsions) while the studio 'head-and-shoulders' portraitist usually goes for the warmer tones of chlorobromide papers.

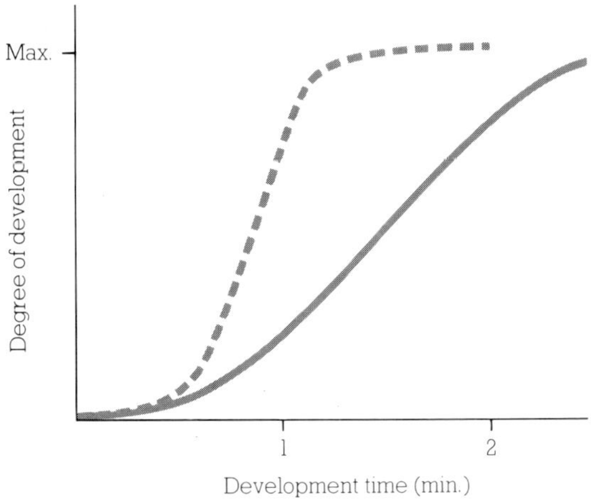

6.7 An indication of development rates for two different paper/developer combinations. The solid line shows a slow gradual development, whereby full development is reached in about two minutes. The other extreme (broken line) shows a rapid initial rate giving almost full development in about one minute and only a slight change thereafter. Most RC papers behave like the latter, while fibre-based papers resemble the more gradual curve.

Paper developers–some practical guidelines

It is not possible to give precise advice on the 'best' paper/developer combination as this must involve largely subjective evaluation. However, it is possible to recommend a series of tests to help you make your decisions:

1 Read the section in this book concerned with paper choice (page 86) and any relevant information from the manufacturers' data sheets, and select perhaps two or three types. It will simplify the choice if you stay with either RC or conventional fibre-based papers. For example, you might buy Kodabrome, Ilfospeed and Multigrade if you prefer RC papers, or Agfa Portriga-Rapid (warm tone), Agfa Brovira (neutral tone) and Ilford Galerie as a range of conventional papers. Buy small amounts of grade 2 paper.
2 From the table of paper developers (fig 6.8), or other literature, select two or three developers and buy small quantities of each. It is a good idea to include one developer recommended by the paper manufacturer.
3 Choose a negative of known high quality which suits grade 2 paper and exhibits subtle shadow detail, a reasonable range of mid-tones, and delicate highlights. If possible avoid subjects which are best printed on specific papers, such as

6.8

Paper Developer	*Properties	Liquid/powder
Agfa Neutol NE	Neutral black	Liquid & powder
Neutol WA	Warm black	Liquid & powder
Metinol	Neutral black. Gives slow image build-up.	Powder
Adaptol	Neutral black. Gives slow image build-up. Recommended as two-dish developer with Neutol WA.	Powder
Ilford Bromophen	Neutral black. Recommended for Ilfobrom paper.	Powder
Ilfospeed	Rapid developer recommended for Ilfospeed paper. Not suitable for Multigrade.	Liquid
Multigrade	Rapid developer for Multigrade paper.	Liquid
LS	Warm blacks.	Powder
PQ Universal	Very versatile GP developer.	Liquid
Johnsons Bromide	Neutral/warm tones.	Liquid
Contrast	Rapid acting.	Liquid
Kodak D-163	GP developer.	Liquid & powder
Dektol	Cold tones. Mainly US availability.	Powder
DPC	Multipurpose developer recommended for Kodabrome papers.	Liquid
Selectol	Warm tones. Mainly US availability.	Powder
Selectol-soft	Lower contrast version of Selectol.	Powder
May & Baker Suprol	GP developer.	Liquid
Paterson Acuprint	GP developer. Recommended for all papers including Multigrade.	Liquid
Tetenal Centrabrom	Lower contrast developer.	Liquid
Eukobrom	Recommended for RC papers including Multigrade.	Liquid & powder
Eukospeed	Rapid processing of RC papers.	Liquid
Neutral	Warm tones.	Liquid & powder

* Image tone is determined mainly by paper choice.

formal portraits on warm-toned papers, as this will bias the tests. It may be necessary to photograph specially for the tests a subject showing all these characteristics.

4 Without burning-in or dodging, make the best possible print from each paper/developer combination. If you have chosen three papers and three developers, there will be a total of nine prints.

5 Examine the finished dried prints (many papers 'dry in' to give subtle highlight detail) under a bright directional light source such as a desk lamp, taking special notice of tonal gradation, especially in shadows and highlights, image colour, clarity of whites, and density of blacks.

Tests of this type will make you more aware of the subtle differences between the reproductions on various papers, but remember that you may decide to standardise on more than one paper/developer combination, selecting the appropriate one for the subject being printed.

Other paper processing steps

The stages after print development (stop, fixer and wash) are always carried out to completion, but it is important to ensure that chemicals are not near exhaustion, otherwise there is a strong possibility of staining. You should use relatively fresh solutions at the beginning of each printing session.

Using an acid stop bath after the developer does prolong the life of the fixer by neutralising the developer's alkalinity and thereby maintaining the acidity (effectiveness) of the fixer. However, some photographers prefer simply to use water as this gives them extra control over development (page 102).

It is more economical, and more efficient, to use two fixing baths, with the last fixer being made up fresh at each printing session and, in turn, becoming the first fixer for the next printing session.

The two main types of fixer are those containing ammonium thiosulphate which are fast working, and the slower sodium thiosulphate formulations. Both types are available with, or without, hardener to toughen the processed photographic emulsion. A hardener formulation is recommended for film processing but is generally not suggested for paper processing because it means that longer washing times are needed to remove processing chemicals from the hardened emulsion. Always follow precisely the paper manufacturer's recommendations for time, dilution, and type of fixer.

You should ensure your prints receive sufficient fixing time, ie. about five minutes in both fixing baths when using fibre-based papers and sodium thiosulphate fixers and about one minute for 'rapid processing' papers and ammonium thiosulphate formulations. But do not leave them for much longer than recommended (up to about 4X the stated time is acceptable) because the fixer will start to dissolve silver from the print, making delicate highlights disappear. It is therefore safer and more convenient, if you are unable to use the shorter times of rapid fixers, to employ the slower sodium thiosulphate fixers for paper processing, enabling you to leave prints in the fixer until it is convenient to transfer them to the wash.

The wash after the fixer should be efficient, ensuring rapid removal of used water and replacement with fresh supplies of water. If you are unable to use continuous running water, then change the water in the wash tank every five minutes or so. Washing times depend on the water temperature, efficiency of wash, and the type of paper, with the usual recommendations being 30 min. and 45 min. for single weight and double weight conventional fibre-based papers, while RC papers only need four min. washing (or less). Times for fibre-based papers can be considerably shortened by the use of washing aids.

Over-washing of RC papers should be avoided because of the loss of optical brighteners from the paper. These are the chemicals that are responsible for the brilliance of whites. There is also a tendency for RC papers to curl at the print corners with prolonged washing.

Archival processing

The processing procedures and times for photographic papers are sufficient to ensure, as the manufacturers say, 'satisfactory permanence for most purposes'. If you want to achieve archival permanence then you must follow a rigid processing pattern, for example as described for Ilford Galerie paper in fig 6.9. You should only print on fibre-based paper if you require archival permanence.

Another method of achieving archival permanence is to use (after a short wash) hypo clearing solution. This improves the efficiency of washing by a factor of about eight times, ie. three minutes in hypo clearing agent is equivalent to about a 24 minute wash. After this, a hypo eliminator solution converts the remaining thiosulphate to the more soluble sulphate form, which can then be washed out quite rapidly.

Now free of all thiosulphate which could cause the image to fade if it were not removed, the silver image is made more stable by use of a gold protective solution. The archival process (fig 6.10) is completed by a final wash, and drying in a dust-free atmosphere.

6.9 Archival processing of Ilford Galerie paper

	Time (min.)	Comments
Developer	1–4	eg. Ilford PQ Universal or LS.
Stop bath	½	Can use water bath
Fixer	½	Rapid type without hardener. eg. Ilford Hypam 1 + 4.
Wash	5	Good supply of fresh, running water.
Washing aid	10	Intermittent agitation in Ilford Washaid (1 + 4).
Final wash	5	

6.10 Processing for print permanence

	Time (min.)	Comments
Develop / Stop / Fix / Fix	As recommended by manufacturer.	Use fresh solutions. Two fixing baths are more efficient than one
Rinse	½	Running water
Hypo clear	2–3	Frequent agitation (eg. Kodak Hypo Clearing agent)
Hypo eliminator	6	Occasional agitation
Wash	10	Running water
Gold protective solution	10	Occasional agitation
Wash	10	Running water
Dry		Clean, dust-free atmosphere

6.11 Thiosulphate test solution

Water	750 ml
*Acetic acid (28 per cent)	125 ml
Silver nitrate	7.5 g
Water to make	1 litre

*Made by diluting 3 parts of glacial acetic acid with 8 parts of water.
Store test solution in a dark glass bottle; avoid contact with negatives, prints, hands and clothing, otherwise staining occurs.

To ensure maximum permanence (ie. for centuries) the print should be stored in low humidity, low temperature conditions. Correctly sepia-toned prints (page 139) have even greater stability than gold-toned prints. But not every image suits the warm brown tones produced by this conversion of the silver image to silver sulphides and selenides.

Test for residual thiosulphate

If you are unsure of the efficiency of your washing in removal of thiosulphate, you should perform a residual thiosulphate test. This involves taking a 'spare' print from the wash and removing most of the water from its emulsion surface.

Place one drop of the test solution (fig 6.11) on

59 Choice of paper type and developer are far less important in photojournalism where content is what counts. However, if several photographs are to be shown at the same time, for example as an exhibit, they should all be reproduced on the same paper type and surface.

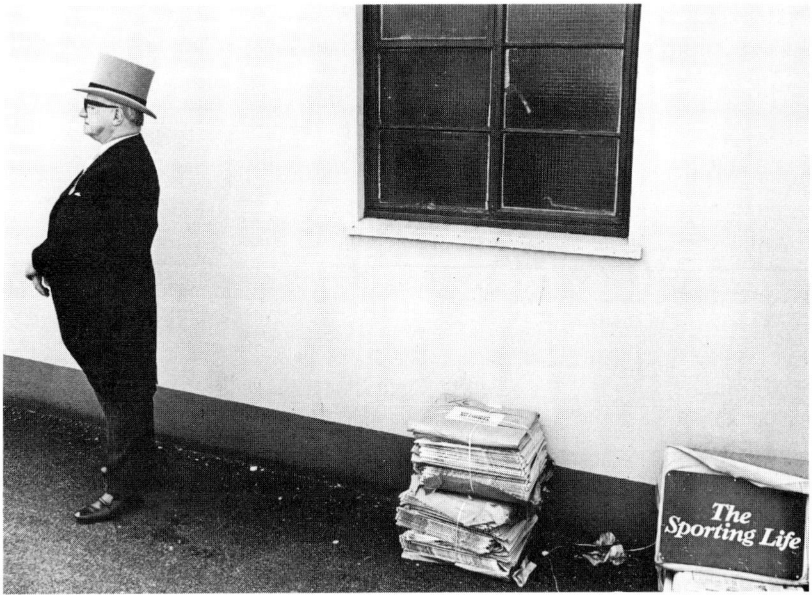

60 Complex subjects containing considerable fine detail and a wide tonal distribution should be printed on glossy paper. If printed on a matt-surfaced paper this scene would possess a compressed tonal range, especially in the darker tones, and important subject details (eg. facial expressions) would be less apparent.

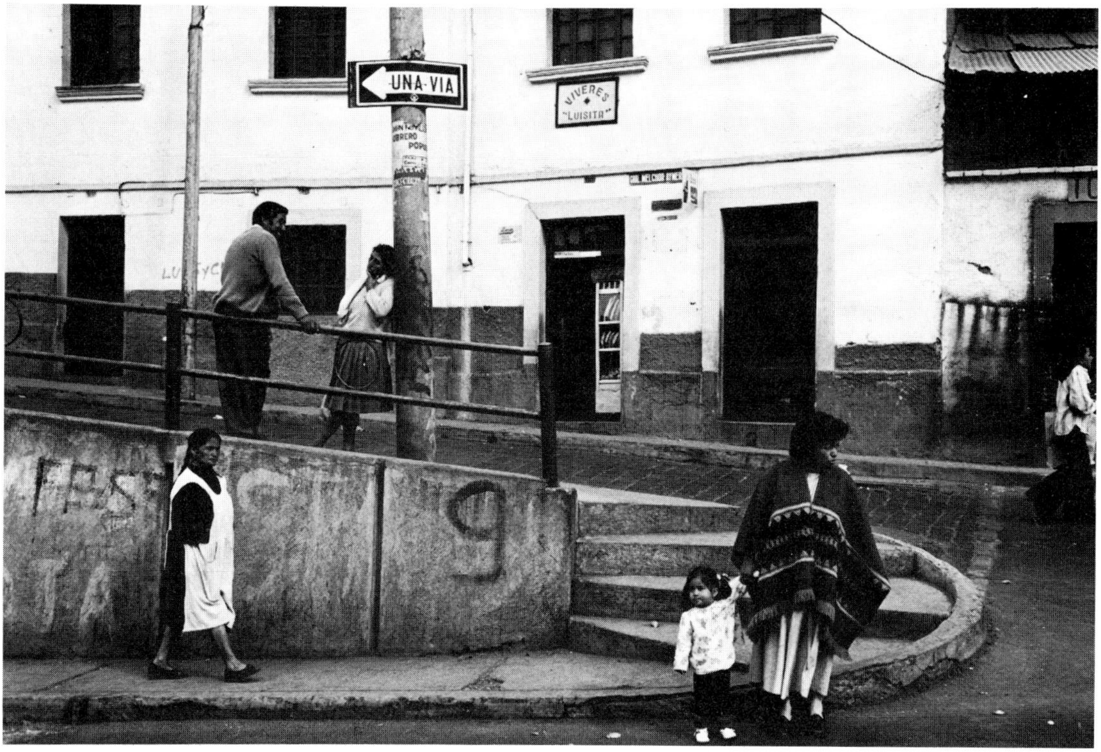

the white unexposed margin of the print, allow it to stand for two minutes and then rinse off the excess reagent. Compare the tint of the stain produced with the reference tints from the manufacturer. Continue washing if the residual hypo is too high and perform the test again after about 20 min.

Transferring information to the print

If it has been correctly exposed and processed, the negative should contain all, or at least most, of the subject's brightness range. The subject's shadow details are recorded as low densities on the long sweeping toe of the D/Log E curve, the mid-tones are on the straight-line portion, and the highlights appear as the densest parts of the negative. When placed in the enlarger and projected, the density range of the negative now becomes the exposure range to be projected on to the photographic paper. The greatest exposures will come from the low density areas (shadows) of the negative, and the least from the high density parts (highlights).

A high quality black-and-white print has clean whites and deep blacks, with an appropriate (in the photographer's opinion) distribution of tones in between. The exposure through the low density parts of the negative should produce a maximum black and tones just lighter than this, while the dark areas of the negative should hold back the enlarger light sufficiently to produce white, and subtle shades of off-white. As previously mentioned, the negative density range should be about 1.0 to achieve a 'perfect' print on grade 2 paper when a diffuser enlarger is used.

Contrast grades of paper

Not every negative 'fits' comfortably on to grade 2 paper, so manufacturers have produced a range of paper emulsions (fig 6.12) which develop to give different contrasts (slope of characteristic curve), thus ensuring that each negative can be printed to give a maximum black and a clean white.

When the density range of a negative is low, the exposure range it projects on to grade 2 paper is also low, resulting in good blacks and muddy whites if the printing exposure is based on reaching maximum black, or giving clean whites but greyish blacks when exposure is reduced to 'hold' the whites. This 'flat' negative needs to be printed on to a higher contrast paper (grade 3, 4, and 5) to realise both maximum black and minimum white (fig 6.13).

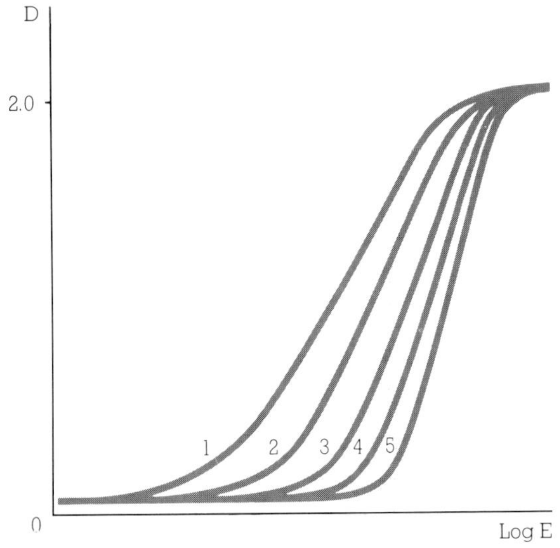

6.12 Representative set of D/Log E curves for one type of paper, showing the five available grades. Grade 2 is considered to be 'normal' and suits most negatives, whereas grade 5 has the maximum contrast and grade 1 the minimum.

The negative with a high density range prints on grade 2 paper to produce good blacks and clean whites but will suffer lost highlight detail if it is 'underprinted' to retain shadow detail. Or, it will exhibit loss of shadow detail if it is 'overprinted' to produce subtle highlights. The solution for these 'heavy' negatives is to print on to lower contrast paper (fig 6.14).

Fitting the negative to the best paper grade is only part of the story. In some cases the use of various paper grades is only an emergency measure to 'save' an otherwise poor negative due, perhaps, to incorrect camera exposure or wrong film development. Chapter 7 examines the relationship of negative to paper, along with other topics, in more detail.

Local density control

In practice, most printers do not necessarily concern themselves with placing shadow or highlight details in correct relationship to the original scene, but simply select the paper grade which gives the subject the best overall appearance and then 'correct' areas of the print with local density control.

To select the most appropriate grade of paper for your negative and your idea of what a good print should look like, you should try your negative on several grades of paper. But remember, it is a

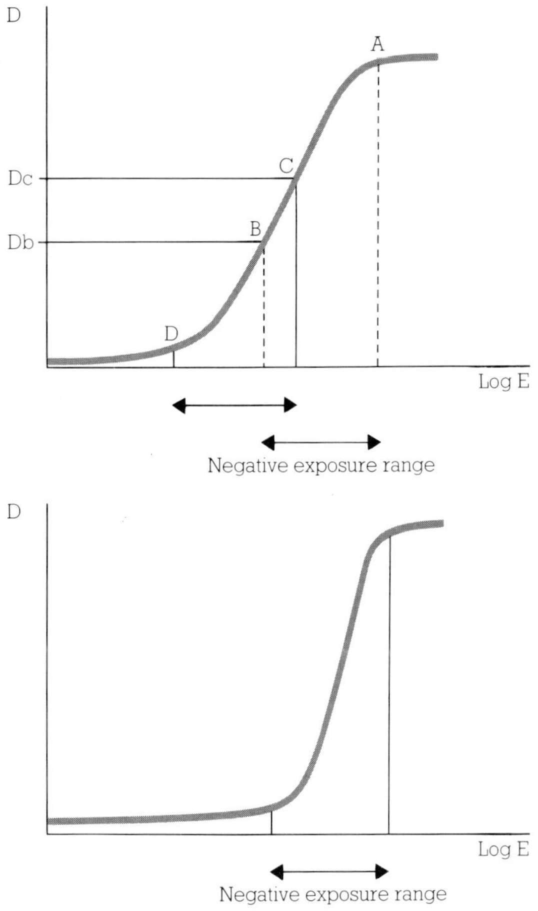

6.13 The top diagram shows the result of printing a negative of short density range on grade 2 paper. If the paper is exposed to give deep blacks (A) the highlights are muddy (B); reducing exposure retains clean highlights (D) but the shadows are not very dark (C). The same negative printed on a high contrast paper (bottom diagram) gives both clean highlights and deep blacks.

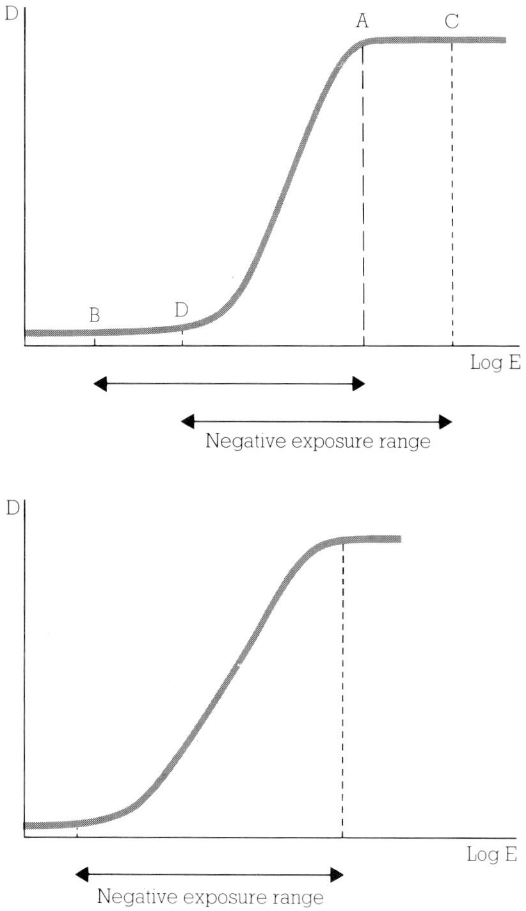

6.14 When a negative of wide density range is printed on to grade 2 paper (top diagram) you either lose shadow detail (B) when printing for delicate highlight detail (A) or, if the shadows are correct (D), then the highlights will lack detail (C), ie. they are 'burnt out'. The bottom diagram illustrates the result when the same negative is printed on a low contrast paper, thus giving good detail in both highlights and shadows.

common fault to select a paper grade which is too low, resulting in grey 'flat' prints, and then to move up to the next highest grade until the best effect is supposedly obtained, but in fact to stop short of reaching the most suitable grade. A far better approach is to start at the other end of the scale, with a paper grade which produces a print that is too hard overall, and then drop down to lower grades to find the best result.

The techniques of holding back ('dodging' or 'shading') or giving extra ('burning-in') exposure to certain areas of the paper are, in principle, the same as each other (fig 6.15); it is simply a matter of adjusting exposure locally compared with what is happening to most of the paper. For some prints, it may be easier to darken small parts of the photograph by burning-in, while with others it might be preferable to shade areas that you would prefer to reproduce as lighter in tone. For complex prints you may have to burn-in some areas and dodge others.

A good set of handmade printing tools (eg. wire with blobs of modelling clay, cardboard with cut-out holes and shapes, small penlight torch, etc.) is

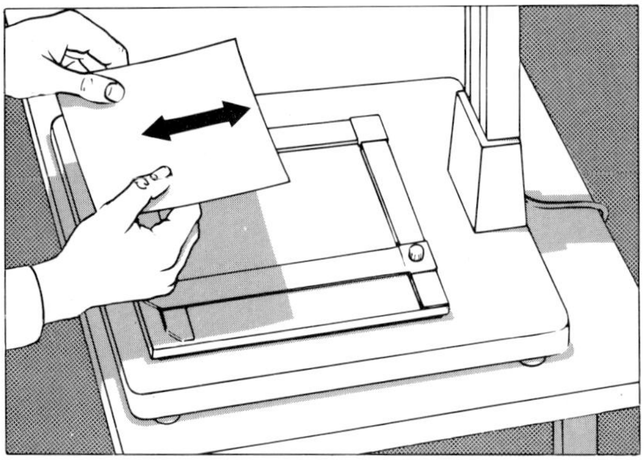

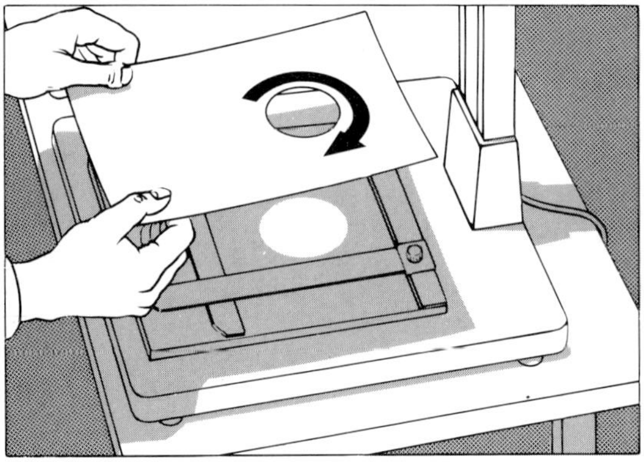

6.15A Local density control Burning-in a relatively large subject area. A piece of black card is held between the lens and the paper, to give extra exposure to the area which is to be made darker; the rest of the image is shaded. To avoid a line showing on the print, you should keep the card moving slowly during the burning-in. Burning-in a small area. The technique illustrated above is used for darkening small areas, except that the card has a suitably shaped and sized cut-out. Practise before you make the print.

6.15B Dodging to make an area lighter. The shaped piece of modelling clay at the end of a piece of wire is moved slowly over the area to be lightened during part of the exposure time.

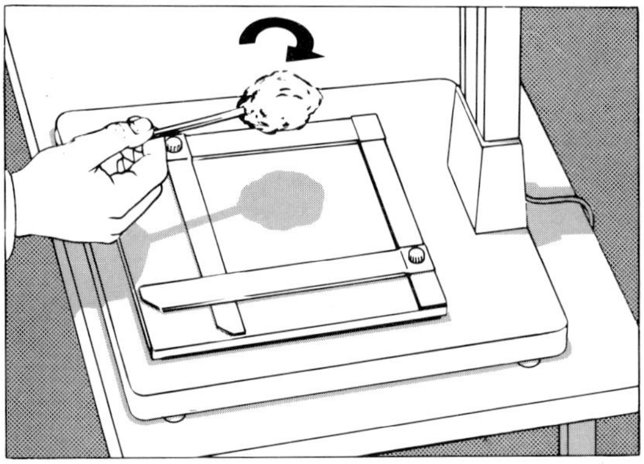

essential for the expert printer, although there are a few masters who can magically contort their hands in the enlarger beam to achieve beautifully controlled printing exposures.

Print tones compared with subject tones

Returning to the topic of tonal reproduction, it may be of interest to some readers, especially those considering the very exacting Zone System, to see how the final print tones relate to the original subject tones (fig 6.16). The maximum brightness range from a print (glossy surface) is about 128:1 (maximum density of 2.1), whereas subject brightness range may be much higher. Therefore, particular attention must be paid to retaining a reasonable separation of tones in the print, with a *similar* distribution to the original subject.

It is theoretically possible for an original subject with the brightness range 128:1 (ie. seven stop variation from shadows to highlights) to be exposed and developed correctly to give a negative density range of 1.0. This negative could then be 'perfectly' printed on to grade 2 paper to give a glossy print where the 'no-detail' shadows appear at maximum density of 2.1 and no-detail highlights as print density of 0.0 (theoretical only). The original subject brightness range (Log E of 2.1) is then mirrored as a print luminance range of 128:1 (density range of 2.1).

The perfect transfer can only occur if photographic films and papers have a straight-line response. However, all materials have S-shaped D/Log E curves. This means that the subject's shadow information is recorded on the toe region of the film's characteristic curve and some compression of tonal range is inevitable. Fortunately, the S-shaped curve for papers to some extent cancels this compression of shadow detail because the low contrast toe of the film is printed on to the upper (high contrast) portion of the paper's curve.

Print tones for non-average subjects

When the subject's brightness range is greater than 128:1 (ie. Log E is greater than 2.1), the final print tones can only be proportional to the subject's tones, assuming that the photographer has been able to capture the wide brightness range on film by careful exposure and film development (page 68). Alternatively, the photographer can choose to expose and process the film for 'standard' conditions, and elect to lose shadow and/or highlight detail but retain a closer relation-

61 An example of a fine art photograph which has been printed to a very high standard and processed for archival permanence. Photographed at night using a long exposure time, the tree is distinguished from the dark sky by means of a single pulse from an electronic flash.

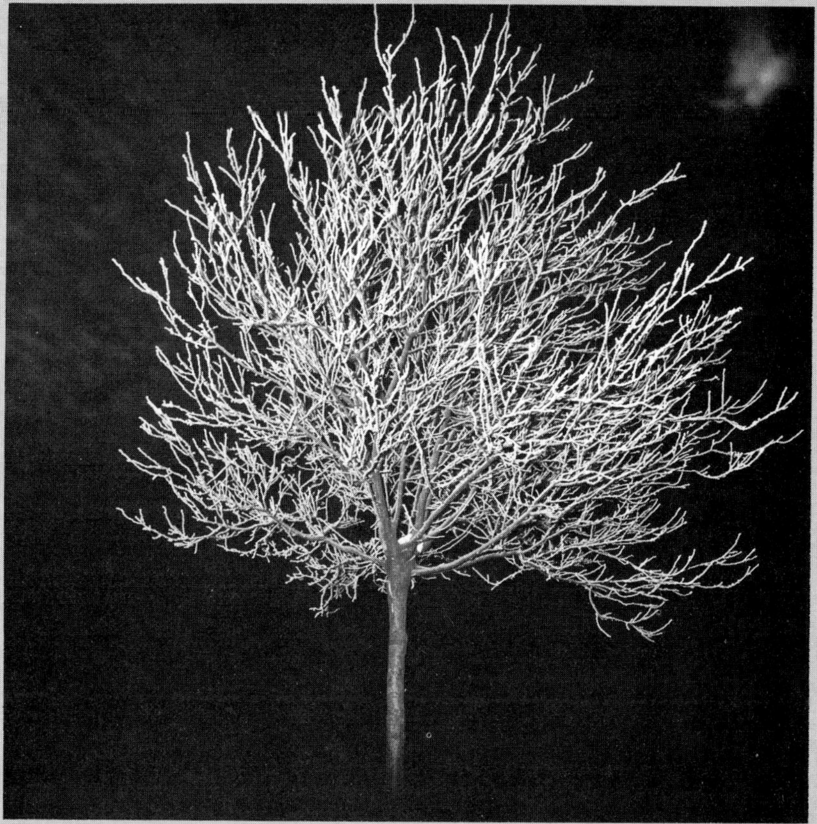

62 Subjects of a gentler nature often look more pleasing on warm-toned paper and printed on to non-glossy surfaces. (The reproduction in this book cannot, unfortunately, demonstrate this.)

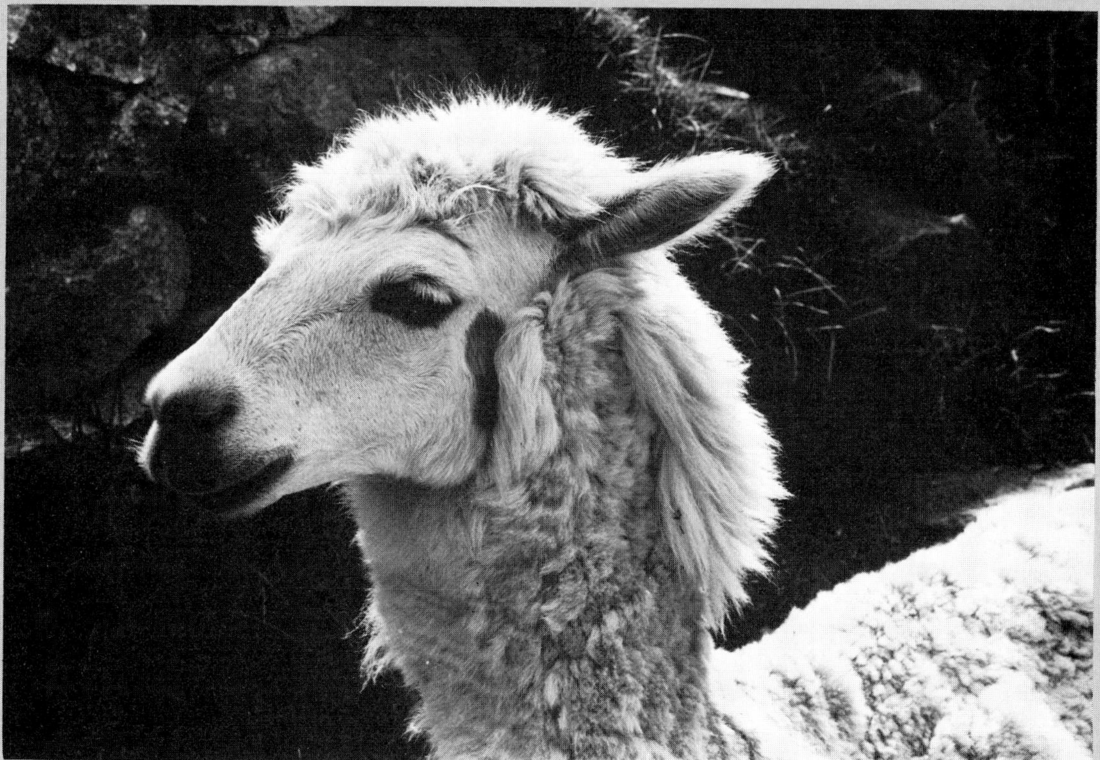

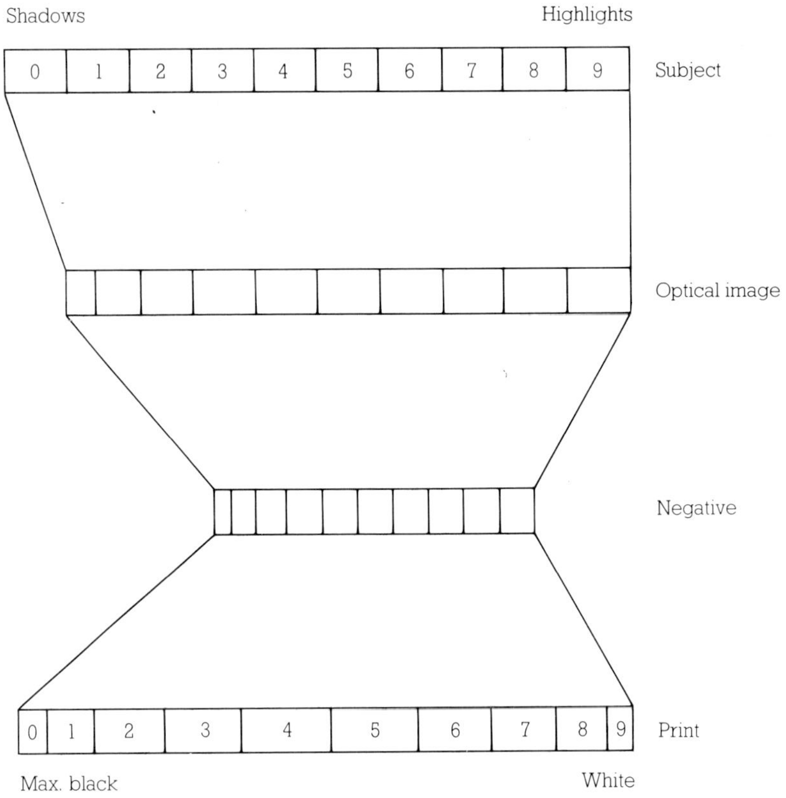

6.16 Representation of how subject tones are recorded and reproduced in the final print. The original subject of 10 equally spaced tones (from black 0 through greys to white 9) is slightly compressed at the shadow end by the flare of the camera lens. The optical image is then projected on to the film and because of the S-shape of the D/Log E curve, the resulting negative shows further compression of the shadows and a slight compression of highlights.
Again, because of the paper's S-shaped curve, there is further compression of both shadows and highlights in the final print, although the higher contrast shoulder of the paper does 'stretch' the shadows a little.

ship between subject tones and print tones.

Subjects of low brightness range are bound to be 'stretched' when printed to give dense blacks and clean whites. For example, a scene on an overcast day with a brightness range of say 1:20 (Log E of 1.3) would normally be printed to give a full density range of 2.1 on glossy paper. Here, the differences between tones in the final print are greater than the tonal differences within the original subject.

Tonal reproduction on other paper surfaces

The discussion above has been based on the maximum density of 2.1 for photographic paper which can only be achieved from glossy surfaces. Most exhibition prints are made on surfaces (eg. pearl) which have a lower density range of about 1.8 and this, inevitably, means that most subjects, including scenes of average brightness range, are compressed on to the paper's limited luminance range. This compressive effect is even more pronounced for matt papers, where maximum density may be as low as 1.4.

The viewer of a print is not concerned with the original subject but only the content and the photographic quality of the image in front of him. Provided that the photograph contains a reasonable black which compares favourably with other printed blacks, from his memory or other surrounding prints, and the tonal distribution is in sympathy with the subject, the viewer accepts the reproduction and enjoys it.

Printing controls

Apart from the basic controls already discussed–paper grade, dodging/burning-in, and developer choice–there are a few more devices other than image manipulations (Chapter 8) which are worth mentioning.

One of the oldest but most effective ways to change the nature of image borders is *vignetting*; a technique in which the printer holds a cut-out card between the enlarger lens and the paper (fig 6.17). The standard example is an oval cut-out which is moved slightly during the exposure to give a portrait shape with 'soft' borders. The softness of the edges depends on the degree of card movement.

There is no limit to the shape of the card and the degree of sharpness in the print borders. One popular method of producing a smallish print positioned within a large sheet of photographic paper is to lay a cleanly cut-out *printing mask* in contact with the paper during the exposure. The card should be black to prevent any scattering of enlarger light and should be held down by weights or designed as part of a hinged printing frame (fig 6.18). The use of glass should be avoided because it can cause optical distortion, and would also need to be kept scrupulously clean.

Some photographers like to surround their pictures with a thin black line, this presentation being especially suitable for subjects which need 'containing', such as the large light areas (sky, sand, etc.) of landscapes. The methods of producing a thin black line around the picture are:

1 Some enlargers project the entire negative image area *plus* some of the clear surrounding area of the film and, if the negative is printed without cropping, it is easy to allow the clear film area to expose the paper to give black. Enlarge your negative as normal and adjust the sides of the paper easel so that a thin white strip is visible around the projected image. The width of the black line on the print can be easily controlled by adjustment of the easel arms, and if your easel has a wide control of image border sizes you can surround your black-lined print with plenty of white. This technique works well when printing a 35mm negative in a 6 x 6cm film carrier, although it is usually necessary to employ glass in the carrier to keep the film flat. The black line is produced adjacent to image borders.

2 When most of your pictures are made to standard sizes and proportion you can construct a printing mask made of two parts (fig 6.19). One cut-out allows only the image area to be exposed, the other is a cut-out line in a separate piece of thin black card which is used in conjunction with a white light exposure (torch, lamp, or enlarger without negative) to give black. To ensure clean, sharp, even lines the mask must be carefully made with clean-cut edges. This technique allows the black line to be at any position outside the image (eg. image edge/white/black line/white) but does mean that a different mask is necessary for each difference in print size and picture proportions.

3 Some special photographic paper surfaces, such as Kentmere Art, allow you to draw a black line on

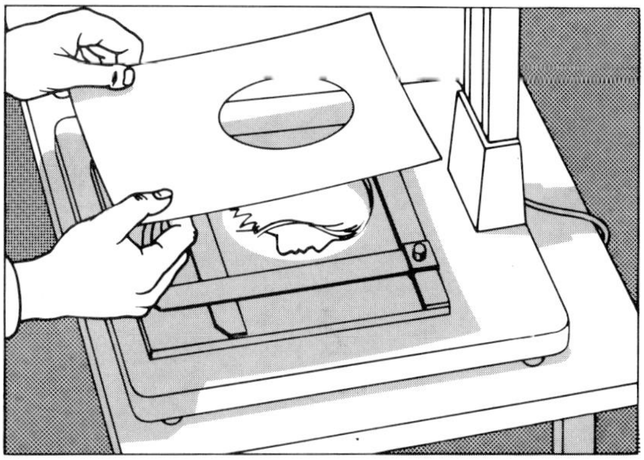

6.17 The technique for vignetting is similar to burning-in (fig **6.15**), except that the oval cut-out is held above the paper throughout the entire printing exposure. The sharpness of the image edges depends on how much the cut-out has been moved during the exposure.

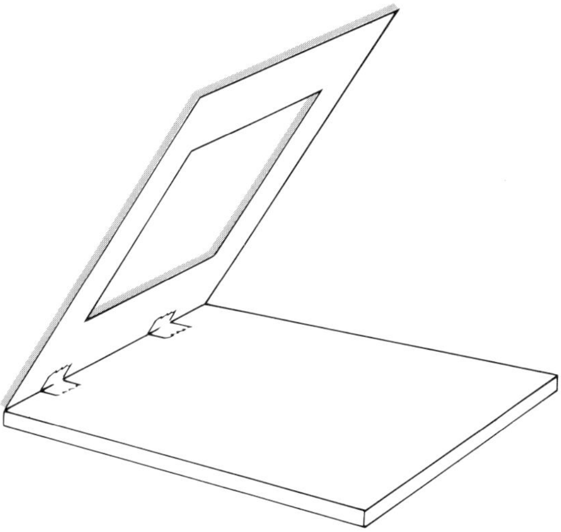

6.18 Simple printing mask. The base should be constructed of a fairly sturdy material such as wood or thick card, while the top is made of a thinner material (such as thin black card) so that it stays in contact with the paper emulsion. Use good quality linen tape for the hinges.

the final print. This method requires a very steady hand and the use of a technical drawing pen if good-looking results are to be achieved.

4 The last method involves mounting the print on black paper or thin card and then mounting once again on white card. See section on mounting, page 108.

Controlling the image shape

If your enlarger has a tilting lens panel and/or a tilting negative holder (usually as part of a tilting

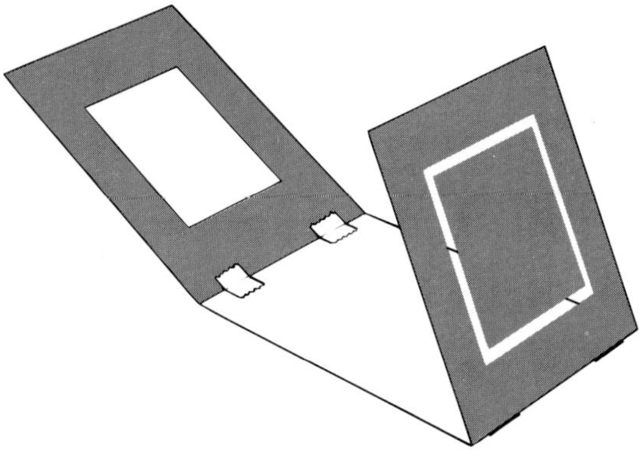

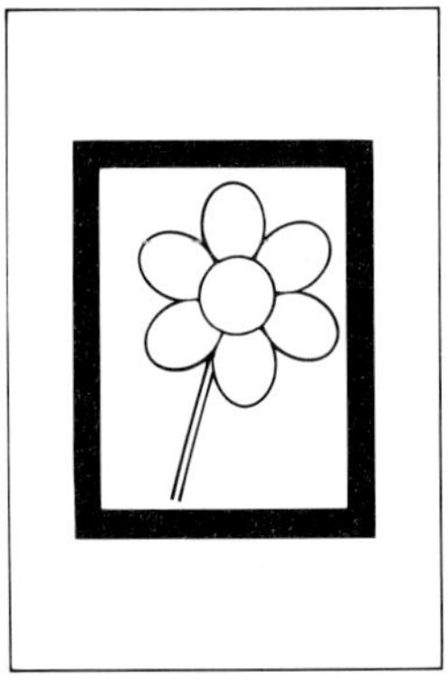

Print

White light exposure

Image exposure

6.19 Double mask printing frame which produces a black line around the print. The first exposure is of the image through the cut-out rectangle, and the second white light exposure is made when the line mask is in place. The line mask can either be attached to a *clean* acetate sheet, or the centre portion can be held separately during the non-image exposure.

head) you can use these facilities to change the shape of the projected image (fig 6.20). The most common application of this technique is to correct converging lines on the negative so that they become parallel on the print. This happens to the parallel sides of tall buildings when you point a small format camera (35mm, 120) or any camera without movements upwards, but there is a limit to the amount of correcting you can achieve by this printing technique.

As the diagram shows, the most convenient method is to keep the baseboard with the paper and easel in their normal horizontal position and use both lens tilt and negative tilt to achieve the required amount of correction.

Although mechanically less convenient than the above, another method is to tilt the lens and paper easel to achieve the same degree of image change. This method is suitable when the enlarger has only lens tilt adjustments.

If your enlarger has only head (negative) tilt, you can still have limited control of image shape, but you need to stop the enlarging lens down to a very small aperture to ensure that you obtain satisfactory print sharpness across the print.

Even if the enlarger has no 'movements', you can tilt the paper easel to produce a limited change of shape, but the amount you can raise one end of the easel is limited by the depth of acceptable sharpness for the projected image–which is controlled by the enlarging lens aperture.

Varying contrast within the printed image

Variable contrast papers (eg. Multigrade, Polycontrast) offer the printer total control of the image. He is able, as with other papers, to control the density of individual areas of the subject by burning-in or shading but he can also vary the contrast from one part of the image to another. In practice, few photographers consider using this extra control, perhaps because only a few negatives actually benefit from it.

The best procedure to adopt for local density and contrast control is:

1 Make a test to find the most appropriate printing grade and exposure for most of the image, and make a full size print.
2 Examine the print critically and decide which areas need to be lighter/darker and which require lower/higher contrast.
3 Carry out tests on these areas to find out the new exposure time (shading/burning-in only) and the new exposure time with new printing filter (contrast changes). Make notes if necessary.
4 Make a print using all extra exposures for local density and contrast control.
5 Refine exposures/contrast filters as necessary.

This procedure may appear complex, but if you are well organised and methodical it should become fairly straightforward with practice.

Control of print development

If you get all your printing exposures (including

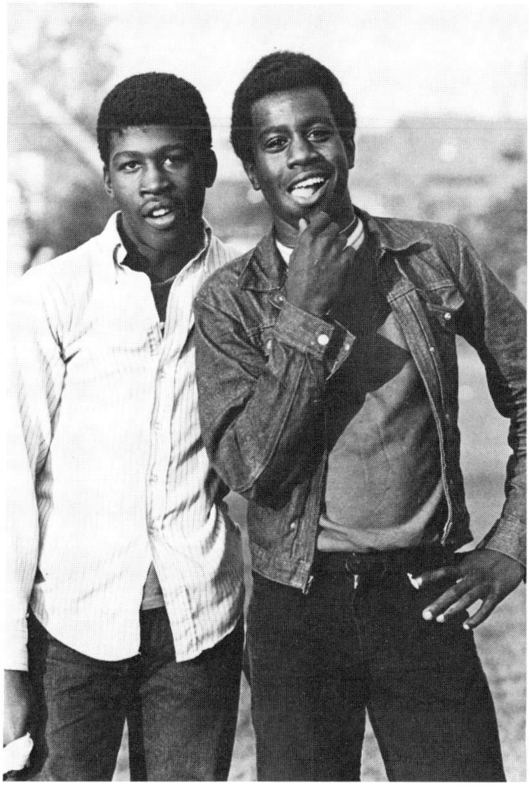

63 A negative usually contains more subject information than can be reproduced in the print. Even though the shirt has been burnt-in, there is some loss of detail here, and also some loss of gradation in the darker tones.

64 A relatively hard grade of paper (4) was selected to emphasise the subject content and make the image more graphic. The edges of the photograph are, consequently, quite dark and force the viewer's attention towards the lighter areas.

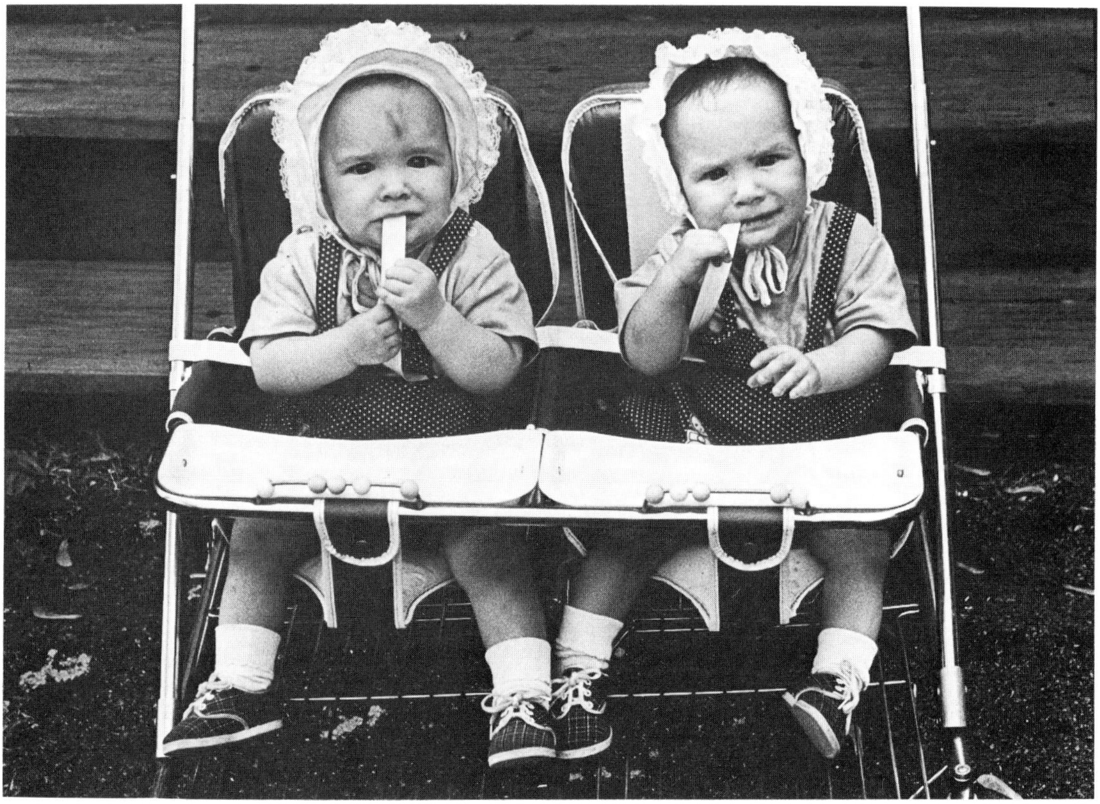

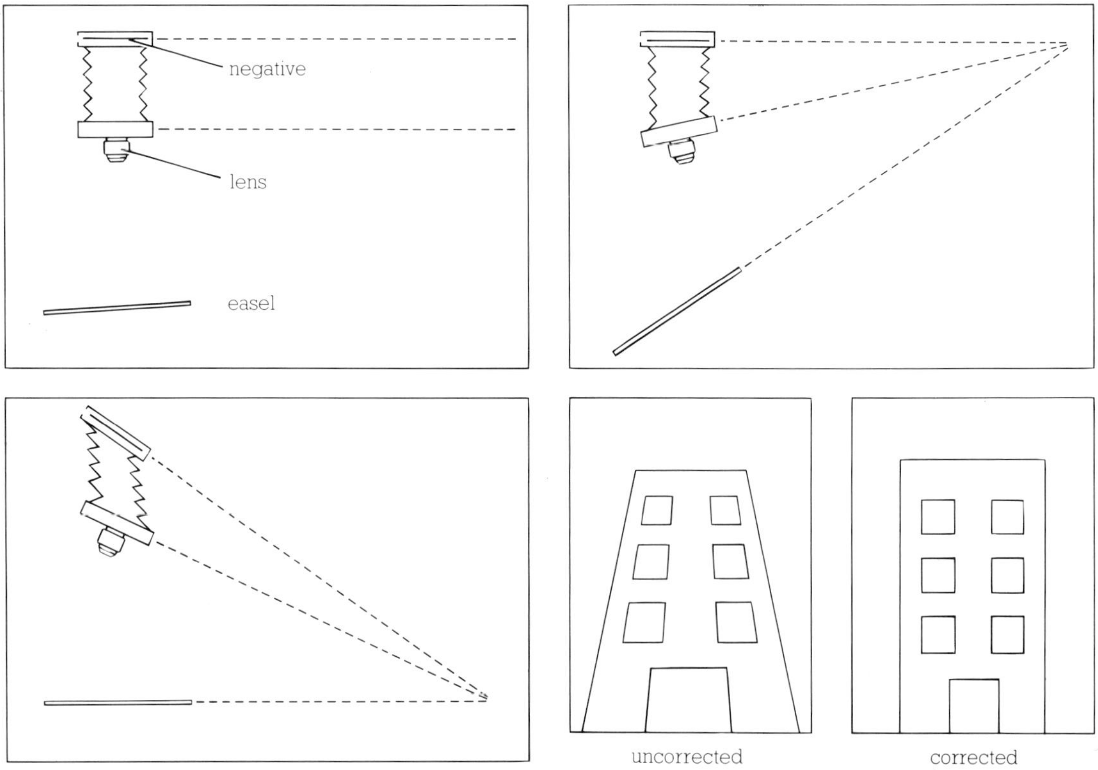

6.20 Three methods of correcting image shape (eg. converging verticals) during enlarging. Top left: easel tilt for enlarger without movements; top right: easel and lens panel tilt; bottom left: lens panel and negative carrier tilt. The dotted lines indicate the ideal situation, in which all planes should meet at the same vanishing point (Scheimpflug rule). See text for full details.

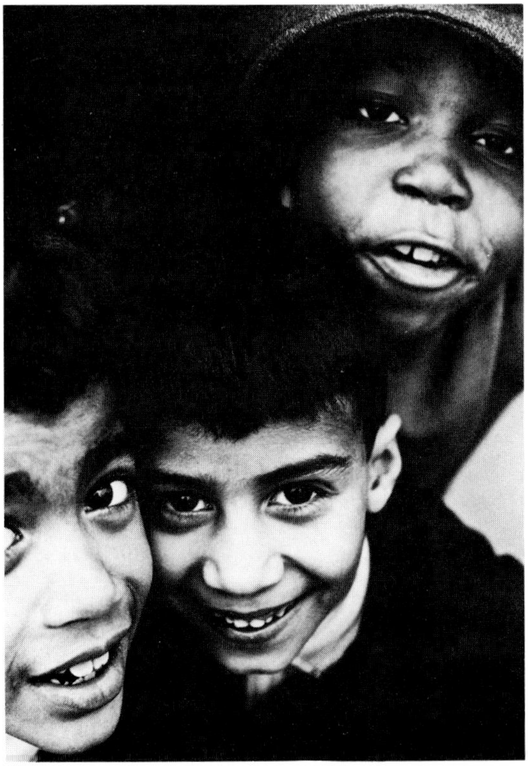

65 Much of the character of this photograph comes from darker image tones, for example in the clothing and hair. To retain the subtlety of these shadow gradations, use glossy paper rather than matt surfaces which compress the darker tones. The top quality fibre based papers are ideal when rich shadow textures are required.

local density control) precisely right, you should be able to develop your paper in the standard manner and obtain a perfect photograph. However, there are times when a sheet of paper is not quite correctly exposed, with perhaps one area going slightly too dark, or another being slightly too light. It is on these occasions that a water bath (instead of a stop bath) after the developer is very useful.

Watch the print carefully as it is developing and look for any areas that are going too dark, or not dark enough. This usually happens with over-

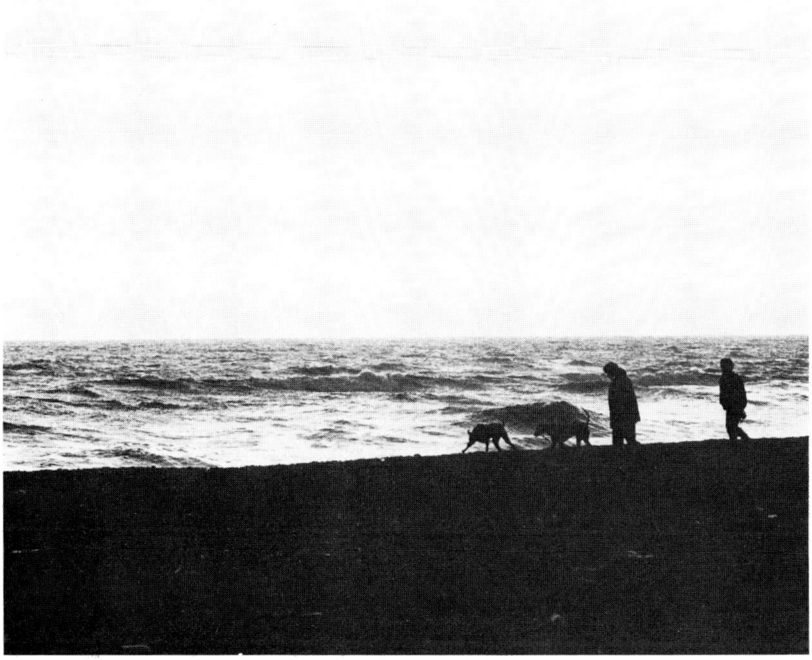

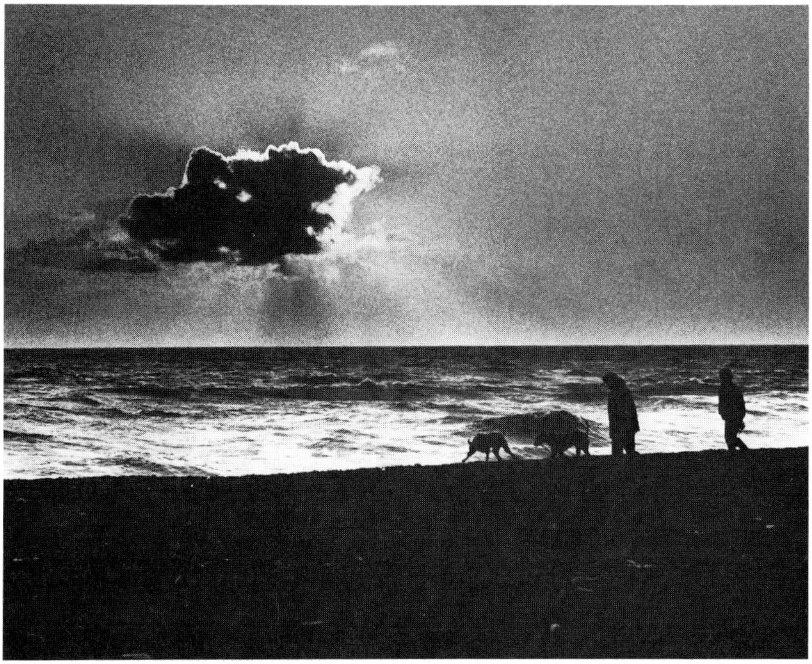

66-67 In the extreme lighting conditions encountered on this stormy day at the seaside, the density range of the negative is likely to be very wide and produce 'straight' prints with considerable loss of subject detail. The sky in the bottom print was burnt-in for three times the overall printing time to produce even more drama than in the original scene.

exposed shadows where detail is starting to disappear and on highlights which are not showing quickly enough. During this initial relatively short development it is important to agitate the print fairly vigorously to avoid uneven development. Place the print in the water bath as soon as any of these 'faults' is noticed and agitate vigorously for about 20 sec

The print now develops very slowly due to the small amount of developer within the emulsion,

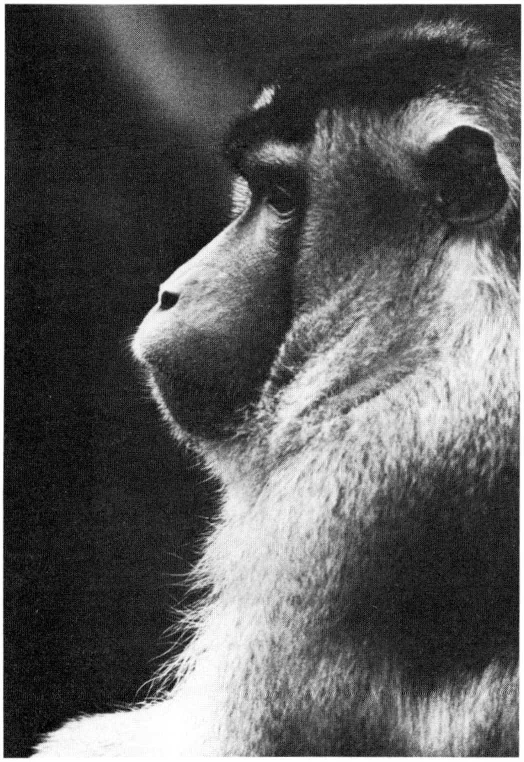

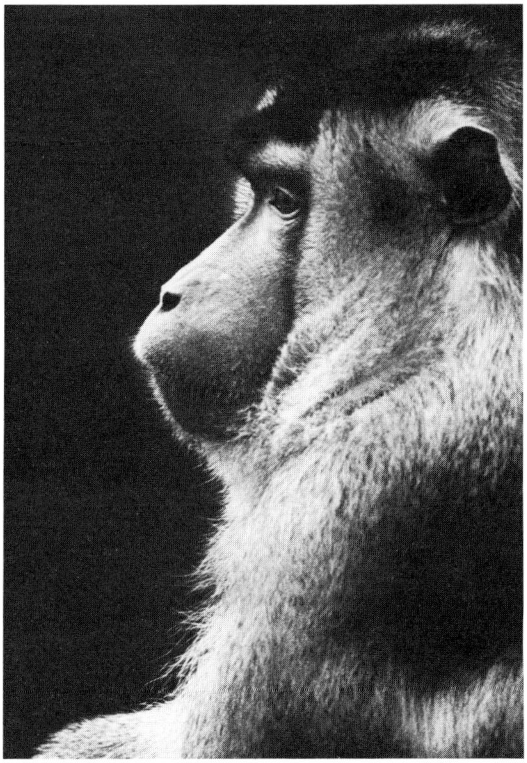

68-69 The left-hand print resulted from a straight exposure, while the print on the right has been adjusted using local printing controls. The bottom left corner and the background of the right-hand picture have been burnt-in, and have received in total about twice the overall printing time. During the initial main exposure, the face was lightened by dodging for about one third of the time.

and any developer in the water from previous prints. If you have 'pulled' the print because some shadows are going too dark, 'paint' the rest of the image with developer, making sure none spreads across the 'overexposed' shadows. You can either use a paint brush or dip your finger into the developer. But if you decide on the latter, use a Phenidone type of developer which is less likely to cause dermatitis, rather than a metol-based formula. Make sure you wash your hands thoroughly after each print is processed. *If you are at all susceptible to dermatitis, use print tongs or gloves and a brush to 'paint' the developer.*

If you have pulled out a print because the highlights were not appearing quickly enough, you should apply developer to the highlights only. The print should be returned to the developer dish for a short period after the 'painting' to ensure that the print develops rich blacks.

Considerable practice is needed before this technique can be mastered, but the effort is worthwhile in giving prints that little extra touch of quality. The technique can only be used for *minor* adjustments to print tone and is not designed to compensate for inaccurate printing exposures. Fast-developing papers (eg. Kodabrome, Ilfospeed) are less easy to control in the developer, so the technique is best applied to the slower-developing fibre-based papers.

Print shape

Traditionally, photographs are rectangular in shape, following the typical format of paintings, and for many subjects this configuration is very suitable. But do not feel obliged to make all your photographs rectangular. Instead, let the composition dictate the format and be prepared to try less obvious shapes.

72-73 The enlarger negative carrier and lens board were both tilted to change the shape of this photograph. By doing this it was possible to square up the bricks so preventing the viewer's eye from wandering out of the right side of the picture. See fig 6.20 for technique.

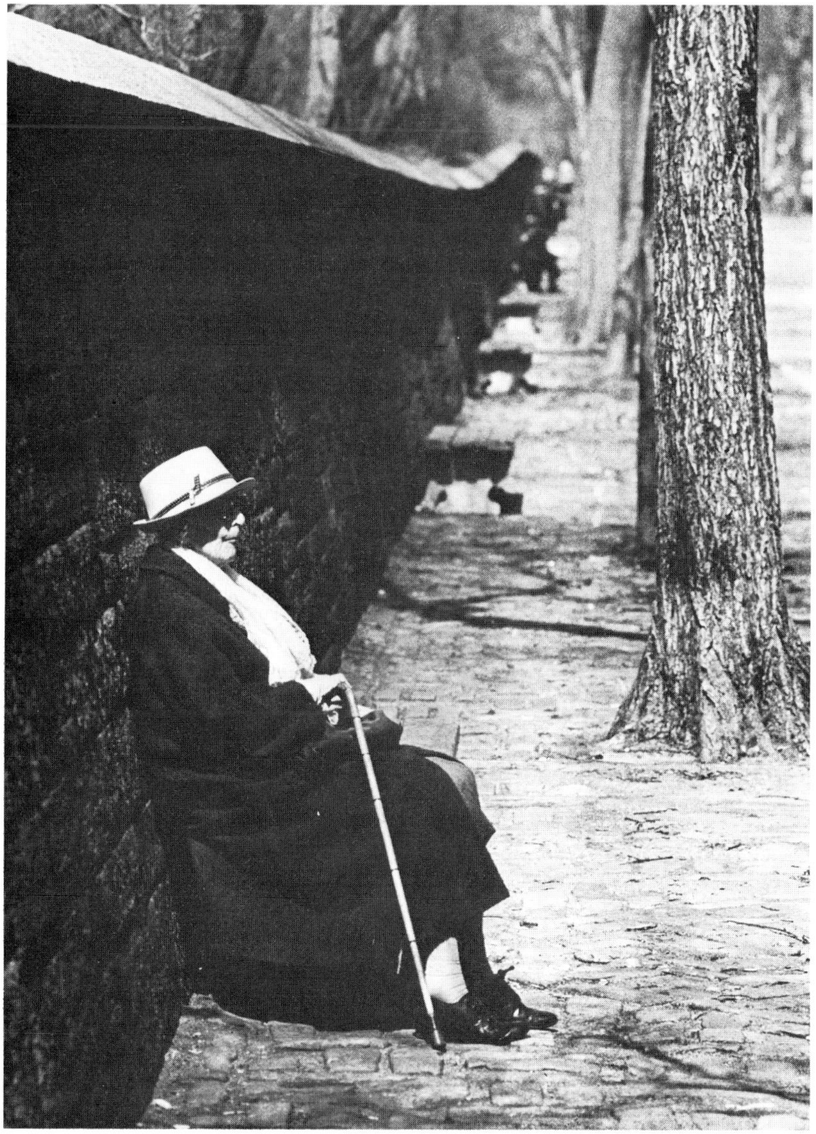

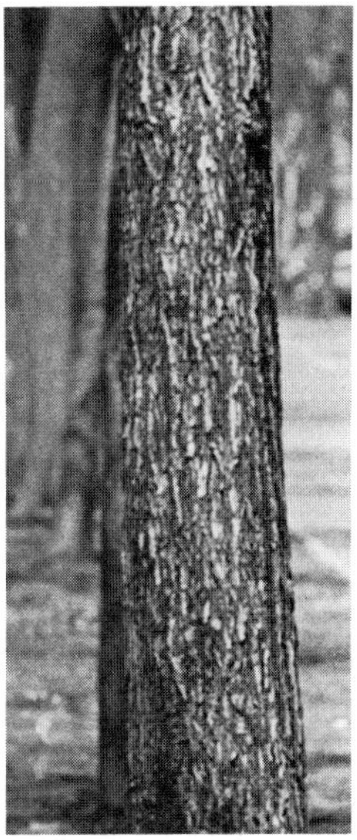

70-71 One advantage of variable contrast paper is that it gives you the ability to vary contrast locally within the same photograph. The original image (above) was a straight printing exposure using Multigrade filter 2. It produced good contrast for the old lady and background but gave a rather flat result on the right side. A second print (left) used a number 2 filter for exposure to the left side, but a number 4 filter to increase contrast on the tree side. A constantly moving card was used during both exposures to shield the half not being exposed.

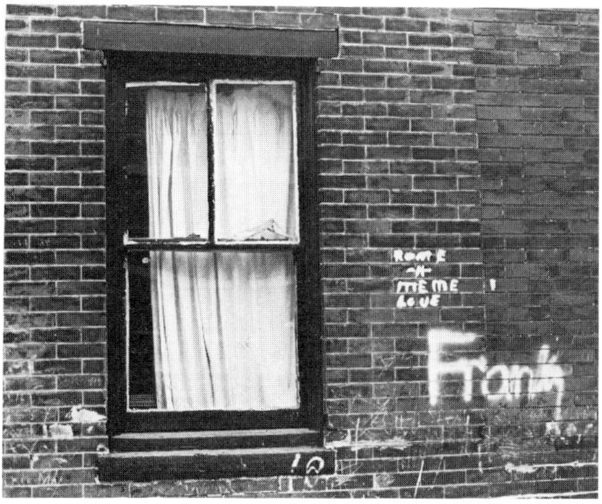

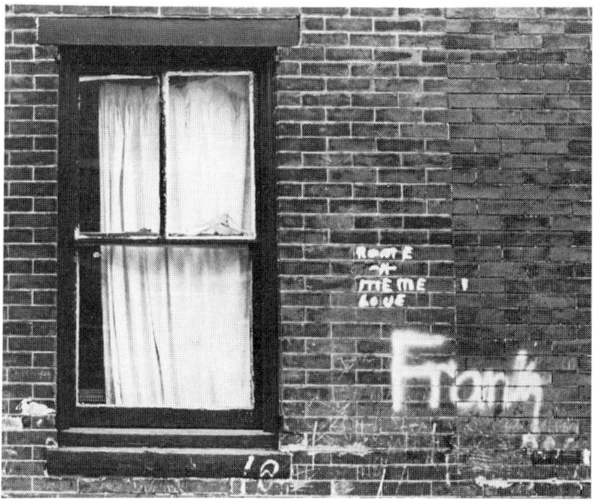

During printing, the question of whether to crop the negative again arises, as it does when considering camera composition (page 17). There are a few photographers who believe that cropping should not be a part of printing but a decision taken in the camera. For most people, however, printing gives a second chance to alter the image.

Size of print

There can be no rule for the size of a print but it is possible to make a few general observations. The purpose for which the print is being produced must be the main influence on print size. For example, most exhibition prints are fairly large (40 x 30cm or larger) so that the viewer can stand well back and get a full view of the photograph. Of course, a small photograph submerged amongst several 50 x 40cm prints will attract greater attention because it is different, and there is always a good argument for not following the accepted norm. However, once your print has drawn the viewer's notice then it must stand on its own merits.

Avoid enlarging a negative to such an extent that the image quality starts to 'break up' (definition is lost, graininess is intrusive), as the viewer is put off by technical considerations and may never really perceive the photograph. The print size should be kept comfortably within the limitations of the negative, which will depend on factors such as subject, lighting (both of the subject and that illuminating the print), camera format, and the amount of cropping.

Small prints can look very 'precious' and 'delicate', especially when they are surrounded by a relatively large area of tone. When this approach suits the subject and the photographer's style, the print can be elevated to 'fine art'. But remember, there is a very thin line between a small print being successful and, on the other hand, simply appearing pretentious.

Mounting prints

For exhibitions, it is usually necessary to mount the print on card so that it is protected and can be pinned to a wall or board. For archival mounting it is essential to use special 100 per cent rag acid-free board, otherwise the chemicals within the board will eventually attack the silver of the photograph. The methods of mounting are:

Dry mounting A special shellac tissue is 'tacked' to the back of the print with a tacking iron and the print and tissue are then trimmed to size. The mounting board is preheated in the mounting press (a kind of large flat-bed heating press), the print placed in correct position on the board and the corners of the tissue are tacked to the board. This board/tissue/print sandwich is sealed together in the mounting press (most photographic clubs have one) or you can use an ordinary domestic iron but you must do some tests to find the best temperature setting. The recommended temperatures for dry mounting vary depending on the paper and tissue used, so check the manufacturer's data. In general, RC prints must not be overheated (above about 80°C) because this causes the polyethylene coating to crack.

Spray adhesive is supplied in pressurised cans and is adequate for quick mounting. It is not suitable for permanent mounting because the solvent can eventually stain the print.

Rubber-based adhesives, such as 'Cow Gum', are ideal for quick work (eg. a 'paste-up') where a permanent display is not required. One particular advantage of this type of adhesive is that the print can be repositioned at virtually any time.

Mat mounting (fig 6.21) involves attaching a print with linen tape to a board and then covering

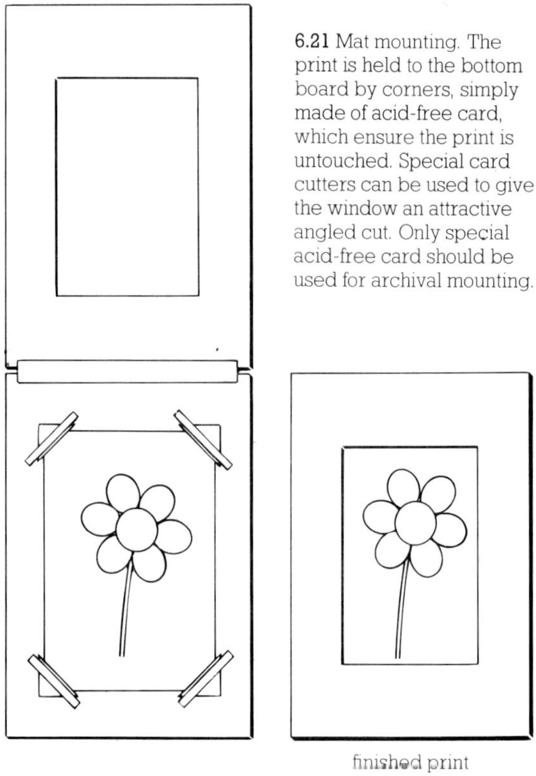

6.21 Mat mounting. The print is held to the bottom board by corners, simply made of acid-free card, which ensure the print is untouched. Special card cutters can be used to give the window an attractive angled cut. Only special acid-free card should be used for archival mounting.

75 Simple subjects are usually best presented in a simple manner; this uncomplex image looks more attractive as a small print. To direct attention to the central band of the photograph, both the top and bottom of the picture were darkened by burning-in.

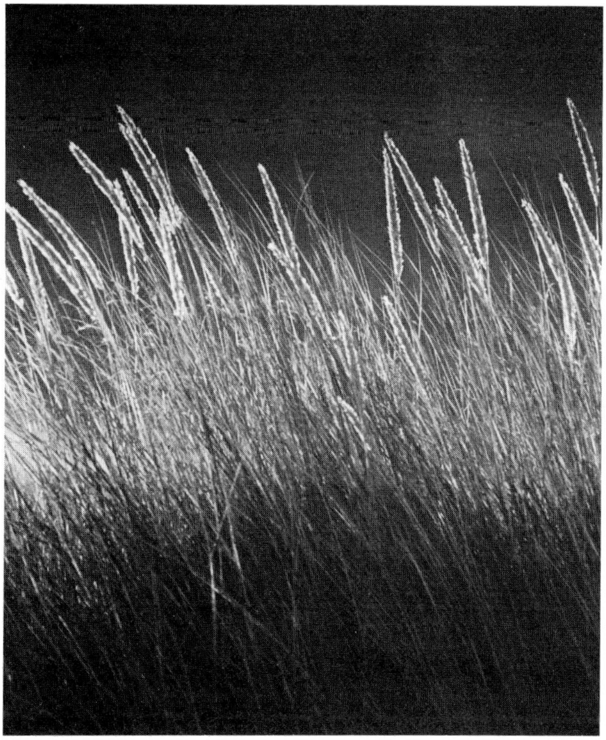

75 The square format is ideal for this graphic night photograph. Notice how the three main compositional elements of rubbish, house and illuminated concrete form a strong triangular relationship.

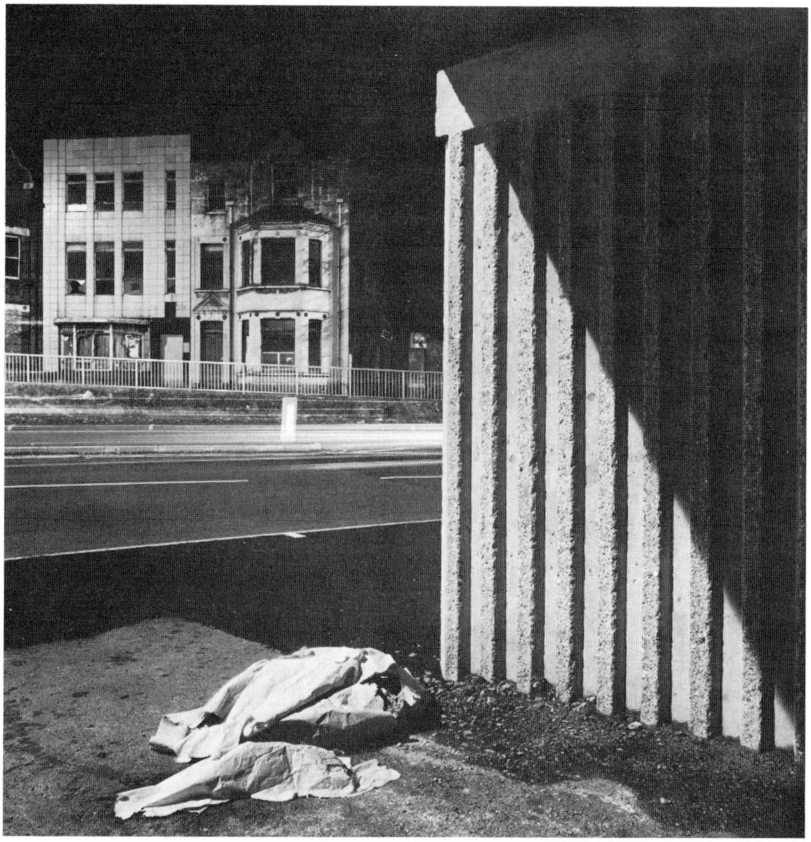

the print with another piece of board (hinged with tape to the bottom board) that has a window cut out to display the photograph. This method is ideal for displaying archival prints because the print is essentially untouched and the window board prevents the framing glass from actually touching the print surface. This could cause adhesion of the photographic gelatin to the glass under hot and humid conditions.

It is a simple matter to surround a print with a black (or white) line by mounting the print twice. The procedure is:

1 Tack dry mounting tissue to the back of the print and trim the two together to the required image dimensions.
2 Place the print on black (or white) heavy paper and tack the corners of the tissue to the paper.
3 Tack a second piece of tissue to the back of the black (white) paper and trim them to give the required width of black (white) surround.
4 Finally tack the corners of the second piece of tissue to the white (black) board, and place the complete double layer sandwich in the dry mounting press.

Print presentation
It is easy to mount a photograph quickly on to card and think that this is all there is to presentation. A print that has taken hours of work to produce, from careful camera composition and exposure, through controlled film development, to painstaking printing can be ruined by thoughtless presentation.

First of all, consider what surrounding material best suits your photograph. For example, a large white surround forces the viewer to look at a relatively small print. This approach usually suits a photograph with dark tones along its print perimeters. Any white detail along the edges of the photograph will fade into nothing if it is surrounded by white. But one solution to this is to have a fine black line around the print to 'enclose' the image.

When a photograph is encompassed by black it gives the viewer the feeling of looking at the subject through a window, and forces his attention to stay within the photograph. This effect is more pronounced when the print is small and the surround relatively large. Substantial black image areas which touch the black surrounds are likely to 'disappear' and in this case you should either consider having a different surrounding or a thin white line around the print to contain it (see mounting of prints).

Grey tones can be used successfully to surround prints, but can sometimes have the effect of 'flattening' the image. As with all possible choices of surround, place the unmounted print against the backgrounds and see which works best.

The simplest way to present a print is to flush-mount it, ie. mount on to card and then trim it to the picture borders so that there are then no surrounds. The drawback to this approach is that your photograph will be viewed against whatever material it is attached to, whether it complements it or not. You have lost control over the perception of your image. If you know the material on which the exhibition is being presented, this approach may suffice but your photograph is still very vulnerable to edge damage from knocks and pins; a photograph mounted inside a surround can always be remounted.

Coloured mounts
Surrounding a black-and-white photograph with a colour can sometimes be successful but it is far more likely to be disastrous. If you are tempted to try coloured surrounds, stick to desaturated colours such as browns and creams, as they are more likely to be pleasing than very pure vivid colours.

As you will have gathered, there is never just one correct way to present a photograph, so always try as many presentation styles as possible and make up your own mind which approach is best in each case. But be careful not to over-present your photograph. Be prepared to let the image stand on its own strengths instead. Remember, presentation is an *enhancement* of the photograph.

Print retouching
Make sure your prints are correctly retouched to hide unsightly white dust marks or small hairs before they are displayed. There is nothing more disappointing than to try viewing an otherwise superb image but to be distracted by these blemishes. Somehow, much of the magic of a good photograph is lost when you are made conscious of the mechanics of production.

The best approach, and the easiest, is to keep the laborious job of retouching to a minimum by adopting a clean working technique. This means careful mixing and use of chemicals, fixing a water filter if necessary, and drying negatives in a dust-free atmosphere. Once dry, the negatives should

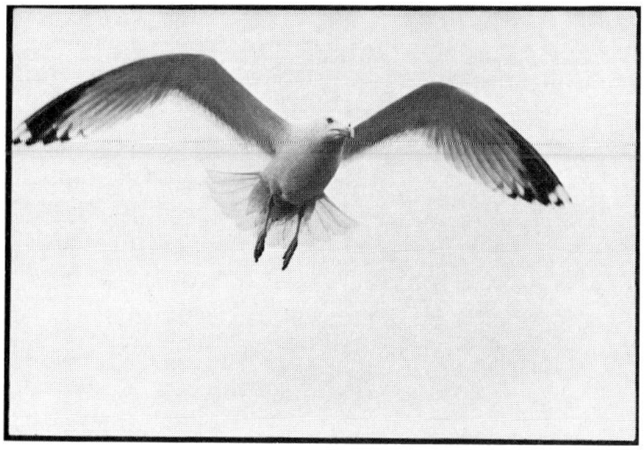

76 To 'contain' the bird, a black line was printed around the photograph. In this case, it was done by printing the full 35mm frame on a 6 x 6 enlarger and projecting the total image plus film perforations. The arms of the printing easel were adjusted to give the required thickness of black line.

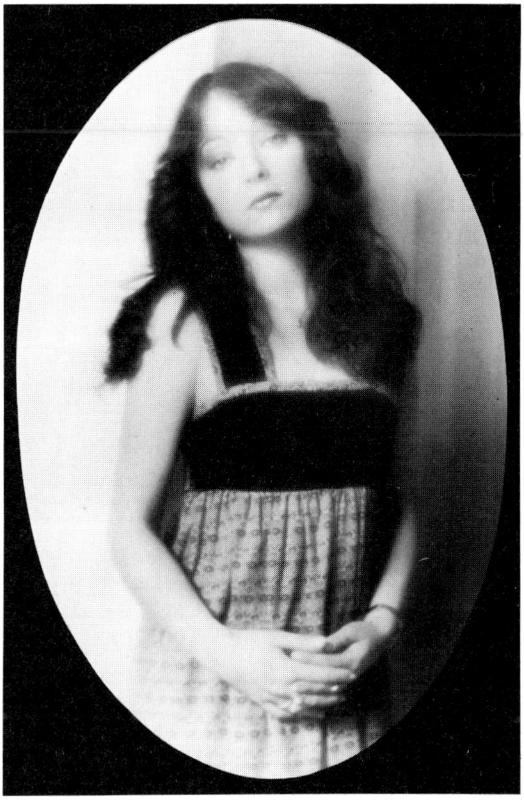

77 To further enhance the charm of this soft-focus portrait, the print was made on warm-toned paper and mounted behind an oval cut-out.

be stored carefully and handled only by the edges. A plastic cover will keep your enlarger free of dust and cleaning the negative with a blow brush or compressed air just before printing will pay dividends.

As we have already been, the easiest prints to retouch are those with non-glossy surfaces, and fibre-based prints are slightly easier to work with than RC prints. Avoid using watercolours for retouching as the colour sits on the surface. Instead, apply photographic dye, which is absorbed into the emulsion and does not leave a mark on the print surface.

The basic steps of retouching white marks are:

1 Work on a comfortable table or drawing board and ensure that there is plenty of light–an angled desk lamp gives ideal illumination.
2 Select the appropriate colour dye (brown-black, neutral black, or blue-black) to match the colour of your photograph and place a few drops on an artist's pallette or glazed tile. Dilute the dye with water until tests on a spare print show that it gives a lighter tone than required.
3 Using a high quality sable brush (0 size for small spots up to 3 for larger areas) collect diluted dye on the brush and wipe on a paper tissue until almost dry.
4 Working from the centre of the white mark outwards apply retouching dye by gently dabbing (not by stroking). It is best to work on several marks at the same time, returning to each and building up density to the required level. Avoid going over the edge of the mark as this leaves a distracting dark ring around it.

Black marks, caused by dust on the film during exposure, are more difficult to remove and are best avoided by ensuring that your camera is kept dust free and using a compressed air can (or blow brush) to clean the film chamber before loading. (Never use a compressed air can on the mirror of an SLR camera because the propellants can affect the surface.) However, if you are unfortunate enough to have black marks on your print, these can be 'removed' by one of the following:

1 Carefully scrape them away with a sharp scalpel. This technique needs a considerable knack to perfect and is not suitable for glossy print surfaces.
2 Apply a white opaque medium mixed with the appropriate amount of black dye to match the surrounding density; the retouched print may have to

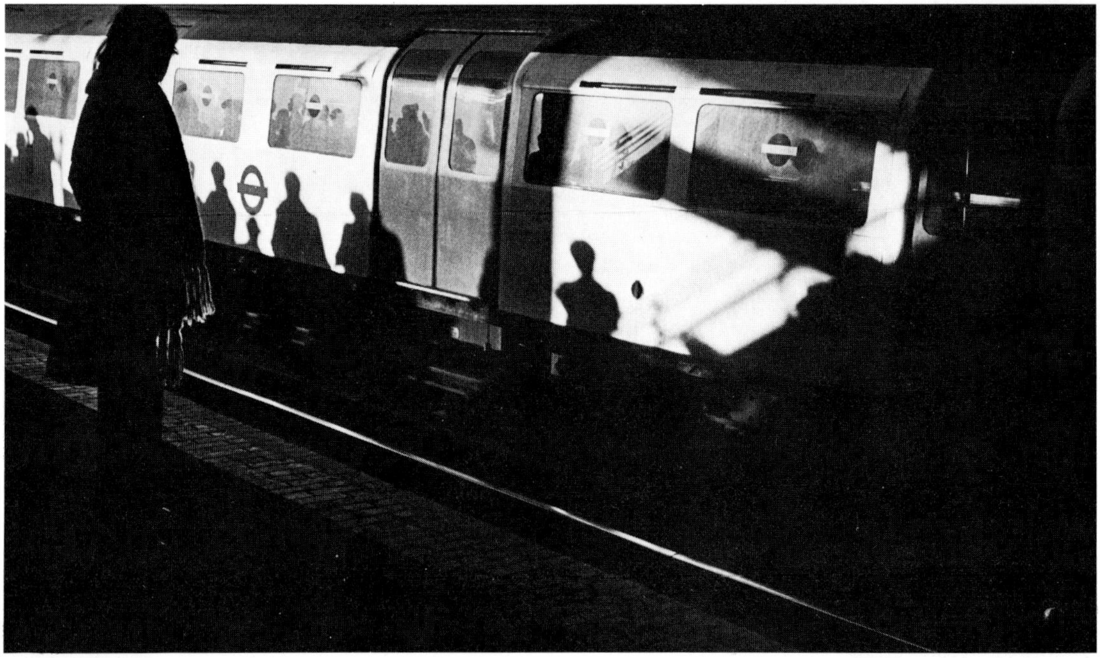

78 Photographs such as this example, which have important but subtle shadow and highlight detail, are difficult for printers to reproduce. The best reproductions require very fine half-tone screens. This particular photograph would lose a good deal of its detailed tonality if it were reproduced in a newspaper.

be sprayed with a sealant (not recommended for archival prints) to disguise retouching.

3 Bleach out the black marks to white with a reducer (page 126) and retouch it, as for white marks. This technique must be done very carefully as mistakes are difficult to rectify.

A great deal of patience is required for retouching, but, if carefully done, it greatly improves the appearance of the photograph.

Prints for reproduction

It is appropriate here to give a few guidelines on producing black-and-white prints for reproduction in newspapers, magazines, books and other printed matter. If you examine the photographs reproduced in this book with a magnifying glass you will notice that they are made up from small black and white dots–this dot pattern is known as a *halftone* reproduction.

The lightest parts of a printed photograph consist mainly of white paper with small regular dots of black ink. When seen from a normal viewing distance these small dots merge with the surrounding white to give a light tone. The middle tones of a photograph are reproduced as dots which cover about half (known as 50 per cent dots) the paper area. The darkest parts of the image are printed as black ink with small areas of white paper showing through. Thus, the tonal scale of the original photograph is reproduced as a series of halftone dots where size varies according to the depth of tone.

The number of dots in a given area is determined by the halftone screen which is used to make the printing plates. For high quality reproduction this halftone screen is very fine (about 133 lines/inch or 50 lines/cm) and for less exacting work is relatively coarse (about 60 lines/inch or 20 lines/cm).

Newspapers with their high printing speeds and low quality paper can only cope with coarse halftones; this restricts the available tonal range so that only modest blacks are possible and also means that very fine image detail is lost. Because of the compression of tonal information at the extreme ends of the tonal scale, it is best to supply photographs which have most of their information in the mid-tones. Also, avoid recording subjects with two much fine detail. Supply prints made on glossy-surfaced paper.

Most *magazines and books* use high quality 'coated' paper which is capable of reproducing a fine halftone image. The quality of photographic reproduction can be extremely high and you should supply only top quality (exhibition standard) photographs of wide tonal range.

7 TOWARDS ULTIMATE CONTROL OF PRINT QUALITY

So far, we have discussed the photographic variables–film exposure, film development and print making–in fairly general terms, allowing the photographer to apply this knowledge intuitively to specific situations. In fact, many photographers become masters of technique simply by careful observation, a good basic knowledge of materials and processes and trial-and-error. They are able to tune their equipment and materials to give very controllable and successful pictures. But, unfortunately, this 'sixth sense' takes a long time to acquire.

This chapter therefore takes the basic knowledge covered so far and develops it into a precise, but practical approach. Not all the techniques to be described are applicable in all styles of photography but the extra understanding acquired will still be valuable.

Zone System

The suggestions that follow are based on the Zone System of black-and-white photography, an exact method of exposing and developing film so that the tonal qualities of the print can be previsualised at the time of pressing the shutter. Mastery of the Zone System means that the photographer can control and predict precisely how the coloured subject reproduces as a series of black tones.

Photographing a scene involves recording a wide range of brightnesses, from the shadows through the mid-tones to the highlights. To simplify the discussion, the Zone System relates everything to a scale of ten greys from black through to white.

Designation of the zones

Ansel Adams defined ten zones in his original Zone System and it is important that you are able to understand what is meant by naming a specific zone. The descriptions given to the zones are, as it were, the universal language of the system (fig 7.1).

Zone 0 corresponds to a clear area of the processed film (density of base + fog only) which has received an amount of exposure which is insufficient to have any effect on the film and which, when printed, gives the blackest black on the print.

The next step on the grey scale is zone I which results from the amount of light which *just* causes a film density above base + fog. The definition for zone I is effective threshold–that is the first part of the subject which just records on the film. For simplicity, let us assume that 1 unit of light crosses this threshold. Zone I reproduces in the print as extremely dark and, for reasons explained later, is often indistinguishable from maximum black (zone 0).

7.1 Designation of zones

*Relative exposure	Zone	Subject	Print
0	0	Black without features.	Zero density (except base + fog) in the negative. Max black in print.
1	I	Effective threshold. Slight density.	First sign of detail but no texture — some papers reproduce this as maximum black.
2	II	Very deep shadows.	First suggestion of texture and detail. Deep tonalities
4	III	Deep textured shadows.	Adequate texture and detail.
8	IV	Blue jeans, dark hair, average dark foliage.	Important dark shadows
16	V	Ground, most shrubs, weathered wood.	Middle grey 18 per cent reflectance
32	VI	Caucasian skin, light stone.	Textured light grey
64	VII	Skin highlights, clouds.	Light grey
128	VIII	White walls, T-shirts.	Very light grey, off-white.
256	IX	Featureless whites, lights.	White, no texture

*A doubling of exposure (1 stop) occurs between each zone.

Doubling the light striking the film (ie. 2 units in our example) produces zone II–the first sign of texture recorded by the film and producing deep tonalities in the print.

Zone III, caused by 4 units of light, corresponds to dark areas of the print which show texture.

Each remaining zone corresponds to a doubling (one stop) of the amount of light reaching the previous zone, eg. zone IV is 8 units, zone V is 16 units (see fig 7.0). The middle zones (IV, V, VI) correspond to the mid-tones of the print, and the high zones (VII, VIII, IX) to the light tones with zone IX corresponding to pure white without any detail.

Practical tests

The easiest way to understand how the Zone System operates in practice is to perform the following experiment:

1 Place an 18 per cent grey card, such as the endpaper of this book, against a firm support and light it evenly with two identical lamps (fig 7.2); it is essential that the lighting is both even and constant. If you use daylight, select a time when the light is even; open shade is ideal.

2 Move the camera close so the grey card fills the viewfinder. Have the lens out of focus (by setting the distance scale to infinity) so that the effect of any slight unevenness in the card or lighting is minimised.

3 Using either a separate hand meter or TTL metering and the film manufacturer's recommended ASA setting, measure the required exposure (see page 58). Note that any reflected reading gives a correct exposure as all meters are calibrated for 18 per cent subject reflectance. This exposure reading will give zone V.

4 Keeping careful notes, calculate the exposures required to give all the other zones, remembering that each zone is different from the next by one stop. Because shutter speeds are less reliable than lens apertures for altering exposures in one stop intervals, you should stay with just two shutter speeds for the ten zone range. Therefore use *f*/2.8 and *f*/16 for zone V (this overlap is explained under **2** below).

5 Fig 7.3 gives one example of possible readings. Note that zones ½, 1½, and X are also included in this test; the reason for this will become clear later (page 116).

6 Using these calculations, make 15 exposures in the following order: no exposure–use lens cap, zone 0, zone ½, zone I, zone I½, zone II, zone III, zone IV, zone V, (*f*/2.8), zone V (*f*/16), zone VI, zone VII, zone VIII, zone IX, zone X. In the example given these exposures would be: no exposure, 1/60 sec. *f*/16, 1/60 sec. *f*/16 11, 1/60 sec. *f*/11 . . . 1/60 sec. *f*/2.8, ½ sec. *f*/16, ½ sec. *f*/11 . . . ½ sec. *f*/2.8.

7 Process the film as *normal,* ie. in your usual developer, time, temperature, agitation, tank, etc.

Evaluation of the test film

Ideally, the film should be placed on a light box and the area not covered with film should be masked off with black paper to make observation easier. If you do not have a light box then hold the film in front of a well-lit lightly coloured wall. Do not evaluate the film directly under a lamp as observations will be extremely difficult to make.

Examine the processed film as follows:

1 Checking the film against your exposure list, mark each frame on the non-emulsion side in one corner, with the appropriate zone number–use a removable marker such as a grease pencil. The numbers should be NE (no exposure), 0, ½, 1, 2 . . . 5, 5 . . . 9, 10 (it is easier to use arabic numerals rather than roman).

2 Compare the two zone V's to see if they are almost identical in tone, as they should be for two equivalent exposures. In the unlikely event that these tones are noticeably different, this indicates that your camera shutter speeds are outside

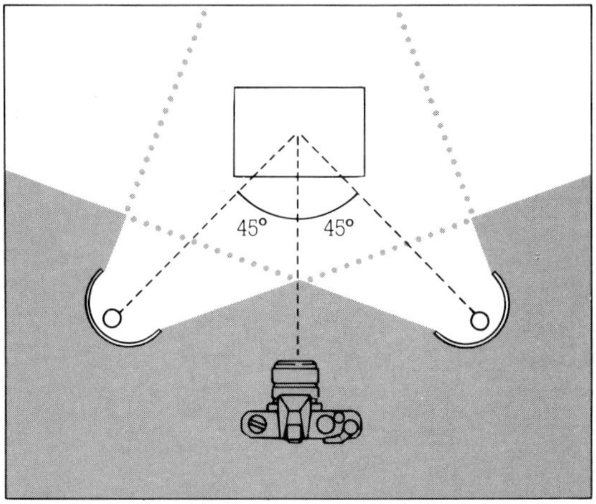

7.2 Position your copying lights so they are at 45° to the camera lens axis and at the same height as the grey card. To check if the lights are of equal brilliance, position a pencil at right angles to the card. The two shadows should be of equal density; if they are not, move one lamp closer or further way until the shadow-tones match.

7.3 Example of test exposures — Meter indicated 1/30 *f*/4

No exposure	Lens cap
Zone 0	1/60 *f*/16
½	*f*/16–*f*/11
I	*f*/11
1½	*f*/11–*f*/8
II	*f*/8
III	*f*/5.6
IV	*f*/4
V	*f*/2.8
V	½ *f*/16
VI	*f*/11
VII	*f*/8
VIII	*f*/5.6
IX	*f*/4
X	*f*/2.8

acceptable tolerances and your camera should be checked out by a specialist repairer who can recalibrate the shutter speeds.

3 Determine which is the first frame to show density greater than clear film (no exposure). If the manufacturer's recommended ASA setting is correct for your camera, meter, and processing then zone I will be the first frame to show a density above base + fog. If zone 0 is discovered to be the threshold frame, this means you should use an ASA (DIN or ISO) setting which is double the manufacturer's guide speed, eg. FP4 which is nominally ASA 125/22 DIN (ISO = 125/22°) should be rated at ASA 250/25 DIN (ISO = 250/25°). If the frame marked zone II is the threshold frame then you should rate your film at half the recommended speed (eg. FP4 should be exposed at ASA 64/19 DIN (ISO = 64/19°)). In both these cases it is unnecessary to repeat your test; instead, simply rename the zones by shifting each number *up* one in the first case where zone 0 is the threshold (0 becomes I, I becomes II, etc.) and in the second case moving each number *down* by one (I becomes 0, II becomes I, etc.).

4 If zone ½ is the first frame to show density, then you must re-shoot the test but this time rating the film ½ stop faster than the recommended speed, eg. ASA 125/22 DIN (ISO = 125/22°) becomes ASA 200/24 DIN (ISO = 200/25°). Similarly a reshoot is required if zone I½ is the threshold frame, this time using a ½ stop reduction in film speed eg. ASA 125/22 DIN (ISO = 125/22°) becomes ASA 80/20 DIN (ISO = 80/20°)).

Negative zone values into print densities

Once a correct zone number is given to each processed frame, wipe off the temporary marks and replace them with a permanent black number, if possible using ink specially formulated for writing on plastic film base (available from graphics shops).

You are now ready to translate these film densities into print tones and thereby check if your standard film development is correct for the Zone System. The procedure for this is:

1 Set up your print darkroom as normal, paying special attention to the correct strength and temperature of the print developer. It is important to develop your prints precisely as recommended by the manufacturer.

2 Place the zone 0 frame in the enlarger and project it to give an 11 x 9cm. (4½ x 3½in.) 'image' approximately.

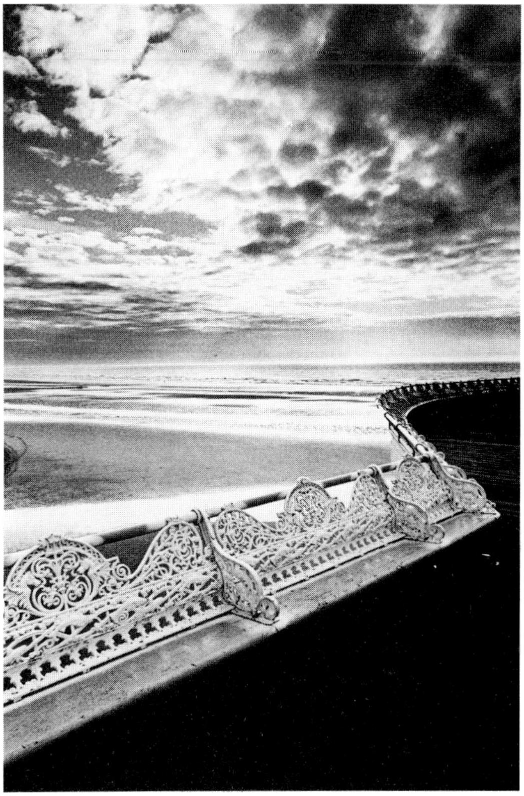

79 Photographs of scenes or images which are not about to change quickly, and which therefore allow time for spot metering, are ideal for the Zone System. In this print, the foreground wooden boards have been placed on zones I, II and III, the bench on zone V, the iron work on zones VI and VII and the lighter parts of the sand on zones VIII and IX (white). Exposure has been based on zone III (foreground) and normal film development has been used.

3 Make the usual test strips to determine the *minimum* exposure time required to give maximum black on your usual grade 2 paper. Remember that the paper must be developed precisely as recommended, eg. Ilford Galerie in PQ Universal diluted 1 + 9 for two min. at 20°C.

4 Using the same exposure time and paper development, print all the zone negatives (except zones ½ and I½). Also, process normally a piece of paper which has had no exposure.

Evaluation of printed grey scale

If your zones are correctly placed (by film exposure and development) the grey prints should have the following qualities (compare with zone definitions in fig 7.1):

There should be a range of tones from maximum black (Zone 0) through dark tones (I, II, III), mid-tones (IV, V, VI), light tones (VII, VIII), and to white (IX). Because of the shape of the characteristic curves (film and paper) the visual differences between the zones are not the same; compression in the shadows and highlights is inevitable.

Zone V should closely match the 18 per cent grey tone (compare with a standard grey card).

Zone VIII should have a very light tone which is only just different to the white of the print with no exposure.

Zone IX should match the white with no exposure.

If your zone prints do not match the zone definitions as set out above, it means your film is either over- or underdeveloped. If zone VIII is pure white (matches no-exposure paper) then your film has been overdeveloped (see page 67). The higher film contrast causes zone VIII to be of higher density than 'normal' and therefore prints as white.

On the other hand, underdevelopment causes a lower contrast than normal and consequently reduces densities, especially in the upper zones. The result is that zone IX does not print as pure white but has a slight density.

Refining film development

If the zones of your negative do not fall on the paper tone scale as they should, adjust your film development time.

In the case of overdevelopment (zone VIII is a pure white), repeat the range of zone exposures twice, each series on a separate film. Develop one film for 15 per cent less development time and the other for 30 per cent less, for example, a 'normal' 10 min. development becomes 8½ and 7 min. (see page 69 for technique). It is important not to alter any other development variables, such as agitation, temperature, etc. for these tests.

As development time increases, its effect on density increase becomes proportionally less. Therefore, an underdeveloped test (zone IX is not white) should be re-exposed on two separate films and developed for 20 and 40 per cent extra on the 'normal' time; a 10 min. standard time becomes 12 and 14 min.

These new test films should be printed (in the same manner as previously described) to give print tones. One of the new films should fit the 'normal' Zone System–ie. zone 0 gives maximum black on the print, zone V as an 18 per cent grey, zone VIII as slight tonality, zone IX as white. It is possible to judge an intermediate development time as the best match to the zone 'rules', eg. between 10 and 12 minutes in the previous example.

Having determined the correct ASA setting and the precise development time for your equipment and processing technique you are ready to apply the Zone System to picture making. It may seem like a lengthy procedure to arrive at this point, but you can now take photographs knowing you have full control of the results.

You will need to recalibrate your system if you add another camera body or buy a second camera, although it is unlikely that there will be any change in film development time, merely a possible slight change in film speed rating for the new equipment. Also, every film/developer combination is different and must be evaluated separately; this is why most Zone System enthusiasts stick to one, or possibly two combinations for all their work.

For most applications, it is unnecessary to recalibrate the system if you buy a new batch of film, although it still makes sense to buy film in bulk to eliminate any possible slight variations in coatings. However, the sheet film user who demands the ultimate in control normally calibrates each emulsion batch for film speed. To economise on film when doing these tests, the photographer using sheet film is advised to make templates so that six exposures can be made on one sheet of film (fig 7.4).

Applying the Zone System to average scenes

As previously stated, the average scene has a brightness range of 1:128, ie. there is seven stops' difference between the shadow detail to be recorded and the highlights which will reproduce as pure white. The Zone System applies a more refined definition to the 'average' scene.

A scene is considered average when an exposure meter gives the following readings: zone VIII areas of the subject (white with texture) indicate three stops less exposure than zone V (mid-greys, such as much stonework), and zone II (darkest part of the scene where detail is required in the

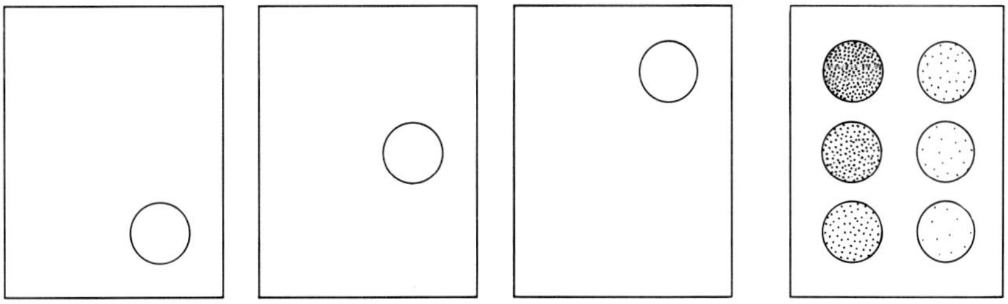

7.4 Templates for sheet film tests. The three templates are inserted into the film holder in place of the dark slide *after* the holder is in the camera. One exposure is made through each of the three templates, as shown, to give the right-hand exposures. Each template is then used again, but this time turned around to give the left-hand exposure. Thus, each processed sheet contains six zones of exposure.

print) indicates three stops more exposure than zone V. An example that should make this clearer might be a person wearing a white shirt standing on a gravel path which has several trees near it. If you take a close-up reading of the path (zone V) and it indicates an exposure of 1/125 sec. *f*/16, the white shirt (zone VIII) indicates 1/1000 sec. *f*/16, and the dark shadow of the tree bark (zone II) 1/15 sec *f*/16, then this can be defined as an average scene. Setting the camera at 1/125 sec. *f*/16, as all meters are calibrated for zone V, and developing and printing for the Zone System, will produce a print on grade 2 which has dark but discernible detail in the tree bark, the path rendered as 18 per cent grey and a white shirt as white but with slight tonality. A further reference point in this example could be the skin (Caucasian) which should indicate an exposure of 1/250 sec. *f*/16 (zone VI).

Zone System and metering

As we have just seen, you require several meter readings to use the Zone System. This is where the spot meter (page 63) with its narrow angle of acceptance comes into its own–it enables you to search the scene and precisely and individually determine the different exposure readings for the various tones. For example, you can compare the reading of one area which you 'see' as zone VIII with, say, a zone IV area, checking if the brightness difference is, in fact, four stops. In this example, you can determine your camera settings (based on zone V) from either a zone VIII or zone IV reading by giving three stops more exposure than the zone VIII reading or one stop less than the zone IV reading–the result should be the same.

Essentially, the Zone System works by measuring key zones and checking that the intervals between zones is one stop in exposure for each zone number. The camera settings can be determined from any one zone reading, although most photographers prefer to base their exposure on the lower zones (II, III, IV) to ensure that full shadow detail is recorded. This is particularly true if there is little time to take a full range of meter readings. To begin with it is easier to use zone IV (important texture detail such as brown hair, dark clothes) to gauge exposure rather than zones II or III which are more difficult to define and locate in the scene.

Subjects of greater than average brightness range

If, after metering say, zone IV and zone VIII, you find there are *five* stops of exposure difference, then if the camera settings are based on zone IV and normal film development is given, the delicate highlights will not record as zone VIII but as zone IX. When the resulting print on grade 2 paper correctly places zone IV, the delicate highlights ('seen' as zone VIII) will appear white without texture (ie. as zone IX).

There are two possible approaches to ensure that an area which is visualised as zone VIII but which gives a zone IX reading is correctly placed as zone VIII on the print. You can either accept the resulting negative but print it on to a softer than normal paper (grades 0, 1, or 0, ½, 1, 1½ for variable contrast papers) or reduce film development so that the high reading zone VIII does, in fact, record as zone VIII on the film.

The 35mm and 120 user, of course, records several scenes on a single roll of film and it is extremely unlikely that they would all have the 'normal' relationship of zones. For most situations, where the majority of exposures on the film are of near-average brightness range, it is best to develop the film normally and accommodate the non-average scenes by printing on paper other than grade 2.

Where each scene is exposed on a separate sheet of film, it is better to adjust development so that zone VIII falls correctly on the processed negative and the print is made on grade 2 paper. This is known in the Zone System as planning development for *one zone of compression.* The sheet film user therefore meters each scene very carefully and makes notes on the required development (see below) for each exposure.

When metering indicates an even wider brightness range (1:500 or greater) then film development should be planned for *two zones of compression.* This means that an area visualised as zone VIII but metering as zone X is forced down to zone VIII by reduced development.

If most exposures on a roll of film are of wider than normal brightness range, then it makes sense to reduce development by one or two zones. The normal scenes on the roll can then be printed on to harder papers than normal to compensate for their reduced negative density scale.

Subjects of short brightness range

When the meter readings indicate that the separation of zone IV and zone VIII is less than four stops, film development should be increased to compensate. For example, if zone IV of a scene meters as 1/250 *f*/5.6 and zone VIII as 1/250 *f*/16, normal development would place our visualised zone VIII as zone VII. The best solution is to plan development for *one zone of expansion.*

For very flat scenes, it may be necessary to expand development by two zones and, in some rare instances, by three zones.

Again, because of each scene's individual control, adjustment of development is best suited to the sheet film user but the 35mm and 120 enthusiast can apply the technique when the majority of the exposures are of low brightness range. Remember, though, extended development rapidly increases graininess and it may be preferable to expand development by a modest amount and also print on hard paper. The occasional flat scene on a roll of otherwise normal exposures is best adjusted by printing controls and the use of harder papers.

Development control for zone compression

To determine the precise development times for zone compression and expansion, you must make new grey scale tests as described on page 114 or re-evaluate your initial trials. This is why it is essential to keep accurate notes of exposure and development tests.

One zone of compression occurs when zone IX of the exposure tests prints (on grade 2 paper) as zone VIII. It is possible that one of your initial tests gave this result, and if this is so simply make a note of the reduced development time to give this one-zone compression. If your initial test was 'spot on' and your normal development time gave perfect 'normal' Zone System results then you will need to expose two more series of exposures on different films–develop one film for 15 per cent less time than normal and the other 30 per cent less (full details have already been given on page 114).

To achieve two zones of compression, zone X of the film test should print as zone VIII on grade 2 paper. The reduced development times described in the last paragraph should also encompass a compression of two zones. When results do not quite match the 'normal' Zone System print scale it is possible to make an estimate between tests to determine the best development time for compression of zones.

Development for three zones of compression (zone X of the test exposures prints as 'normal' zone VII) is rarely practical since development times are likely to be so short as to be in danger of giving uneven development. Also, this amount of development compression is only needed on very rare occasions and can be more easily achieved by the use of a softer grade of paper.

Development control for zone expansion

The procedure for determining the appropriate development times for expansion of zones is identical to that just described for zone compression, except that development times are longer than normal. The essential method has already been described.

Development for one zone of expansion means that zone VII of the test exposures prints as zone VIII, thereby compensating for a subject of lower than normal brightness distribution. Two zones of expansion occur when zone VI of the test exposures prints as zone VIII. In most situations of very low subject brightness range where three zones of expansion is needed (zone V test exposure printing as zone VIII) it is best to develop the film for two zones of expansion and print on to a harder grade of paper to achieve correct tonal distribution in the print.

Once you have determined the development times for your film/developer combination(s)

80 Metering of this scene quickly revealed that the subject brightness range was well in excess of even a two stop compression of zones. Therefore, exposure was based on the immediate foreground (zone IV) and development was for a two zone compression. The print required the holding back of the foreground and burning in of the sky.

81 Although it is possible to take several spot readings of sunsets, it is usually quicker to apply a modified Zone System. In this case, exposure and film development were based on two readings–the immediate foreground (zone I) and the sky away from the sun (zone V.)

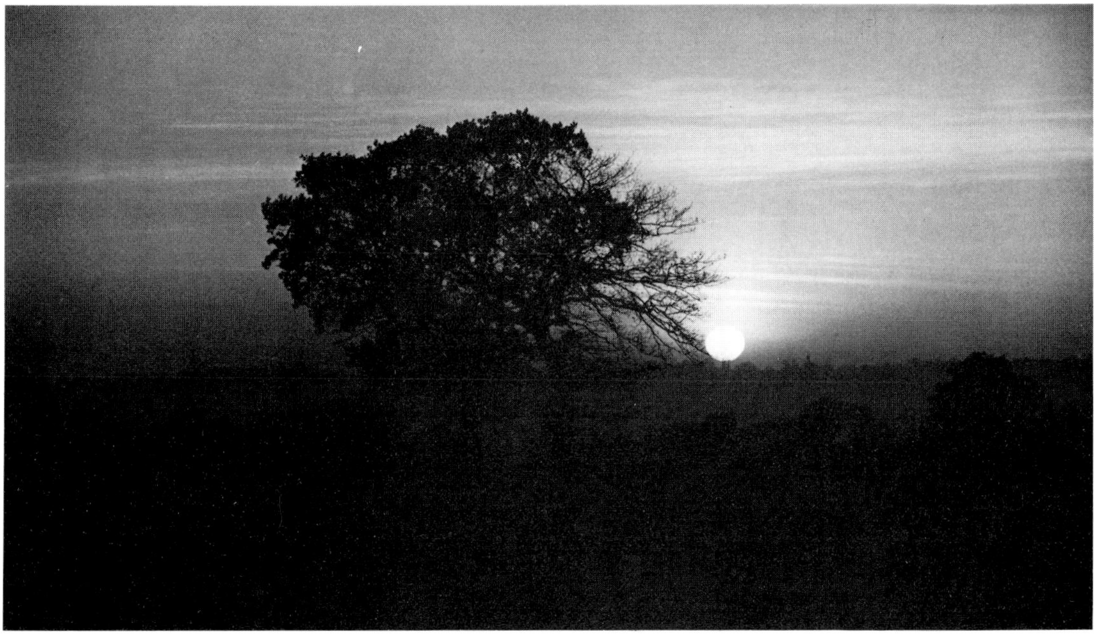

which give one and two zones of compression and expansion, you can apply them to practical exposure situations, such as those described at the end of this chapter.

Summary of the Zone System

Although at first the Zone System may appear complex it is, in fact, a simple and logical method of applying photographic sensitometry (the scientific evaluation of photographic materials and processes) to practical situations. In summary, the Zone System comprises:

1 Exposure tests on film to determine the correct ASA setting for your camera equipment, meter, developer, and processing technique.
2 Finding the correct film development time to ensure that each zone of the test film prints as defined by the Zone System, ie. zone 0 as black, zone V as 18 per cent grey, zone VIII as slight tonality, etc.
3 Determining the variations in development times to achieve one and two zones of compression or expansion.
4 Measuring the brightness of key zones of the subject and from these readings, deciding on camera settings and required film development.
5 Printing to retain your visualisation of the subject.

Various film formats and the Zone System

Only the *sheet film user,* with his ability to expose and process each photograph separately, can practise the Zone System in its entirety. Photographers like Ansel Adams meter several zones of each scene, make careful notes, expose accordingly, and process each sheet precisely as indicated by their notes and previous tests. The procedure is not difficult but it is exacting, and produces prints of superb quality which mirror the photographer's visualisation at the time of photographing the scene.

This style of very controlled working is most successful when the scene can be studied in a fairly leisurely way, such as in most landscape photography. However, this does not rule out the photographer determining the 'precise moment' to press the shutter, perhaps waiting for the clouds to be in the 'correct' position or the lighting to be precisely as metered and visualised. The latter is of course necessary in climates where the weather and lighting is constantly changing.

Because the *roll film user* must process all the different scenes on a single roll for the same development time, he does not have the finite control of the sheet film worker. However, he can follow the Zone System's method of working very closely and use a modified approach. There are many possible modifications he can use and the following suggestions will help you decide which practical option would work best for you:

1 Whenever possible, use more than one camera body/back, as this allows you to keep similar scenes on the same roll. For example, you could expose lower-than-normal contrast scenes on one roll and use another roll for normal and higher-than-normal contrast subjects.
2 Process all the exposed film from one expedition on the same occasion and avoid having a roll containing scenes from different photographic trips. Black-and-white film is relatively cheap and it is also easy to cut 35mm film (in the dark!) half way through the roll.
3 Keep careful notes so that you can process each roll to suit the majority of exposures on the roll. If you also adopt suggestion 1 the small variation of subject brightness range within the roll should ensure that all the negatives produce excellent prints, probably on slightly different grades of paper.
4 Avoid adopting too many film/developer combinations, but concentrate your efforts on thoroughly understanding the chosen one(s).
5 For faster working, base your exposures on one meter reading, eg. zone V (incident reading, 18 per cent grey card), and develop according to the *general* subject brightness range which can be measured at leisure. This method works well for photojournalistic subjects and when lighting conditions are relatively stable.
6 For particularly 'difficult' subjects, such as snow scenes (see page 121) it is best to take several different exposures (ie. bracketing) of each scene on each roll and develop them separately from more conventional subjects. Some photographers like to make a *'clip test'*, whereby a short length of test exposures is developed and evaluated before the main bulk of work is processed.

Some specific examples of the Zone System

The photographs in this book have been selected to illustrate specific technical points which are fully explained by the captions. Because there is, inevitably, some loss of tonal scale when a photograph is reproduced in a book or magazine the reader must take this into account when analysing

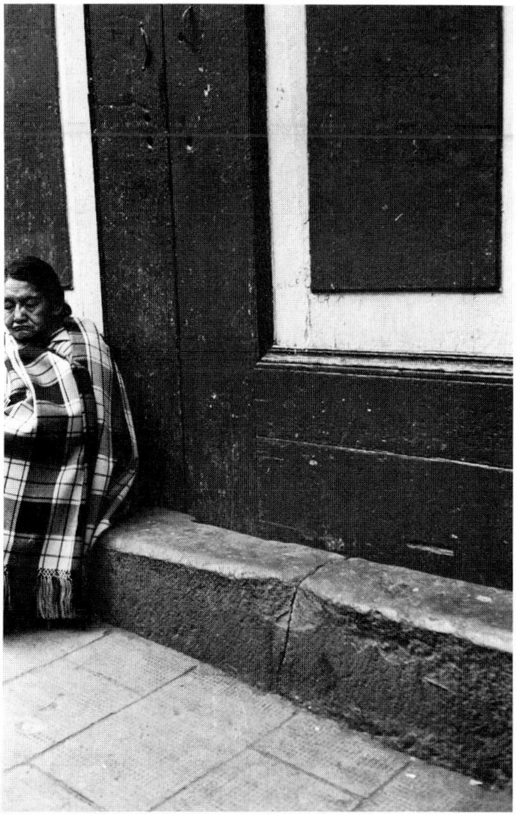

82 A quick metering (undetected) to the right of this subject revealed a scene of average brightness range. Therefore, exposure was based on the dark wood reading to give zone III and development was 'normal'. Notice the unusual framing which has produced a stronger composition than a straightforward photojournalistic image.

the caption comments.

However, to augment the photographs in this book it is worthwhile discussing some specific types of subject and the 'problems' they cause.

Landscapes generally have a wide tonal distribution and include large areas of mid-tones. Most photographers like to place delicate highlights, such as white clouds and light stonework, on zones VII or VIII, and base their camera settings on zone III which might be the darker detail of trees. If you take a general reflected reading of the scene tip the meter downwards and thereby prevent the lighter toned sky from biasing the reading. Filters (page 40) can be used to darken and lighten tones; for example, a light orange filter has the effect of reducing the sky in most landscapes by the equivalent of about one zone, a red filter reduces it by about two zones. A green filter can be used to lighten foliage by about one zone.

Seascapes are a similar case, except there is usually a larger proportion of lighter tones (VI, VII, VIII) than in landscapes. It is essential to prevent these highlights from 'burning out' to white (zone IX), especially on sunny days, and often film development needs to be compressed by one or two zones. On the other hand, some photographers like to base exposure on zone VIII, develop for normal zone reproduction, and let the darker areas fall into zones I, II and III–this gives the seascape a very sombre and dramatic appearance.

Snowscapes obviously consist mainly of higher zone values and it is important to ensure that exposure and development places these on zones VII and VIII. It is very easy to end up with underexposed negatives where the snow has been recorded as an 18 per cent grey (zone V), especially with automatic metering cameras. One

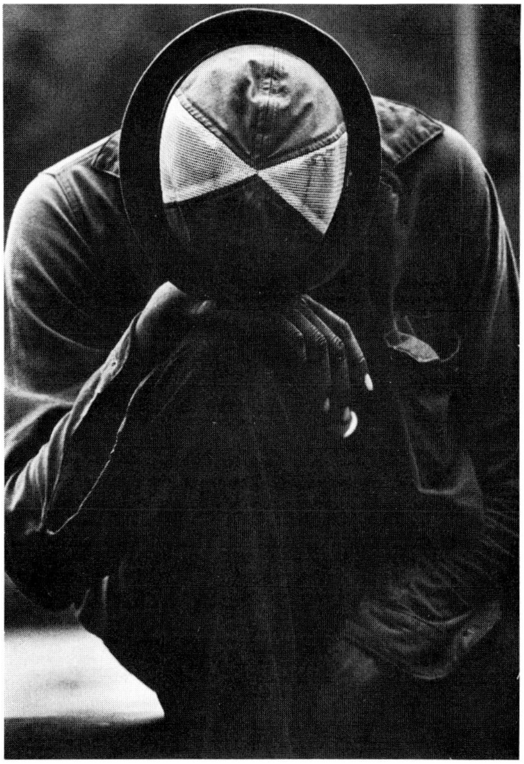

83 Most of the zones of this subject are between II and IV and exposure was based on these areas. In practice, it was more convenient to take one carefully judged exposure using the camera TTL meter and basing development (in this case for one zone of expansion) on more leisurely readings taken from surrounding comparable subjects.

method of avoiding this, if no separate hand meter is available, is to reduce the film's speed rating by two or three stops, eg. ASA 125/22 DIN (ISO = 125/22°) becomes ASA 32/16 DIN (ISO = 32/16°)) or ASA 16/13 DIN (ISO = 16/13°) and metering off the snow highlights–essentially you are adjusting the metering system to read for zones VII and VIII instead of its normal zone V. Whenever possible, avoid reducing film development time to compensate for a wide subject brightness range, as this has the effect of flattening highlight detail–an essential ingredient of good snow pictures. It is usually preferable to sacrifice some shadow detail.

Portraits in which the lighting is controlled by the photographer, such as in a studio or using window light which is balanced with reflectors or fill-in flash, are ideal for use of the Zone System. Adjust your lighting until you get the correct meter readings for the various tones. Normally-lit Caucasian skin should fall on zone VI, black hair with some detail on zone III, highlights on zone VII or VIII. It is sometimes helpful to place an 18 per cent grey card in the frame and measure for zone V. Non-Caucasian skin tones are best placed on zone V or IV and must not be placed on too low a zone, or delicate details will be lost. Avoid lighting the sitter with too much contrast as the facial areas in shadow may appear very dark (zone I or II) in the print. Use your meter to check subject brightness range, which should ideally be about 1:128 (seven stops).

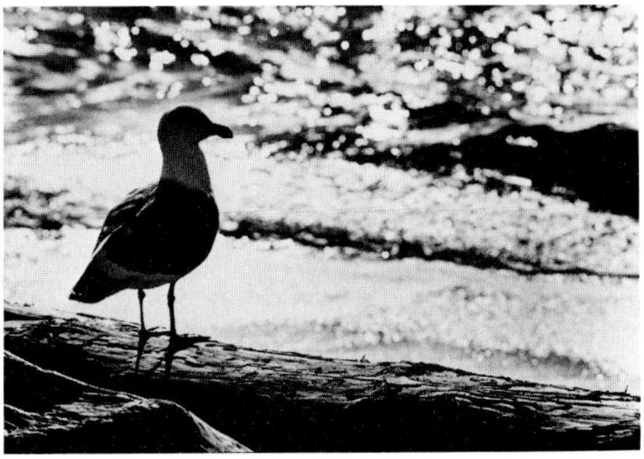

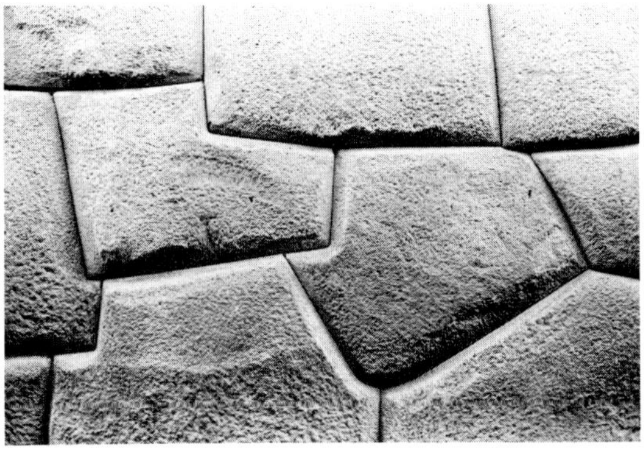

Photojournalistic portraits (or any form of subject where full tonal scale metering is impossible due to lack of time) are best judged for exposure on an overall zone V, such as given by an incident or general reflected reading (see page 58). Development can then be adjusted according to readings of the general lighting conditions taken

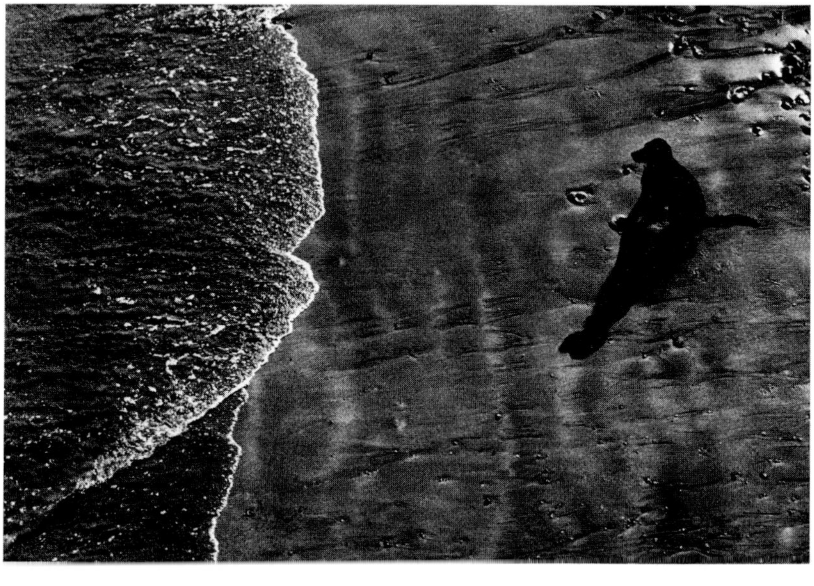

84 The large area of sand makes an ideal surface from which to take a meter reading, and on which to base the camera settings. The sand was placed on zone IV and because of the wider-than-normal subject brightness range (dark shadow to water highlights) the film was developed for one zone of compression.

85 Because the photograph was taken on roll film (35mm) it was not possible to apply the Zone System strictly. However, a spot meter was used to meter the highlights on the water and the tones of the driftwood. Exposure was based on the darkest areas of the wood (zone II) and the whole roll of film was developed for one zone of compression. The final print still needed considerable burning-in for the water highlights.

86 Static subjects of this type are ideal for the Zone System of working, as spot readings can be taken at leisure. Exposure here was based on the lightest areas of the stone printing as zone VII, and development was found to need one zone of expansion.

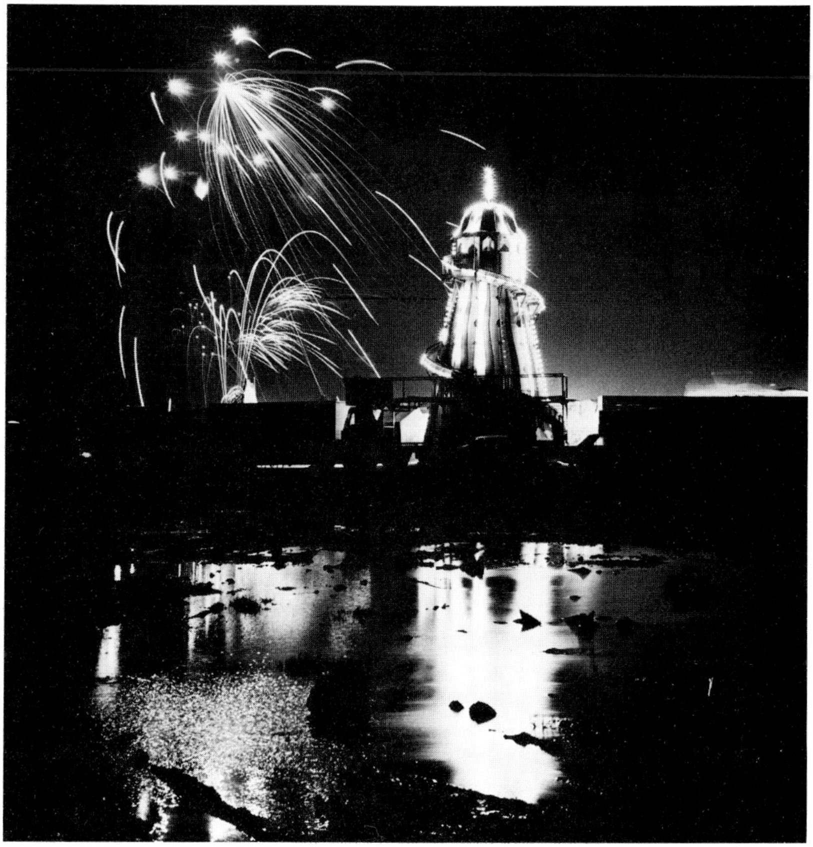

87 A sensitive spot meter was used to take readings off the highlight reflections (zone IX), and camera exposure was based on this. Allowance was made for the film's reciprocity failure.

at greater leisure.

As with portraits, *still-life* work in the studio is best controlled by precise adjustment of lighting and lighting contrast, to fit the subject perfectly into the Zone System.

Some scenes which are low in subject brightness range, such as *fog, mist and rain,* rely on a 'dreary' appearance for their photographic appeal. You must avoid the temptation to increase the contrast by too much extra film development which will make the print look too 'bright' and false. However, if you do not develop for *some* expansion of zones you are likely to produce a flat print. A good guideline is to expand the zones by about half that indicated by the subject brightness range. For example, if the meter indicates a brightness range of 5 stops (1:32), expand development by one zone. The extra graininess achieved by this slight 'forcing' of development often adds greater mood to the print.

On the other hand, with subjects displaying extremes of contrast, such as on sunny days with a clear blue sky, you must avoid the temptation to reduce development by so much that the graphic quality of the subject disappears. Again, moderation is required and mild compression (by one or possibly two zones) of the tonal scale is quite adequate.

Subjects which have large areas of a single tone, such as *deserts,* are best metered so that the predominant tone is placed on the tonal scale where you want it. For a realistic rendering of the subject, this means placing the sand on about zone VI, but there is no reason why you should not 'interpret' the scene and place the sand on different zones (eg. III, IV, VIII). Remember that graininess is more noticeable in large areas of even light tone and this is one of the reasons why many sandscapes are taken on slower film and/or larger formats.

When photographing under conditions of *low levels of illumination* you need to use either a sensitive meter or restrict your readings to the higher zones–a common practice is to meter off a white card (zone IX). This means that the Zone System can only be used at low levels of illumination when a sensitive meter is available; many TTL metering systems are not sufficiently sensitive to be able to read the lower zones under dark conditions.

You should also be aware that many available-light situations exhibit relatively high contrast and increased development times should be avoided or the prints will resemble line images. All these factors go against 'push processing' and, wherever possible, you should use faster films rather than higher film speed settings.

Night scenes are best photographed to retain highlight detail and you should use a sensitive meter to place these highlights on zones VII and VIII. Many night scenes include the light sources themselves which will inevitably fall on zone IX in the print. For metering purposes you should ignore them. The reciprocity characteristics of the film (see below) must be understood if you are going to use exposure times that are longer than one second, or thereabouts.

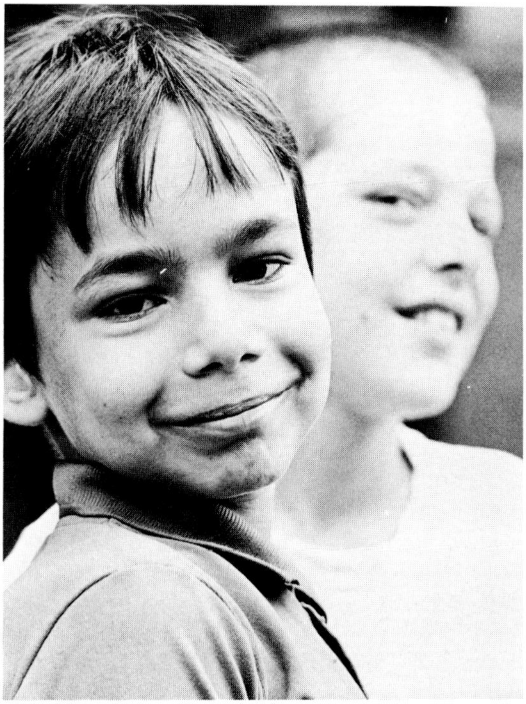

88 Exposure here was based on a TTL reading of the face and sweater (averaging to about zone V). Because general light readings indicated a shorter than average brightness range, the 35mm film was developed for one zone of expansion.

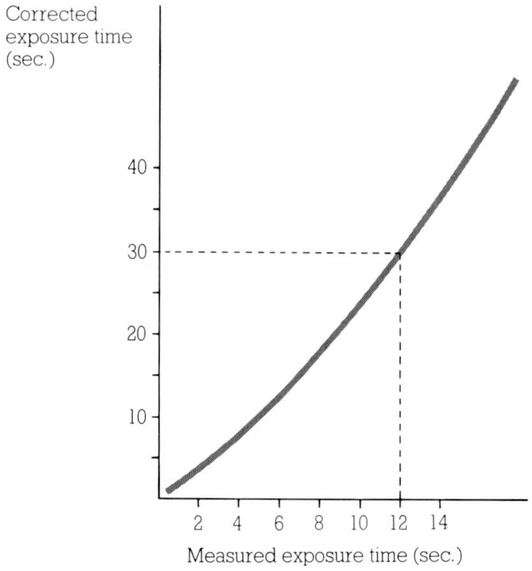

7.5 Reciprocity characteristics of films. Typical graph indicating the required exposure compared with the metered exposure. The example (dotted line) shows a metered exposure time of 12 sec, which needs to be 30 sec for correct exposure.

Reciprocity characteristics of black-and-white films

The law of reciprocity states that:

Exposure = Intensity x Time

where intensity is the brightness of the image on the film (controlled by *f*-stop) and time is the shutter speed setting. For most camera films, this law holds true for exposure times of between 1–1/1000 sec.; for example 1/125 sec. *f*/8 is equivalent to 1/250 sec. *f*/5.6, 1/60 sec. *f*/11, etc.

With exposure times longer than one second (as often occurs in night scenes or when photographing still life subjects, where small apertures are used) then it is normally necessary to give longer times than those indicated by the meter. Manufacturers supply charts (fig 7.5) for each film indicating the required exposure time relative to the time indicated on the meter.

There may also be a slight change in reproduction characteristics for these long exposure times–the relationship of mid-tones and highlights may subtly alter. The best solution is to shoot an extra small length of film (or one more sheet) and use this as a 'clip test' to determine the best processing time.

8 IMAGE MANIPULATION DURING PRINTING

A wide range of printing techniques can be used to alter the appearance of a 'straight' photograph. These manipulations can involve many stages of production and possibly several days of work before the final print is made, or they may be completed in a few hours.

For purposes of clarity, the techniques are explained separately as distinct processes, but they can be intermixed to produce any result the photographer wants. There are no limitations–you can let your imagination take over.

The results of some of the techniques are less predictable than others, but you should approach each technique in a methodical manner and make careful notes as you go along. It is extremely annoying to have produced a masterpiece which cannot be repeated simply because no data was recorded at the time of discovery.

Distorting the tone scale

Much effort may go into producing a photograph which has a full range of tones from black, through various shades of grey, to a pure white and for many subjects this endeavour is justified. But sometimes the elimination of some, or most, of the subject's tonal scale can improve the photograph, and give it greater impact. The viewer can then concentrate on form and content.

Some people may, in fact, photograph a subject with the 'previsualised' idea of distorting the subject's tonal scale and in this case the camera exposure and/or film development can be adjusted to accommodate the required result. However, most ideas for printing manipulations are conceived after the contact sheet is examined and, in any case, it gives you more control and selection if you have recorded as much of the subject information as possible. It is relatively easy to eliminate subject tone and detail, but it is much more difficult (and requires very skilled air brushing and/or montage techniques) to add these elements once you are in the darkroom.

Deliberately misprinting the negative

The easiest way to distort the subject's tonal scale is to deliberately over- or underprint the negative. After examining the contact sheet or your first 'normal' print, you may decide that either the shadow or highlight details recorded in the negative are not important and the photograph would be improved by eliminating them.

If you overprint your negative, the darker parts of the subject will get even darker until they reach maximum black and, depending on the degree of extra printing exposure, you may force some of the darker mid-tones to become blacks on the print (fig 8.1). As you are really using only part of the available negative density range, to obtain a print containing clean whites you need to print on a higher contrast paper (grades 3, 4 or 5). This type of approach is appropriate, for example, if you want to accentuate the highlights of backlit subjects such as sun striking a winding road or 'tone down' the brilliant highlights sometimes found on water. Often the 'overprinted' image looks like a photograph taken at dusk or at night-time.

Underprinting the negative causes the print to appear much lighter in tone overall with the subject's highlights burnt out; there is also a full range of shadow detail which looks grey rather than black. To compensate for the grey shadows, which are the result of only part of the negative density range being used (fig 8.1), you should print on to a higher contrast grade of paper. The underprinting approach works best for light,

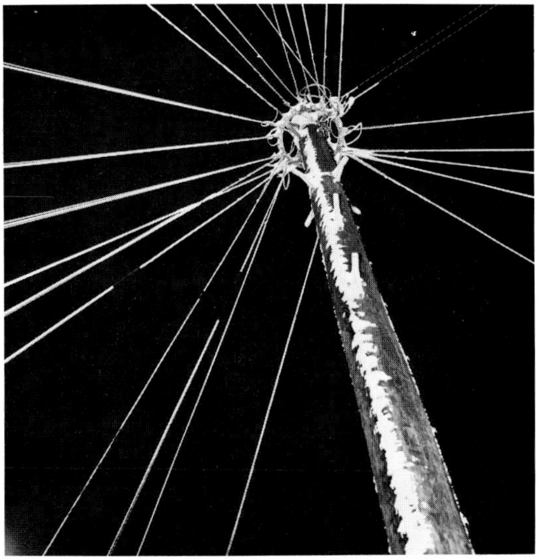

89 Not all image manipulations require complicated techniques and, in fact, some ordinary images may appear derivative when a 'straight' print is made. This example resembles a posterisation, but in fact is a night photograph taken by electronic flash.

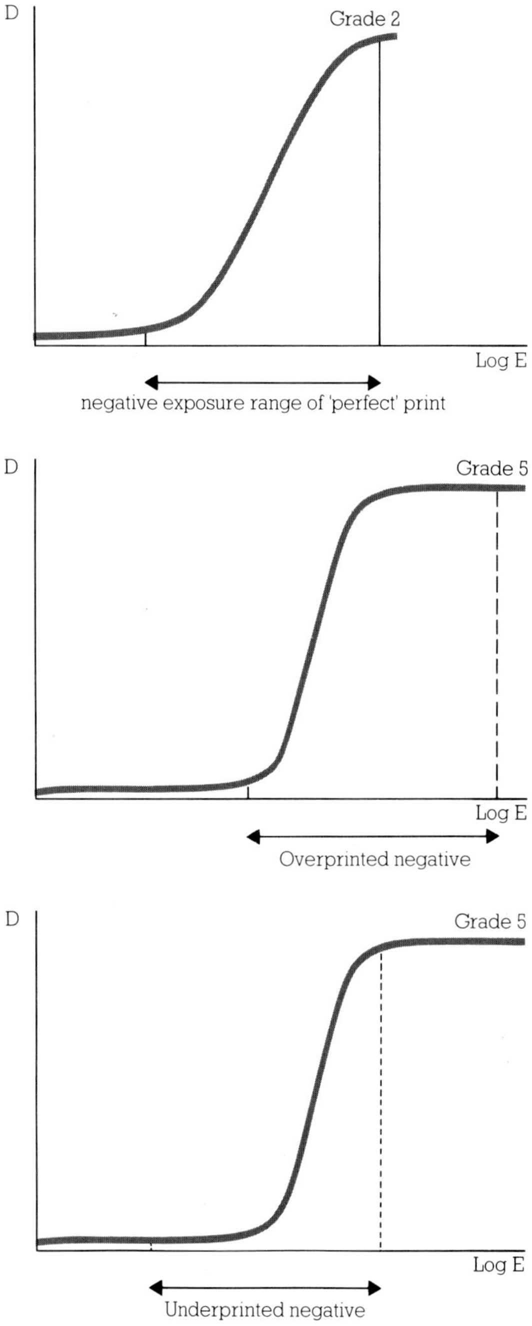

8.1 The top diagram shows a negative exposed on grade 2 paper to give a full range of image tones. When overprinting on to a harder grade of paper (eg. grade 5), more subject tones become black and the print has higher contrast (centre diagram). Underprinting the same negative (bottom diagram) on grade 5 forces many lighter tones to be printed as white.

delicate subjects, such as some female and child portraits, and produces a high-key effect.

Chemical reduction of image tones

It is relatively easy to lighten areas that have printed too dark by carefully applying a chemical reducer to the area. For small adjustments of tone you should make up a fresh solution of *Farmer's reducer* (fig 8.2), and make a preliminary test of its activity by applying it to a spare print. For easy application the reducer should not work too rapidly.

The print should be fully washed and the excess water removed from its surface. Support it on the back of a processing tray or similar flat object, and either brush or swab the Farmer's reducer on to the over-dark area. Care must be taken to prevent the solution running into adjacent areas, and you should rinse the surface every minute or so to prevent yellow stains from forming.

Farmer's reducer is not suitable for large reductions of density and if you need to remove heavy densities, it is better to use an *iodine* reducer (fig 8.3). This formulation can transform black into white without the possibility of staining.

If you want to remove a large area of tone, such as by converting the grey background of a still life subject to white, you can coat the areas of the picture which are to remain unchanged with a special rubber solution. When dry, this mask protects the area covered and means that the entire print can be immersed in the appropriate reducer until the required degree of lightening is obtained. After the print has been washed the rubber mask can be carefully removed with adhesive tape.

High contrast prints

Eliminating all or most of the mid-tones of a photograph will produce a very graphic image containing, basically, black and white only. This type of photograph is very effective as part of a display poster for example, as it is extremely eye catching.

The way to achieve this *tone elimination* technique is as follows:

1 Enlarge the negative image on to high contrast film (usually 'lith' film) to produce a fairly high contrast positive image.
2 Project this positive on to another sheet of lith film to obtain a high contrast negative.
3 Print the high contrast negative on to paper.

8.2 Farmer's reducer

Stock solution A	
Water	250 ml
Potassium ferricyanide	37.5 g
Water to make	500 ml
Stock solution B	
Water	1 litre
Sodium thiosulphate	480 g
Water to make	2 litre

For use: 1 part A + 4 parts B + 27 parts water

8.3 Iodide reducer

Stock reducing solution	
Water	100 ml
Potassium iodide	30 g
*Iodine (resublimed)	10 g
Water to make	200 ml
Stop and clearing bath	
Water	500 ml
Sodium thiosulphate	200 g
Water to make	1 litre

*Iodine is harmful and should be used with care.
For use: Dilute reducing solution 1 + 10 with water
Clearing bath to be used undiluted.
1. Soak print in water; remove excess.
2. Apply reducer as needed.
3. Clear iodine stain produced in stop bath.
4. If further reduction needed, wash print and repeat process.
5. For removing dark spots, use reducer undiluted.

During step **1** enlarge your original continuous tone negative up to the maximum size your enlarger can handle eg. 35mm up to about 6 x 4cm (2¼ x 1½in), if you own a 6 x 6cm (2¼ x 2¼in) format enlarger; a 12.7 x 10.2cm (5 x 4in) format enlarger is ideal for this type of work. If you have only a 35mm enlarger then it is better to produce a same-size positive by using an enlarger than by contact printing, otherwise you are very likely to introduce dust marks on the resulting positive. During this initial step you can, of course, crop the image and/or adjust local densities, although burning-in/dodging is quite difficult for such small enlargements. The printing exposure of step **1** must be controlled in the same manner as paper printing to produce a film positive which contains all the required image detail.

The second step produces a same-size high contrast negative but, again, this is best achieved by projection and not by contact printing. Exposure is still critical and is best determined by test strips.

Printing is reasonably straightforward for this type of photography in that all contrast grades of paper give very similar prints and exposure needs to be judged on the basis of giving sufficient time to produce maximum black. Slight overexposure does not alter the image, although a very excessive exposure usually causes the edges to blur ('bleeding' of the image).

Lith materials

Lith films are generally employed in the lithographic printing industry to make the large film negatives and positives which are used to produce the printing plates for the presses. To generate maximum contrast from these films you should develop them in lith developer, a solution made up from two stock solutions just before use. Once mixed, lith developers are only usable for

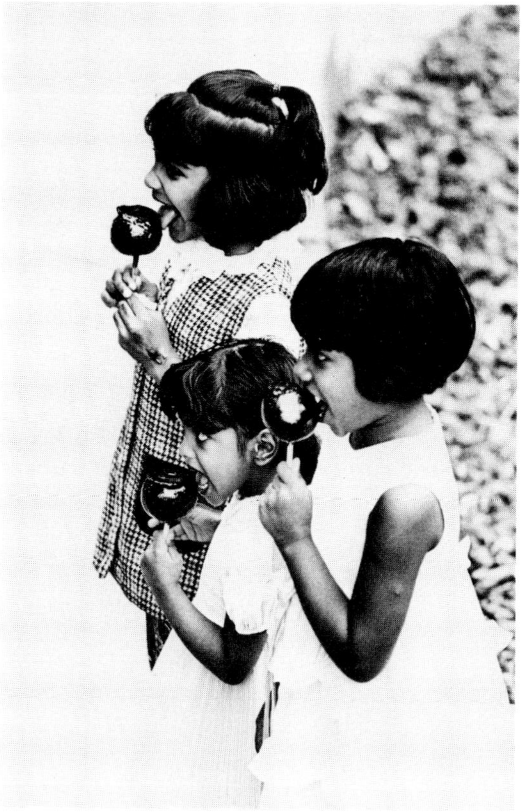

90 To simplify the composition, Farmer's reducer was used (in combination with dodging) to bleach large areas of this print out to white. Dilute solution was brushed on to selected areas and painstaking repeated applications between washes were used to produce the desired photograph.

about two hours and then lose activity.

Lith developers produce very high contrast results by 'infectious' development, the process whereby the byproducts of a slowly developing area act as catalysts and cause a sudden increase in development rate. Do not overagitate the developer, as this will remove these catalysts too quickly from the developing site. Some workers use a 'still bath' technique, where agitation is very infrequent after about 15 seconds of initial vigorous agitation to ensure the film is thoroughly soaked.

Most lith films have orthochromatic sensitivity and can be handled in red safelighting. As printing exposures are likely to be very short for this type of work you should, if possible, use an enlarger timer and set the enlarging lens to its minimum aperture; never use an enlarging lens below the last marked stop because diffraction will cause loss of image definition.

Line films are high contrast materials but do not give as high contrast as lith films. They are developed in very active high contrast developers (eg. Kodak's D-19) which are relatively stable (cf. lith developers), can be replenished and do not involve infectious development. For occasional use, the lith materials are more useful than line films. There are a few high contrast films (eg. Agfa Rapidoprint) which can act as both line and lith materials when processed in the appropriate developer.

Working with lith materials

It is important to carefully read the instructions given by each film manufacturer on the best exposure and processing methods for their materials. However, a few general guidelines given here will help you to obtain the best results from lith materials. General working practice is:

1 For most applications described later in this chapter, it is preferable to use sheet film. As this is fairly expensive, you should cut it up for use as test strips, or cut it down to the maximum film size that your enlarger can handle. The sheet film lies flatter than 35mm lith film and is easier to process.
2 Handle the film under the safelights recommended by the manufacturer (usually red) and, because of its higher sensitivity than paper, do not hold it for more than a couple of seconds in front of safelights.
3 Set the easel for wide borders around the projected image as this ensures that the lith image will sit in the middle of the film carrier when enlarged in later steps.
4 Place the film in a small dish, eg. 18 x 13cm (7 x 5in) of developer which is freshly made up and at the correct temperature and dilution; agitate the film as recommended. You may like to try the still bath technique (15 sec. continuous agitation, followed by one gentle rock of the dish at 30 sec. intervals) for some applications.
5 Always use a stop bath to halt development sharply and fix the film for twice the clearing time (total of about five min. for slow fixers).
6 All your dishes, etc. must be kept scrupulously clean as dish processing can cause scuff marks on the film. Use a wetting agent before carefully drying the film.
7 Lith films are liable to develop 'pinholes' (small clear spots on the film) and for some applications it is necessary to spot these out with *photo-paque* (or blocking-out fluid), a brown paste which blocks out the covered area. To minimise pinholes you should not underexpose the film or give less than the recommended development time.

Posterisation

This is a very popular technique which converts a continuous tone image into several (usually three or four) distinct tones, for example, white, mid-grey, and black. Because of its large areas of a single tone, the photograph then resembles a poster.

Posterisation is generally most successfully applied to uncomplicated subjects without too much fine detail, such as images with bold graphic shapes. A black-and-white posterisation can be derived from almost any original continuous tone image, including colour negatives and slides and both colour and black-and-white prints. The procedure described below uses a black-and-white negative, but other possible routes are shown in fig 8.5.

Technique of posterisation

Starting with a black-and-white negative there are several possible routes to making a posterised print and each has its own merits. The author finds the following approach (fig 8.4) successful for a three-tone posterisation:

1 Place your negative in the enlarger and project an image which is the same size as the largest film format that your enlarger can handle. For a 35mm enlarger this is 36 x 24mm; for a 120 film enlarger this is at least 6 x 6cm and possibly up to 6 x 9cm. If you are fortunate enough to have a sheet film 12.7 x 10.2cm (5 x 4in) or equivalent enlarger you can use most of the sheet film of this format (allowing for a ¼in border on all sides). If you have already decided on the boundaries of your final posterised print, then you can crop the image at this early stage but it does limit your choice for later–it is safer to retain all, or most, of the available image area and trim the photograph before presentation.

2 Place a sheet of lith film in the print easel, stop the lens down to the minimum aperture, and make a test strip exposure. As a guide try times of 1, 2, 4, 8 and 16 sec.

3 From the processed test strip, select two exposure times and produce two reasonably different film positives. For a three-tone posterisation, the lighter positive indicates the black parts of the final posterised print and the darker positive indicates the final white areas. The mid-grey will come from whatever areas are left (fig 8.0).

4 Project each of the two positives on to lith film to give two high-contrast negatives. It is important to ensure that the two high-contrast negatives are of the same magnification, ie. the enlarger must not be adjusted (apart from focusing) during step **4.**

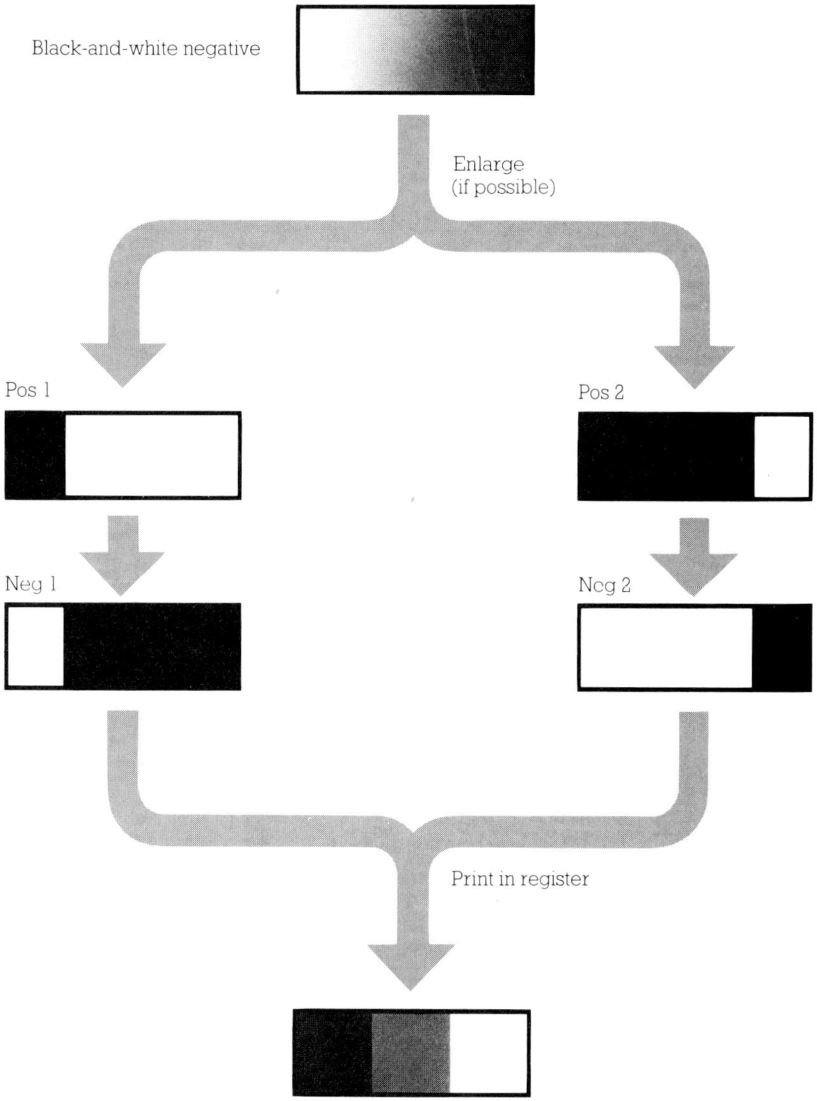

8.4 Procedure for making a three-tone (black, grey and white) posterised print. Full details are given in the text.

5 Place the darkest high-contrast negative in the enlarger and project it to give the full print size. Place a strip of paper in the easel and give a test strip exposure at a small aperture (see step 7) to determine the times necessary to produce a mid grey and a maximum black.

6 Still with the darker negative in the enlarger, expose a full sheet of paper for the time necessary to give maximum black.

7 Without moving the enlarger or the paper easel, replace the darker negative by the lighter one and make sure that it is correctly aligned (see registration techniques, below). Give the paper a second shorter exposure, sufficient to produce a mid grey. The small printing aperture should ensure accurate focusing but if you find that you have to refocus each negative then this should be done as quickly as possible at full aperture through a red filter.

8 Examine the three tones of the posterised print and make adjustments to printing exposures to darken or lighten tones and/or refine alignment technique.

A successful posterisation depends largely on careful control at each stage and on good registration of the two printing exposures. With practice, you should soon be able to visualise how a continuous tone image will convert into a posterised photograph, and to judge the intermediate steps to achieving your visualisation.

Registration techniques

The best technique for ensuring perfect registration is to use a registration punch, a registration board and a film carrier with matching registration pins. These can be purchased but are also fairly easy for the DIY enthusiast to make. The simplest system is to use a good quality paper punch which puts two good clean holes in film at about 7cm apart. Next adapt a spare enlarger film carrier to take two round pins separated by 7cm; this is obviously easier for a large sheet film carrier than smaller formats. Finally, fix two round pins to a flat board to hold the film during exposure. This board should be clearly marked with the useful image area and be equipped with some means to anchor itself to the baseboard.

Registration of 35mm film is more difficult and needs to be much more accurate because of the greater degree of enlargement. It may be possible to adapt the pin registration of a 35mm film editor, so experiment with this.

The other method of registration uses some type of visual marking system which is automatically transferred with every stage of production. One such method is to use the four corners of the original negative by making sure that at each stage the four corners are placed within the projected image. For total 35mm working this would mean a slight reduction of the image to make the two 35mm positives so that they sit comfortably inside the 36 x 24mm format; subsequent stages could be at same-size reproduction.

To make the final double exposure on paper, mark the four corners on the photographic paper in black, and align each negative in turn at full aperture, using a red filter under the enlarging lens. This alignment should be done as quickly as possible, because there can be some print-through of the bright image on to the paper if the time is lengthy.

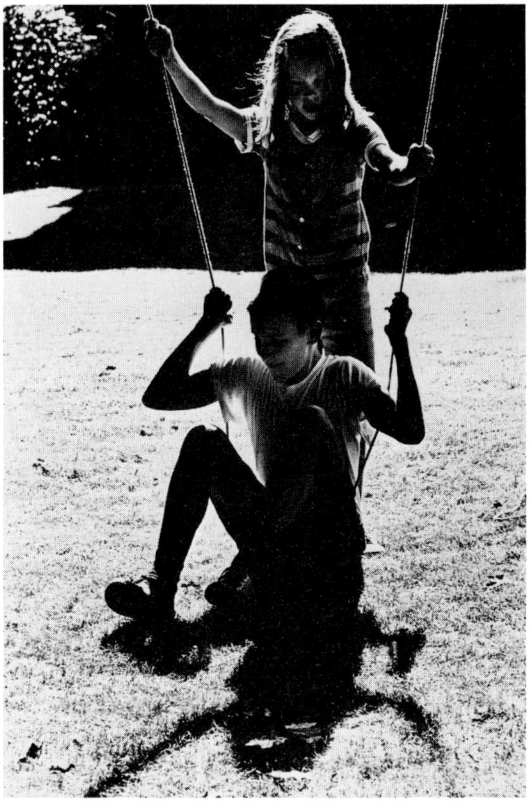

91 This dramatic image was made by simply printing on to grade 5 paper, and using a high contrast developer to process the print. The faces of the children were lightened by dodging.

8.5 Alternative routes to producing a three-toned posterised print.
A Colour slide must first be converted to a black-and-white continuous tone negative by projecting on to *panchromatic* film–for the remaining steps follow fig **8.4.**
B colour negatives can be projected on to *panchromatic* lith film to give lith positives directly, which are then used to give two lith negatives for printing.
C Alternatively, a colour negative can be projected on to *panchromatic* black-and-white film to give a continuous tone positive, which is then used to generate two lith negatives for printing.

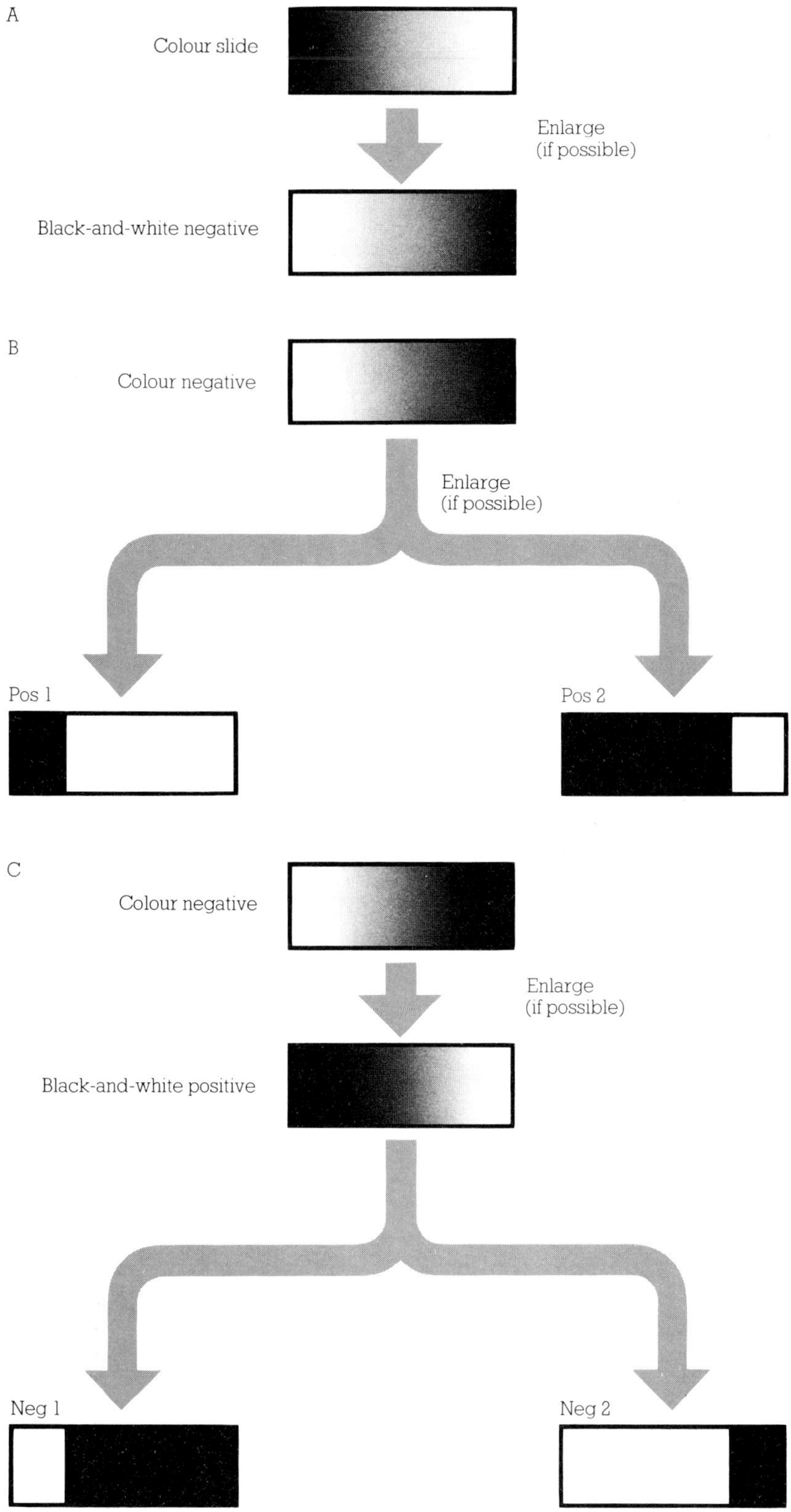

Posterisations with more than three tones

To create a four-tone posterisation consisting of black, white and two greys, you need to produce three positives from your original continuous tone negative (fig 8.6). Remember, the lightest positive indicates the final blacks and the darkest positive the whites, while to estimate the two greys you must compare the middle positive against both of the others and judge their tonal differences. From the three positives, you next generate three high-contrast negatives which are then printed in register. The darkest negative is exposed to give black, the middle negative to give dark grey and the lightest negative to give light grey, while white will result from any remaining unexposed area.

It is possible to produce a five-tone posterisation by generating four positives and then four negatives for printing, but the result will look very similar to a continuous tone print made from the original negative!

Do not destroy your intermediate positives because they can be used to produce other print modifications such as bas relief and colour posterisations. If this is your intention you will have to

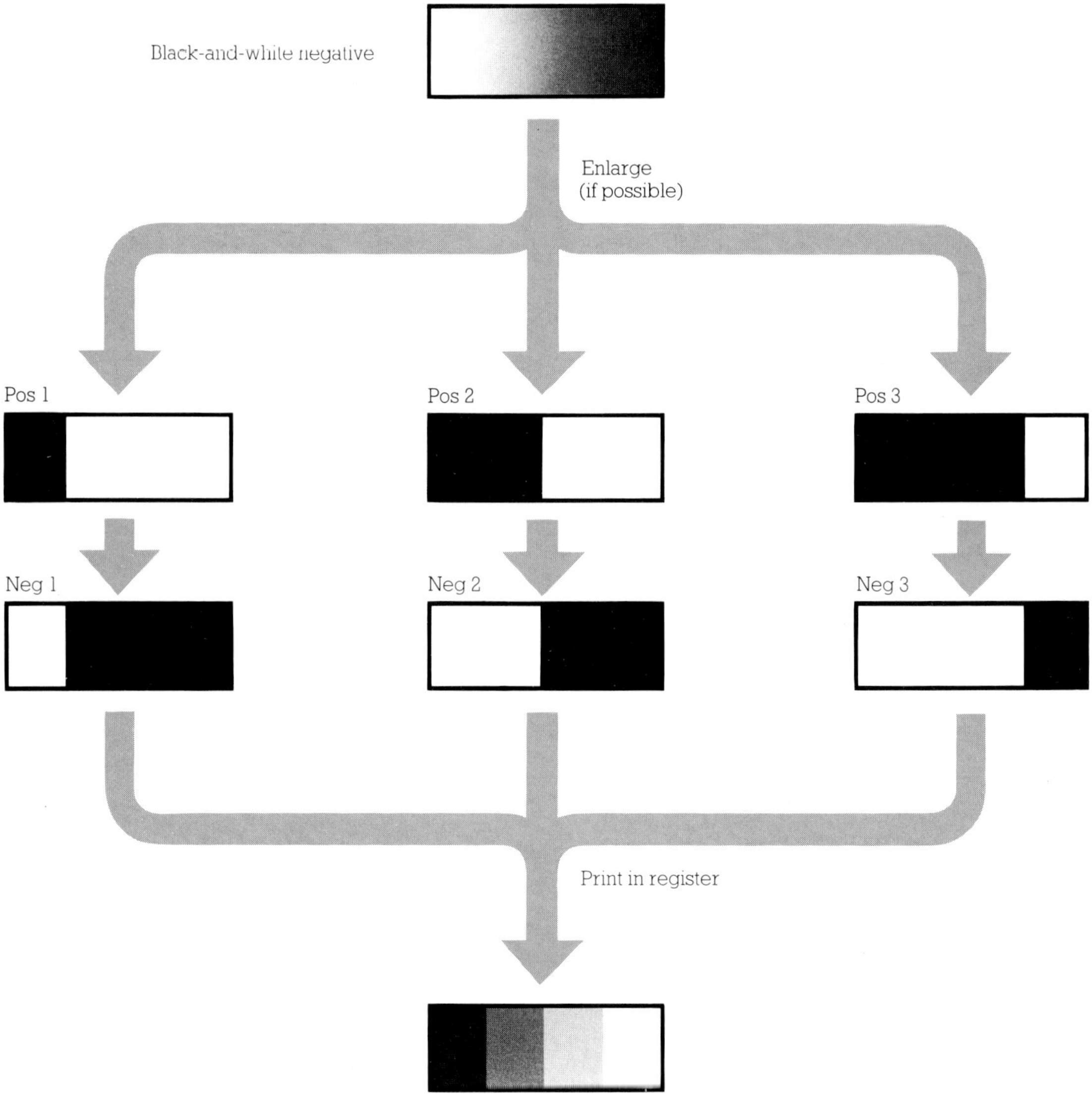

8.6 Procedure for making a four-tone (black, dark grey, light grey, white) posterised print. For complete details see the text.

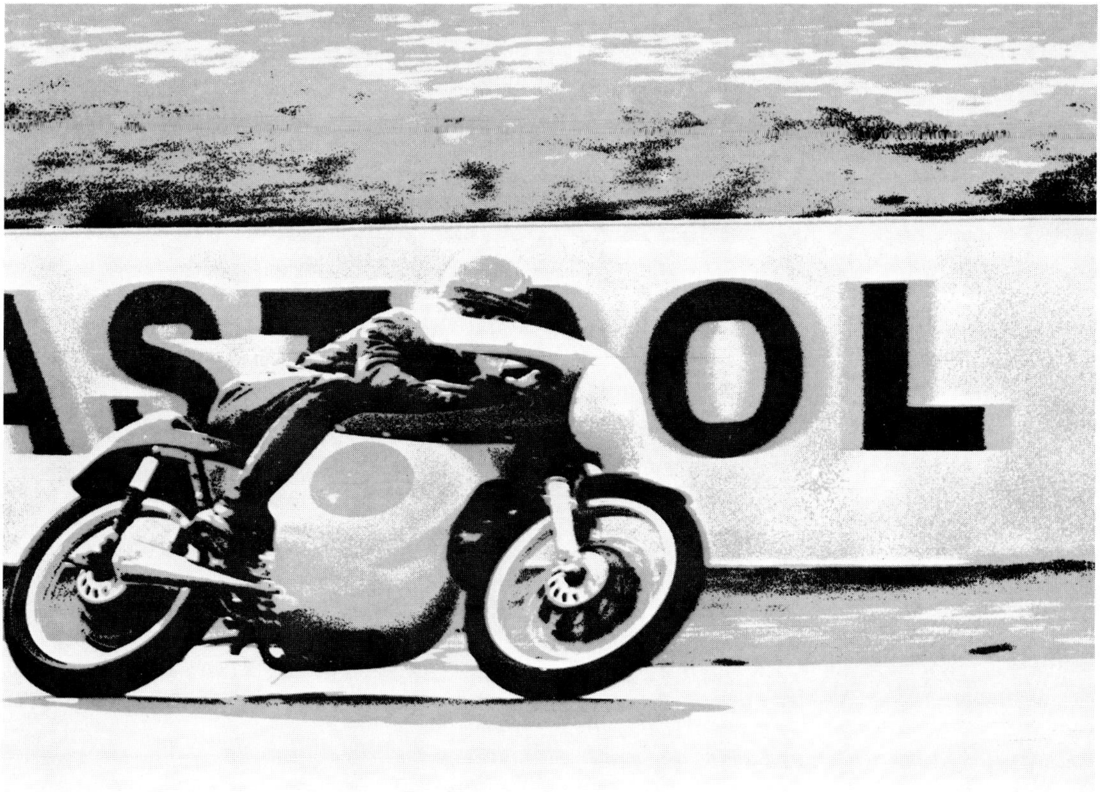

92 A posterisation derived from a 35mm black-and-white negative. To achieve the three tones (white, mid-grey, black) two lith positives were made from the original negative, and from these two lith negatives were produced. The latter were printed sequentially and in register on the paper; see text for full details.

produce new high-contrast negatives by contact printing rather than by projection.

Modifying image lines and shapes

There are a number of printing techniques which change the image lines and shapes and which can be used to produce slightly modified photographs or to generate almost new pictures.

As we have already discovered, these techniques can produce unpredictable results, so always be ready to improvise and try capitalising on any 'mistakes' which would produce exciting pictures. As always, try to keep detailed notes of your more successful experiments so that you can apply them to other images.

Bas relief

One of the simplest printing manipulations is through the process known as bas relief. This technique produces a pseudo three-dimensional image not unlike a relief painting; the amount of 'relief' produced can be altered to suit each picture.

There are several slight variations to the technique of bas relief, but the basic procedure is as follows:

1 Contact print your black-and-white negative on to lith film and process; this results in a high-contrast positive.
2 Sandwich together (emulsion to emulsion) your original black-and-white negative and the high-contrast positive, but make sure the two films are misaligned. This is most successfully achieved on a light box, where you can judge the required amount of image distortion. Tape the two films together at one edge.
3 Enlarge this film sandwich on to photographic paper and make a print.
4 After examining the first result, adjust the printing exposure, grade of paper, and degree of misalignment to obtain an improved image.

Be very careful during step **1**, as with any contact printing, to keep all materials and equipment free of dust. Use of a compressed air can is invaluable for removing the last specks of dust. Normally, the best results are obtained by aiming for a lightish positive image. If you cannot obtain good contact between the two films (step **3**) then use a glass film carrier (which must be kept scrupulously clean). Stop the enlarging lens down as far as is practical for reasonable exposure times, this will ensure that any slight separation of the two films does not affect the sharpness of the photograph.

One variation on this basic procedure is to use a lower contrast film, such as Kodak Gravure Positive (handle in orange safelight), in place of the lith film. The 'softer' positive may suit some gentler types of subject. Another variation is to contact print the lith positive against another sheet of lith film to give a high-contrast negative. The lith positive and the lith negative can then be sandwiched together slightly out to register to produce a high-contrast bas relief photograph.

The overall appearance of the bas relief print is 'positive' if the sandwich positive film is weaker than the original negative (or any second generation negative). If you think your subject would look better as a predominantly negative bas relief, either make a fairly dense positive, or generate a weak negative from the positive and sandwich the latter two together for printing.

Bas relief works best with simple, uncomplicated subjects and is usually more pleasing when the degree of misalignment of the two films is quite small, creating thin 'shadow' lines around subject outlines.

Sabattier process

The sabattier process, sometimes incorrectly described as solarisation, produces delicate lines around the subject shapes and sometimes results in a photograph resembling a contour map. It is one of the most exciting photographic derivative techniques, but is also probably the most unpredictable and most difficult to control. However, if you follow a few simple guidelines you should soon be able to create some very strong images.

The most crucial stages of the process are the momentary turning on of a light while the photographic material is in the developer, and the development for a short while after this light 'fogging'. The characteristic image lines of this process result from a build-up of chemicals at contrasting image boundaries.

Because the results are so unpredictable, it is unwise to try and sabattier any camera exposed film. Instead, project the processed negative on to sheet film in the darkroom. It is possible to fog photographic paper during development but the sabattier print which results from this will be too dark for display. However, working with film gives you an opportunity to transfer any sabattier image(s) on to a subsequent sheet(s) of film.

Sabattier process–step by step

1 'Enlarge' the black-and-white negative on to lith film to give the largest image size which can be handled by your enlarger film carrier. For example, a 35mm negative should be projected up to about 55 x 37mm (allowing a small safety margin) if you have a 6 x 6cm enlarger.

2 By the usual test strip method, determine the correct exposure to produce the film positive; as a guide, stop your lens down to *f*/16 and try exposures of 1, 2, 4, 8 and 16 sec. For initial experiments use lith developer.

3 Using the time found from step **2**, expose a strip of lith film and develop with *constant agitation* until a clearly defined image is just formed–this works out to be half the recommended development time, ie. about ½–1 min. Stop agitation and wait until the film is stationary. Switch on a hand torch for about five sec. and move it constantly (to avoid uneven illumination) about 25cm (1ft) above the film. (If the torch has a strong 'hot spot' of illumination you should diffuse it by placing a tissue over the light.) Allow the film to develop *undisturbed* for about a further minute or less.

4 Transfer the film rapidly to the stop bath and then to the fixer. When the film is clear, examine the image by holding it up to a strong light. The image will be very dark, but this is inevitable; look for evidence of sabattier lines.

5 If the film is virtually black and no lines are visible, repeat the test using about one sec. of fogging exposure. Insufficient fogging exposure is indicated by lack of lines and a low density margin outside the image area; increase the fogging time to about 15 sec. or use a more powerful light source (page 135).

6 Repeat tests until you are happy with the image, and then expose a full sheet of film.

7 Because the film is too dark for printing, project it at the same size on to a sheet of continuous tone copy film (eg. Kodak Gravure Positive) and produce an image of printable density.

8 Print the negative/positive from step **7** in the usual manner.

Some sabattier variations

The process described above is only a guide and

can be modified in many ways. For example, the film/developer combination can be changed to almost any fairly 'active' system that gives a reasonably high gamma. Films worth trying include lith, line and copy films which can be developed in 'active' solutions such as lith, line film and paper developers.

You may also like to experiment with alternative fogging lights such as room lights but if you decide to try this, make sure to use a pull cord rather than placing wet hands on switches which is *potentially lethal*. Another light source you can use is a portable flash gun, preferably of the automatic type so that you have more control of output. *The flashgun must not be handled with wet hands.*

You can also project your sabattier film on to another sheet of film and perform the sabattier process on this image to produce a double sabattier image. There is no reason why you could not try further sabattiers to give triple and even quadruple sabattier images. Prints from multiple sabattiers can be quite remarkable.

Optical printing effects

The enlarging process gives you another chance of optically modifying the image, after the camera exposure. There are many possible effects, ranging from slight image distortion such as 'softening' the picture with a diffuser, to a quite drastic alteration of the image.

Placing a special effects filter (page 44) over the enlarging lens is one straightforward method of producing interesting images. Because a black-and-white negative is projected, the effect on the subject may be the opposite of when the same filter is used on the camera. For example, a diffuser placed in front of the camera lens has a greater effect on the subject's highlights, whereas the same diffuser over the enlarging lens mainly softens the shadows.

Use the more dramatic effects filters with caution because they can produce very obviously contrived images; some of the effects filters have already been overworked and they need to be used with subtlety to avoid clichéd photographs.

Paper distortion

One way to create an optical distortion is to bend the photographic paper into an unusual shape and to project the negative on to it.

A simple curving of the paper, either towards the lens at the paper's centre or away from it at the centre, can produce startling images. Adjust the printing exposure across the paper, to avoid producing either very dense areas close to the lens or very light areas further away. The paper must be rigidly held in its contorted shape by supports.

The sharpness of various parts of the photograph depends on the degree of paper distortion and the enlarging lens aperture; for maximum sharpness stop the lens down to the minimum aperture. There is potentially much greater control of sharpness if the enlarger has a lens panel and/or film carrier that can be swung away from the square-on position (page 101).

Moving the paper during exposure

If the paper is moved during the printing exposure the photograph will be blurred, the degree of blur depending on the amount of movement and whether it is even throughout the exposure. Generally speaking, it is more pleasing to produce an overall sharp image with a streaked background, which is done by keeping the paper stationary for part of the exposure.

To move the paper in a straight line (ie: in one direction only) support the paper easel on rollers and try pulling the easel along with a piece of attached cord. Try various speed patterns from the same continuous speed to gradual acceleration of the easel and, for smoother results, adjust the exposure time to around 10 sec. Experiment with non-linear paper movement, such as zig-zag, rotational (eg. on a turntable), or a combination of several movements.

While we are discussing paper movement, it is worth mentioning a specific example of multiple printing exposures which is covered later in this chapter. Print a negative once on a sheet of paper, move the paper to another stationary position and print the image or part of it again. This process can be repeated several times, and the result is a series of sharp repeating images.

The technique works well if one of the images is printed 'correctly' and the others either lighter or darker, giving the photograph a strong main interest. Uncomplicated subjects are the best choice for this printing manipulation, and you might consider photographing a subject against a white background specifically for multiple printing.

Montaging several images

Combining several images on the same sheet of photographic paper is an exciting, albeit lengthy,

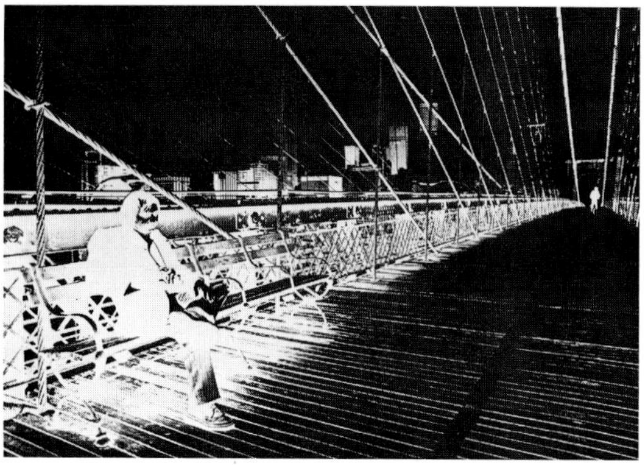

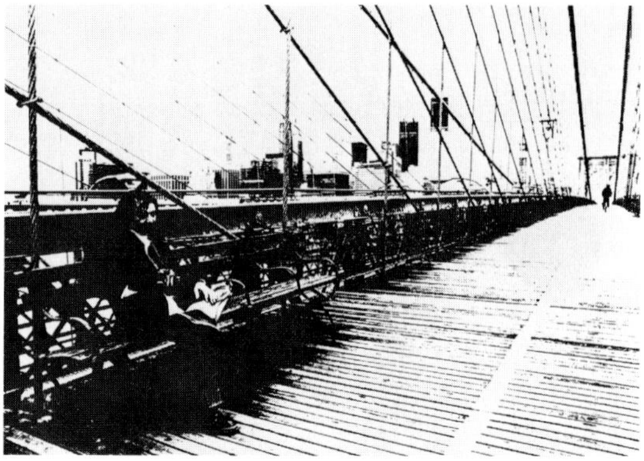

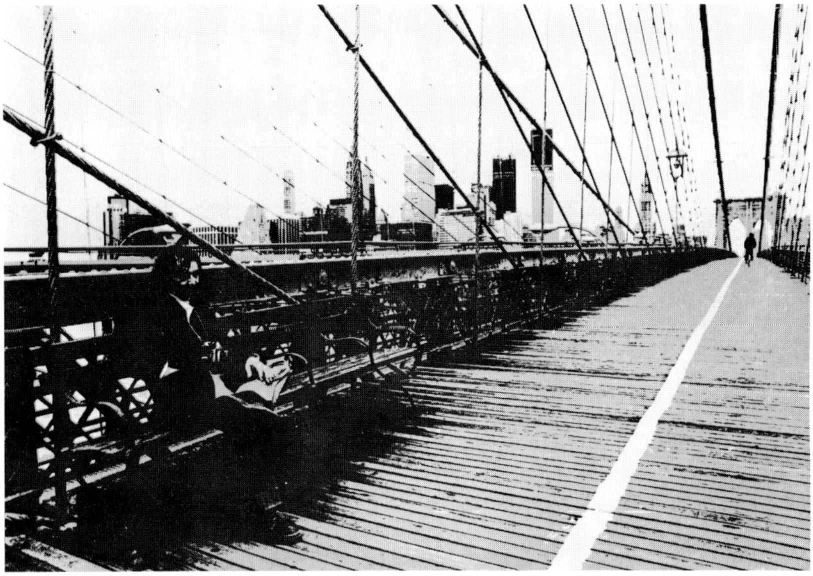

93-98 A series of prints, all of which derive from the same original 35mm black-and-white negative. The negative was enlarged on sheet lith film to give two lith positives of different density (ie. from two different printing exposures). One of these lith positives was printed to give a high-contrast negative print, **93**. From the two cut film positives were made two sheet lith negatives (by contact printing); one of these was printed to give a high-contrast positive print, **94**.

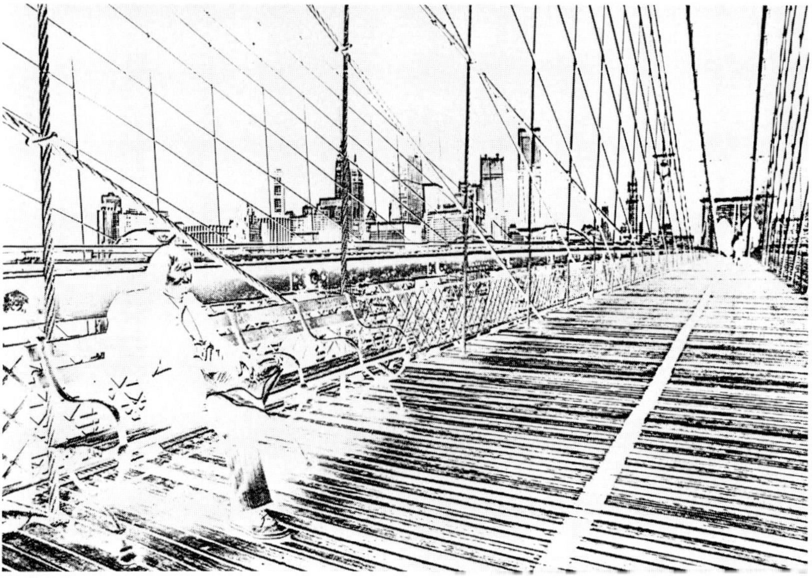

process which can produce surrealistic photographs. Sometimes these montage images can be planned in advance, while others result from seeing separate photographs and then deciding to unite them in one print. Jerry Uelsmann's pictures are outstanding examples of montage photography.

The three main techniques of combining several images in one photograph are sandwich printing, multiple printing, and collage. Each technique has its pros and cons and the choice of method is usually dictated by the subject and its surroundings.

Sandwich printing

This technique involves placing two negatives on top of one another and projecting the sandwich on to paper. To keep the two images in close contact you may have to use a glass carrier. The easiest way to position the two images with respect to one another is to line them up on top of a light box; once aligned they should be taped together along

The two lith negatives were printed sequentially on to one sheet of paper to give a three-tone posterisation, **95**. The bas relief print, **96**, was obtained by sandwiching together, slightly out of register, one lith negative and one lith positive and placing the sandwich in the enlarger and printing from it. The sabattier process was used to produce print **97**; in this case a positive image was solarised to give a predominantly negative print. The result of solarising a negative image is print **98**.

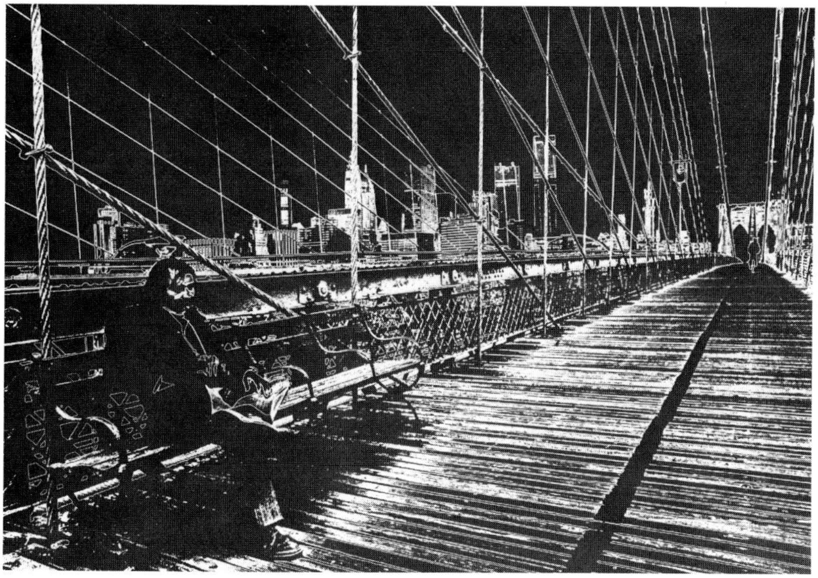

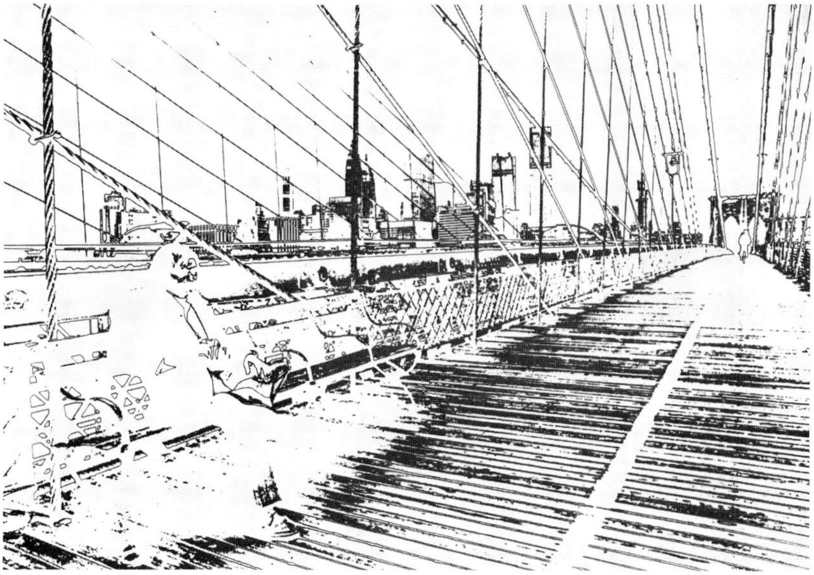

one side. Keep the two emulsions as close together as possible; ie. for normal orientation the two negatives are separated by one thickness of film base, but if one image is 'flopped' (ie. turned over) the two films should be emulsion to emulsion.

Sandwich printing is most suitable for negatives with large clear areas which then have 'space' to accept the other negative's image detail. This technique, therefore, suits subjects which are surrounded by dark tones. To complete a sandwich it may be preferable to photograph the second subject against a black background and at the same time adjust the size of the object on the negative to fit into the composition.

If you have two subjects that are suitable for montage but the size relationship of the two negatives is wrong, you can make a duplicate negative (via a film positive) of one of them at a different magnification so that the images match.

Besides a negative/negative combination, you can also try a sandwich of a negative with a positive (enlarged or reduced to the appropriate size) to give a print whose overall character (negative or positive) depends on which film image is the most dense. Another possibility is to sandwich high-contrast (lith) negatives or positives (page 127) made from the original continuous tone negative, to produce high-contrast photographs.

Or, you can try sandwiching three films together, although in this case a glass carrier would be needed to ensure that all three films are in contact. Also, because at least one film will be separated from the others by one or two layers of film base, you should stop the enlarging lens down to its minimum aperture to ensure that all images are sharp.

Multiple printing

Several images can be projected on to a single sheet of photographic paper to build up a montage. There is no limit to the variety and number of images that can be combined but there is a greater chance of success if you can plan all or some of the images. If you have planned an image, you can leave 'space' for another subject which may be photographed specifically for multiple printing, or just a stock picture which needed something extra added.

Because you are adding exposure to the photographic paper, the technique works best with darker negatives, ie. for subjects which are surrounded by lighter tones, as there is then less chance of one subject printing on to detail in the other. When photographing an object specifically for multiple printing, you should have the subject on a white background and also try to match the lighting to the other subject(s).

The illusion created by multiple printing only succeeds if the various images look as if they belong together. Careful attention should be given to matching image definition and grain, by enlarging all negatives to similar magnifications and, as we have just discussed, to selecting similar lighting conditions. For example, if the main scene has been photographed on an overcast day with 35mm HP5 film then all other subjects should, ideally, be photographed in 'flat' lighting on the same film and format.

To succeed at multiple printing you must be methodical and well organised, and have a clear idea of what you want the final print to look like. It may be helpful to sketch out the images on to plain paper by drawing around the outlines of the projected images. Keep detailed notes of exposures, degrees of enlargement (ie. record enlarger column height), shading or burning-in, paper grades, etc.

Multiple printing–step by step

The basic procedure for printing two negatives on to a single sheet of paper is as follows:

1 Place negative one in the enlarger and adjust the controls to give a correct size image which matches your sketch.
2 In the usual manner, determine the correct printing exposure and grade of paper to give a good quality print. Make a note of the exposure time, lens aperture, column height, and any burning-in or dodging.
3 Replace negative one with negative two and repeat steps **1** and **2** for the new image.
4 Expose negative two to the photographic paper and remove the easel with the paper still firmly in position to a safe place clear of the enlarger light. Replace negative two with negative one.
5 Using your sketch, align negative one and set it up for exposing. Replace the easel and paper and position them correctly with respect to image one by using the enlarger's red filter to protect the paper. Expose negative one.
6 Examine the double-exposed print and make any necessary corrections to either or both of the exposures.

Should the two negatives not print equally well

on the same grade of paper, you must either produce a 'duplicate' (but slightly different) negative of one of the images which does then give a good print on the chosen paper grade, or, more simply, use a variable contrast paper so that the printing filter can be changed to suit each exposure.

Printing more than two negatives on to one sheet of paper involves essentially the same procedure, but it obviously takes longer. If you are contemplating a fairly frequent use of multiple printing, consider purchasing an extra enlarger, so that each negative can be left in its enlarger, correctly adjusted and ready for exposure. It is then a simple matter to transfer the paper easel across from one enlarger to the other.

If you want to experiment further with multiple printing, you could try printing positives, negatives and positives, or high-contrast (lith) negatives and/or positives. Lith film images offer the opportunity to 'block out' areas of the subject with *photo-opaque* (blocking-out fluid), which is painted on to the non-emulsion side of the film.

Collage techniques

Another method of combining several images on one sheet of paper is collage. This involves producing separate photographs which are cut out and pasted together. The technique is extremely versatile, allowing you to refine each individual photograph, move the separate images around until the collage looks right and reprint small sections if necessary. There is also the possibility, if you have painting skills, of adding brushwork to the composition.

Although any type of photographic paper can be used for collage, it is best to use matt or preferably art papers (such as Kentmere Art) as they are easier to cut out and paste up and accept retouching and/or brushwork very readily. Rubber-based adhesives, such as Cow Gum, are ideal for paste-up work because they allow you to stick the images down in one position and then later peel them off and reposition them elsewhere on the sheet. Remember, most adhesives contain unpleasant volatile solvents and should always be used in well-ventilated areas.

Your collage should have a high quality finish, and to achieve this it should be re-photographed to obtain a copy negative (see fig 7.2 for lighting set-up); the final print should then not look like a paste-up. If possible, use a film specifically designed for copy work such as Gravure Positive. Note, however, that most copy films are not easily available to the amateur. However, reasonable results can be obtained with pan camera film if it is developed to a higher contrast than normal. For initial tests try a slow pan film, in order to conserve as much image quality as possible, and develop it to a gamma of about 1.0.

Image colour

As we have already discovered, the colour of a black-and-white photograph can be varied within a small range from blue-blacks to brown-blacks by the appropriate choice of photographic paper and developer (see page 86). There are, however, a few techniques which can be used to broaden this range and include more saturated colours.

Chemical toning is an old technique for converting the metallic silver image of a print to other chemicals which are coloured; the range of colours is limited by the number of reacting chemicals which produce stable colours.

Some manufacturers produce photographic papers which have a conventional black-and-white emulsion coated on to a coloured paper base. These papers are used extensively in exhibition and poster work.

Another method of producing a coloured monochrome photograph is to print a black-and-white negative on colour paper; for the colour enthusiast this offers a quick method of obtaining a wide range of effects.

The details given below will help you experiment with a great variety of techniques and chemicals. If you are particularly interested in this subject, you should consult some of the older photographic textbooks, such as Clerc's *Photography Theory and Practice* and the former *Ilford Manual of Photography*.

Sepia toning

There are many published formulae which will convert a black-and-white image of neutral tone into a coloured image. The most popular toners are those which convert the image to brownish silver sulphides or selenides and, as we have previously mentioned, they also improve image stability to archival standards (page 94).

Sulphide toning is best achieved as a two-part process. First, the print is soaked in a rehalogenating bleach (fig 8.7) to convert the silver image to silver halides, given a short rinse in running water (about one minute), and then placed in the sulphide toner (eg. May & Baker Embesol,

Kodak sepia toner). After toning, the print is washed for 10 min. and dried in the usual manner.

8.7 Rehalogenating bleach

Potassium ferricyanide (anhydrous)	40 g
Potassium bromide (anhydrous)	40 g
*Potassium oxalate	100 g
**Acetic acid (28 per cent)	20 ml
Water to make	1 litre

*Potassium oxalate is harmful and should be used with care.
**Made by mixing 3 parts glacial acetic acid to 8 parts water.

The final shade of brown depends on many factors including the paper type, print developer, and toner formulation. Be prepared to try several combinations before settling on one. On the whole, chlorobromide papers give more pleasing results than bromide emulsions, and the effect is more successful with fibre-based papers than RC types.

To achieve high quality results it is essential that the prints be correctly processed and washed thoroughly to remove all chemicals before the toning process commences, otherwise there is likely to be some staining on the print. Some sulphide toners emit hydrogen sulphide fumes which are not only unpleasant for the user but also fog photographic materials. These toners are toxic and must be used in a well-ventilated area away from photographic film and paper.

Metal toners

There is a wide range of 'heavy' metals, such as cobalt, copper, iron, nickel and vanadium, that can form coloured metal complexes; the silver black-and-white image of the processed photograph can be converted by a one- or two-bath process to one of these coloured complexes. Unfortunately, most of the resulting prints are relatively impermanent and will fade in time. However, reasonably stable and attractive images can be obtained by using blue toners (iron) and red-brown toners (copper).

As with sepia you will probably get more successful results if you use chlorobromide fibre-based papers rather than resin-coated bromide papers, but it is still worth experimenting with different paper types. Before starting the toning process, you should ensure that all your prints are thoroughly washed and that your processing trays are clean and free from any contaminants. You can either mix your own toners or buy them already made up (eg. Berg's toners)—do take careful note of any health risk warnings given by the manufacturer.

Dyed images

Another approach to colouring a black-and-white photograph is to 'mordant' a dye to the image (ie. the silver image is converted into a form that acts as a *mordant*, which holds dyes in the image areas but allows them to be washed out of others). A good way of doing this is to use a mordanting bath (fig 8.8), followed by a wash to restore all whites and then by immersion in a one per cent acetic acid solution containing the chosen dye (about one per cent or more). Finally, to clean out the whites, the dyed print should be immersed for a short time in a weak solution of household bleach (sodium hypochlorite).

8.8 Mordanting bath

Copper sulphate	20 g
Neutral potassium citrate	80 g
Acetic acid (glacial)	30 ml
*Ammonium thiocyanate (10 per cent)	100 ml
Water to make	1 litre

*Dissolve in a small amount of water and add slowly (with agitation) to the main solution. For occasional mordanting the ammonium thiocyanate is best stored separately and added when needed.

These dyed images are not particularly stable but should keep for several years if stored in fairly dark conditions. There are one or two kits available, such as Berg's 'colour conversion kit for black-and-white images' and one from Colorvir, but if you want to mix your own solutions the following dyes have been used successfully: fuchsine, malachite green, methylene blue, methyl violet, and thioflavine.

Printing on colour paper

A broad choice of prints of different colours can be obtained by printing a black-and-white negative on colour paper. If you have colour printing facilities, you may find this method easier and more versatile than toning techniques.

The basic procedure for printing a continuous tone black-and-white negative on to 'negative' colour paper, such as Ektacolor, is as follows:

1 Compose and focus the black-and-white negative on the paper easel, and stop the lens down by, say, three stops from maximum aperture.
2 Adjust the filter pack or colour head to OY OM OC and expose a small test strip at 5, 10, 20 and 40 sec.
3 Expose further test strips (or other corners of the

same sheet of colour paper) at the same times, but using the widest range of colour filter settings possible. For example, you could try 120–00–00 (Y–M–C), 00–120–00, 00–00–120, 120–120–00, 120–00–120, and 00–120–120. Keep careful notes.

4 Use your standard procedure for processing the colour paper.

5 Evaluate results, remembering that for 'negative' colour paper longer times give darker images and printed colours are complementary to the filter colours, ie, a setting of 120Y 120M 00C (red) gives a cyan print.

Other possibilities with colour printing

To obtain more saturated (purer) colours, try using narrow-cut filters below the enlarging lens ie. Wratten 47 (blue), 58 (green), 25 (red), 12 (yellow), 32 (magenta), and 44 (cyan). If you want less saturated colours, perhaps to simulate sepia tone, the best approach is to find the colour filter pack for a neutral print and to deviate slightly from this. Once you have produced a range of colour test strips, you can use these for any future black-and-white negatives you wish to print in colour.

The procedure for using an additive colour enlarger is essentially the same as that described above for the subtractive type, except that you will probably obtain a wider spectrum of colours, especially if you are able to turn the three colour channels on or off independently.

For further variations, try printing the following:

1 Continuous tone black-and-white positives on negative colour paper to give monochrome negative prints.

2 Black-and-white continuous tone negatives or positives on reversal colour papers, such as Cibachrome and Ektaflex, to give monochrome negative and positive prints.

3 Lith negatives or positives on either negative or reversal colour papers to give high-contrast monochrome prints.

4 Posterised or sabattier negatives/positives on colour paper.

These and other techniques are fully covered in the book *Colour Printing in Practice* in this series.

9 PUTTING ALL THE VARIABLES TOGETHER

The purpose of this chapter is to link all the photographic variables together and to give some guidance on developing a personal style. It is very easy to think of camerawork, film processing, printing and presentation as separate topics, which must be completely finished before embarking on the next. However, the good photographer knows before he presses the shutter how he wants the final print to appear; he has mastered the technology and can control all the stages to produce his 'visualisation'.

In the first chapter we briefly discussed the various stages needed to produce a good quality black-and-white photograph. We are now able to link these steps in much more detail and discuss how they may be modified to suit each photographer's ideas and style.

From 3D colour scene to 2D monochrome print

It is extremely difficult to look at a 3D colour scene in front of the camera and visualise precisely how it will appear as a 2D black-and-white print. This ability can only be achieved by experience; there is no substitute for taking a large number of photographs and 'discovering' how the scene translates into a monochrome print. To be truthful, even an expert in the Zone System is sometimes surprised on seeing the final print, and much of the magic of black-and-white photography is this degree of uncertainty.

However, you should now be able to examine the scene and ask some key questions, basing your practical camerawork on the answers you get. The main questions to ask are:

1 What is the best composition for the subject? Examine all the possibilities — where to place the edges of the frame — the best viewpoint ie. perspective — is it better to photograph from a distance with a 'narrow-angle' (tele) lens or to work close to the subject using a wide-angle lens? — what is the perspective change when you move slightly to the left or right? — is it worth viewing the subject from a very low or very high position rather than the standard eye height of a standing man? — does the horizontal or vertical format suit the subject?
2 How much tonal detail should be recorded? Scan the subject's tonal distribution — are the shadow details important and should exposure be based on them, or should exposure be determined by critical highlight detail? — are there any key tones, such as skin, which must be accurately reproduced in the print? Can you visualise the scene and place the zones of the finished print?
3 What is the best aperture to use? Is it important to have most of the subject reasonably sharp, ie. a large depth of field, or is the subject improved by using a large aperture to separate the main centre of interest from the surroundings? — how does this 'ideal' aperture relate to the shutter speed?
4 Is the choice of shutter speed critical? If the subject is moving, how much blur (if any) do you want? — can you hand hold the camera at the 'ideal' shutter speed or should you use a tripod or a faster film?
5 Should you change the lighting? Would auxiliary lighting such as flash or a reflector be helpful or practical? — does the light change (eg. cloudy days) and is it worth waiting for the best lighting?
6 When should you press the shutter? Is there one best arrangement of the moving elements (including cloud movement)?
7 Are you unsure of any decisions made so far? Should you take more than one exposure, perhaps to vary depth of field, or degree of subject blur, and select the best frame in the darkroom? — is exposure difficult to gauge and should you bracket exposures?

Film processing decisions

Most of the decisions that influence the *structure* of the final photograph are taken before, or during, the camera exposure. However, processing affects the way that elements of the image are presented in the final print.

8 Do you plan to process the film in your usual developer or is there an advantage in using another 'special' developer, such as one which gives slightly increased speed?
9 Should the development time be your normal 'standard' or is there an advantage in extending the time and developing to a higher gamma? — or should you reduce development to give a lower gamma? Have you planned development for zone compression or expansion?
10 Do all your films need the same degree of development or should you separate them and vary their development?

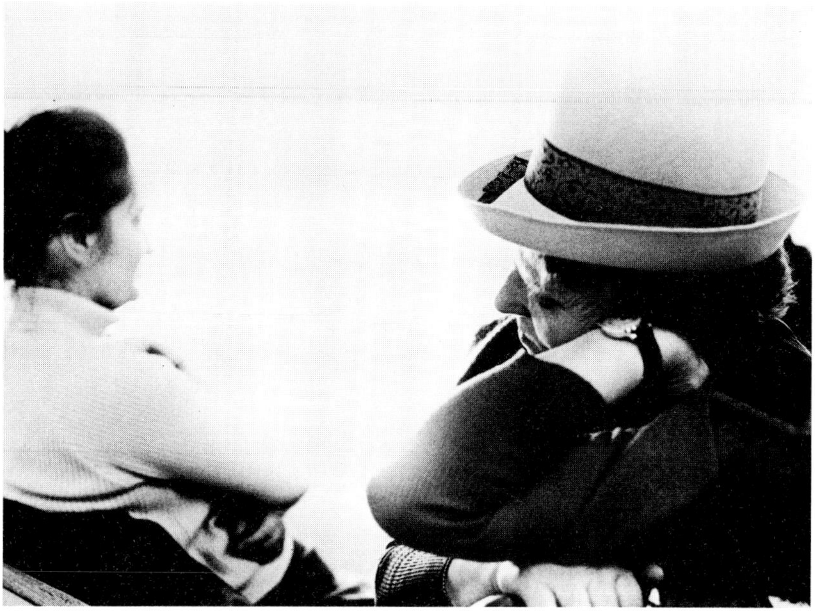

99 At the time of taking the picture, these two tired ferry passengers were not visualised as they appear here. It was only at the printing stage that the idea came to remove all the background detail and surround the two people with white. This effect was achieved mainly by dodging during the whole printing exposure, and the last traces of background detail were removed by bleaching.

11 Do you intend the negative(s) to be the starting point for a print-derivative technique such as the sabattier process, and does this affect the 'best' development time?

Printing decisions

The main advantage that printing has over the other, previous, stages of camerawork and film processing is the amount of time you now have to reflect on the image. You can study the negative and contact print carefully and then, at leisure, decide which is the best way to print the negative. You can even change your mind during the printing session.

The main questions that should be asked when printing a negative are:

12 Should the negative be cropped to improve composition? — which is the best shape and size for the photograph?
13 Does the overall mood dictate darker or lighter tones than 'normal' or should you reproduce the scene as you remembered it? — which contrast grade best suits the subject and your interpretation of it?
14 Should you 'tamper' with the recorded tones and control local density on the print by dodging/burning-in?
15 Which monochrome colour is most suitable for the photograph — blue-black, brown-black, toned prints, colour monochrome prints?
16 Can your image be improved by derivative techniques — high-contrast, posterisation, etc or would these methods 'overembellish' the photograph?
17 Finally, what is the best method of presentation? — simple flush mounting, elaborate borders, framed or unframed, coloured backgrounds? — is the print exhibited on its own or with others? — how will the final photograph be viewed? — exhibition, in a private house, as part of a portfolio book?

So many decisions

The more you understand about black-and-white photography the more decisions there are to be made! But looking at it another way, the more knowledgeable you are about the technology and how you wish to apply it, the more flexibility you have. There are few limitations to 'choke' your ideas, and you can manipulate the equipment and materials in the way you want.

Defining a personal style

When starting any serious hobby, it is inevitable that you will copy the work and style of those exponents of the art or craft you admire. This is an excellent motivating force and, in fact, encourages you to learn new techniques quickly. The difficulties arise when you have reached a competent standard and need to develop a style of your own.

Finding a personal style of photography has more to do with psychology than photography and relies on your mental attitude to picture making. First of all, decide why you want to take

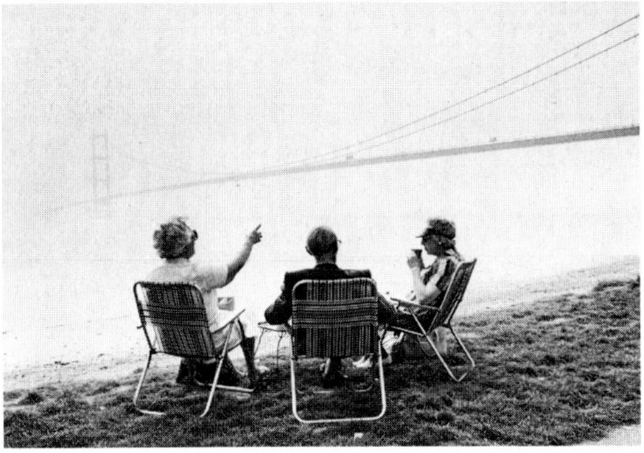

100 One of those well-observed strange occurrences which nobody believes has happened, and which has to be photographed to prove that it did and that you were there. Prints like this are always welcome in any exhibition.

photographs. Is it to win the approval or admiration of others or is it a desire to record images that you find fascinating? Obviously, we all want our photographs to be seen by many people, for there is little point in taking pictures and then storing them in a box which is never opened. But should we take photographs *just* for the approval of others?

As soon as you have confidence in your own photographic ability you will start to produce exciting photographs, those which are uniquely yours and not a copy of someone else's style. When this happens, your photography is raised to another level and becomes a strong outlet for your artistic and emotional ideas.

To 'find' your own style be prepared to experiment with a fair degree of recklessness. Do not be inhibited in what you attempt and expect to make many mistakes which will nevertheless prove worthwhile when you produce the occasional outstanding picture.

Maintaining inspiration

Like all creative people, photographers have 'dry' periods when good photographs are difficult to come by; your inspiration seems to have evaprated and you wonder whether you can rekindle whatever makes you creative. Do not despair. Depending on how serious you feel your 'block' is, either keep going until a breakthrough occurs, or perhaps you should remove the creative pressure for a short while by temporarily giving up photography.

But one of the best methods of maintaining or regaining inspiration is, in fact, to join a group of like-minded photographers who inspire you with new ideas and approaches. There are many excellent photographic societies, clubs and small groups which have been set up for this purpose. Before you join a group, visit their annual exhibition or a club night to see if you are in general sympathy with their photographic approach. There is nothing more frustrating than to join a club where the members enthusiastically produce photographs which you consider dreary and unexciting. The best clubs encourage a wide variety of approaches and thrive on active debate and controversy.

Self-motivated projects

If you join a photographic club or group, you should be motivated by the general atmosphere and by club competitions, some of which will be on specific themes. But if you prefer to work alone, or just want to pursue an individual course, you might consider setting yourself projects to help direct your photography.

There are any number of themes to choose from, and the list below is given only as a guide. Try to design a project which is neither so large and all-embracing that you will never complete it, or one which is so insubstantial that you cannot work up any commitment or motivation to it. The best projects are those which you can come back to after a couple of years and approach from a completely different angle from your earlier attempt.

Some project ideas

As just mentioned, the list below cannot be comprehensive and can only help you formulate your own projects. Many good ideas can be 'discovered' in photographic magazines, or from television and films.

Photojournalistic themes: Groups of photographs which tell a story are an excellent way of involving you in events and perhaps giving you a chance of helping others to promote their activity. Some possible ideas might be:

1 Theatre groups — documenting a stage production from rehearsals, stage setting and backstage work, publicity, through to the final production.
2 Community centres — describing what they do, perhaps concentrating on one aspect (eg. youth work, sports, music).
3 Local sports clubs — sailing, soccer, cricket, cycling, etc. Try to record the personalities and their interaction with their pastime and other members. Always try to adopt a specific approach (eg. one member, or one specific event)

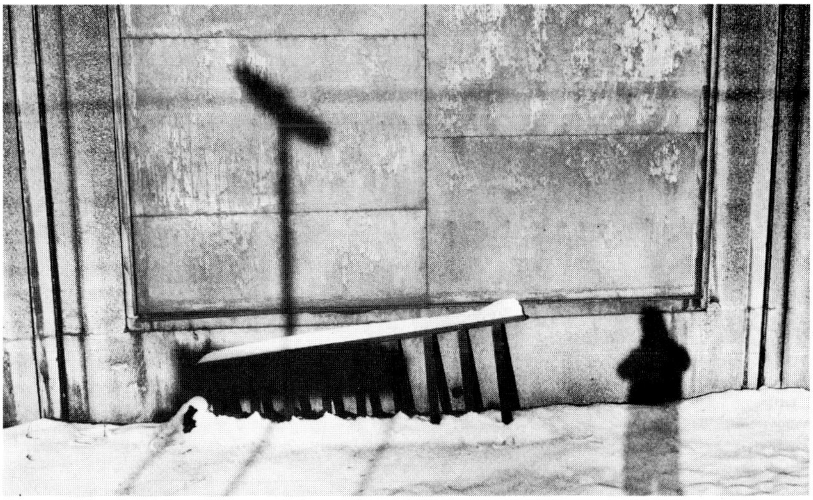

101 A very personal photograph which, when shown, has received a very mixed reception, either strongly for, or against. If you honestly produce personal images, then at least no one can accuse you of following the crowd, but must admit that you are prepared to find your own way.

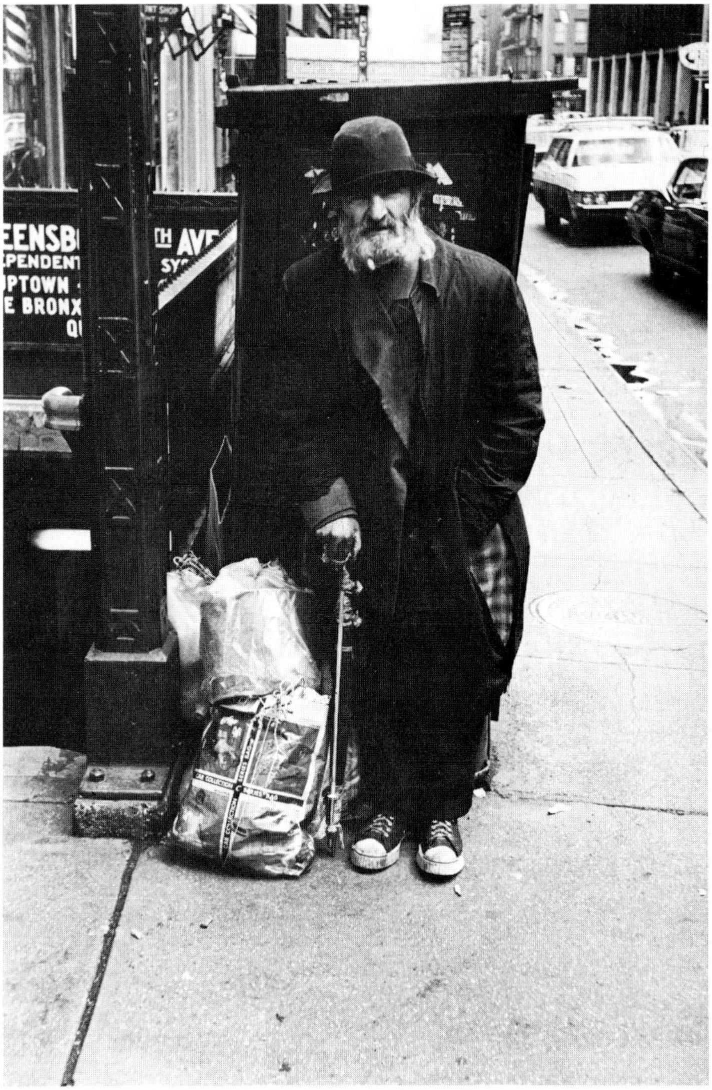

102 An honest, straightforward approach to photojournalism, in which the subject is allowed to portray himself, without being influenced by the photographer's ideas.

rather than a general overview.
4 Demonstrations — always very exciting but can be hazardous!
5 Events — eg. national holidays, carnivals, circuses, flower shows, major sporting events (Derby day, football games). Before you go to the event decide which approach you are going to take; from a purely practical viewpoint this helps determine which equipment and film is most suitable.
6 Documentaries — eg. the story of one person or a group of people (family, minorities, etc). These can cover serious social problems (housing, environmental decay, concern for the aged, etc) or be more light-hearted (eg. local resident who has gained national recognition in his field).

Pictorial themes: You could concentrate your efforts for a period of time on one specific pictorial aspect; this gives you a chance to examine one visual idea in depth and, at the same time, give your photographs a cohesive theme. Some ideas:

1 Specific landscape details — eg. skies, water, horizons, trees, seascapes.
2 Detailed subjects — these may encompass quite small subject areas, even close-ups, eg. doors or gates, boats, cars (or more specifically, for example, car headlights), houses, farmyard tools, old wood.

More abstract themes: An interesting exercise is to explore less realistic ideas and tackle abstract themes. The one major advantage of this approach is that it forces you to look beyond the commonplace reality of a subject and examine it in a completely different context, a sort of visual 'lateral thinking'. Some possible themes:

1 Shadows and reflections — instead of being a subsidiary part of a photograph you could try to make them the main subject element.
2 Movement — analyse movement not as related to a specific solid object but as a subject in its own right, perhaps concentrating on one aspect only, eg. graceful motion, generation of movement patterns, comparative analysis of movement.
3 Time lapse — indicating how slowly moving or developing objects get from one point to another eg. plants, snails, sun or moon. Perhaps a sequence of pictures to describe a complete event.
4 Grouping objects or scenes in unusual combinations can be an interesting surrealistic exercise, eg. unusual size relationships, strange lighting. Derivative techniques, such as sandwich or multiple printing, are ideal for this kind of work (see Chapter 8).
5 Tonal distortions — converting the subject into abstract shapes and textures (see the techniques discussed in Chapter 8).

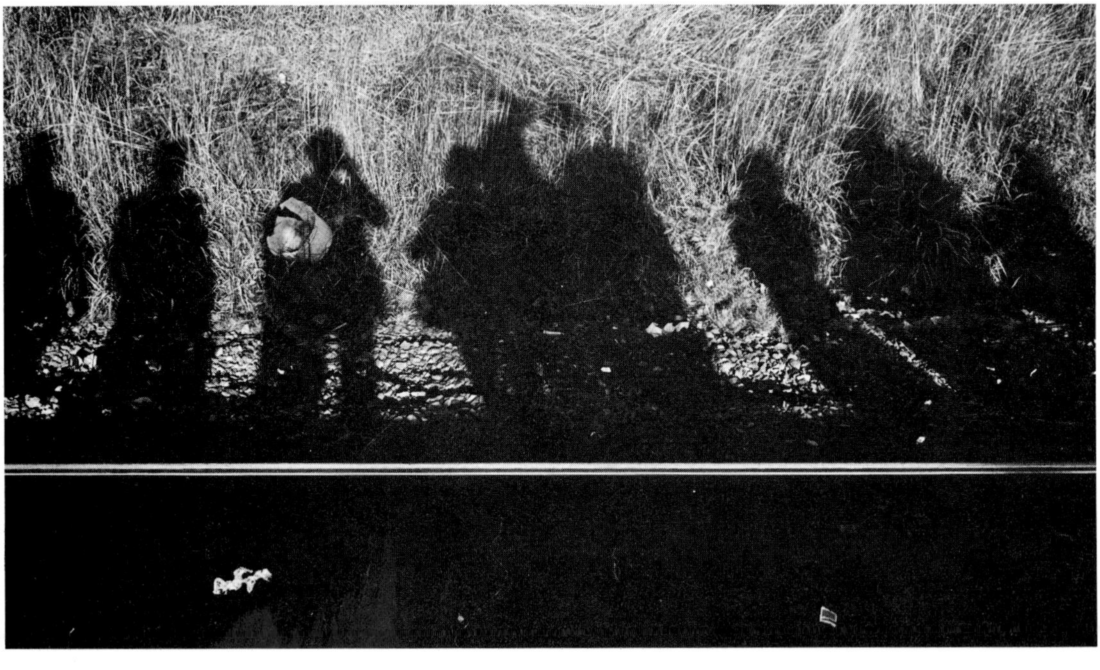

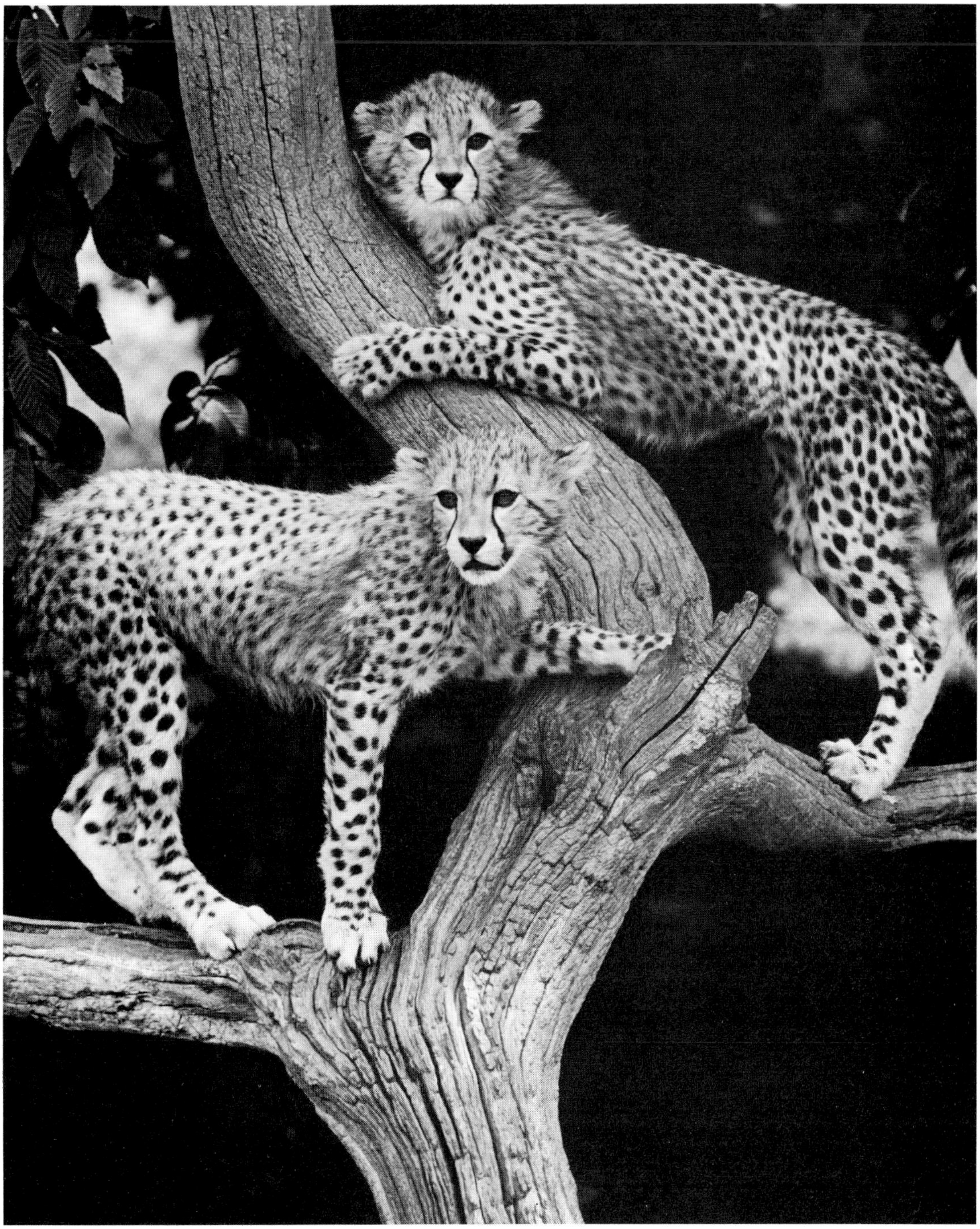

103 I had stood at this single-track railway station in the early morning sun many times before, but had never before 'seen' this image. During its printing, I toyed with the idea of removing the rubbish by dodging and retouching, but discarded that possibility because I felt that the image would then lack realism and become 'over designed'.

104 A very sensitive pictorial treatment of two cheetah cubs. Patience was needed to wait until the two subjects themselves decided to form the 'best' arrangement.

6 Familiar objects converted to abstract photographs — this type of approach can, perhaps, include close-ups or unusual viewpoints or, maybe, unnatural lighting. Studio lighting gives more control in this type of photography.

Showing your photographs

As we have already noted, there is little satisfaction to be gained from producing photographs that are never seen. There are several outlets besides camera clubs and societies which will give you an opportunity to display your work.

Some publishers are constantly searching for good and interesting photographs to reproduce; it is simply a matter of getting in touch with the right outlet for your kind of work. Start by examining magazines and journals critically, to see what kind of pictures they already publish and then get in touch with the editor or art/picture editor if you feel your approach is sympathetic to their needs. To find the right book publishers for your style of photography have a good look through your local library or bookshop and try to gauge the particular market of each publishing house. Directories are available which give this information together with addresses.

A number of banks, building societies, town halls, libraries, department stores and other outlets have window or wall space which is used for exhibitions. A display of photographs with a specific theme, or with strong local interest, will be particularly popular.

Galleries are now receptive to exhibitions of photographs although they tend to specialise in 'art photography'. But there are also photographic galleries, especially in the major cities. If you do have an idea for an exhibition get in touch with the gallery and arrange for them to see your portfolio. Most galleries have a fairly long waiting list for exhibitions and if they accept your idea you will probably have plenty of time to complete your project.

Whichever method of showing your photographs appeals to you, do be positive and get your work seen. Remember that both adverse comments and compliments amount to constructive criticism if given in the right spirit. Learn from other people's opinions of your work but keep the strength of your convictions and follow your own ideas. Black-and-white photography is not only a highly satisfying pastime, it also gives you the chance to express your view of the world to anyone who cares to look.

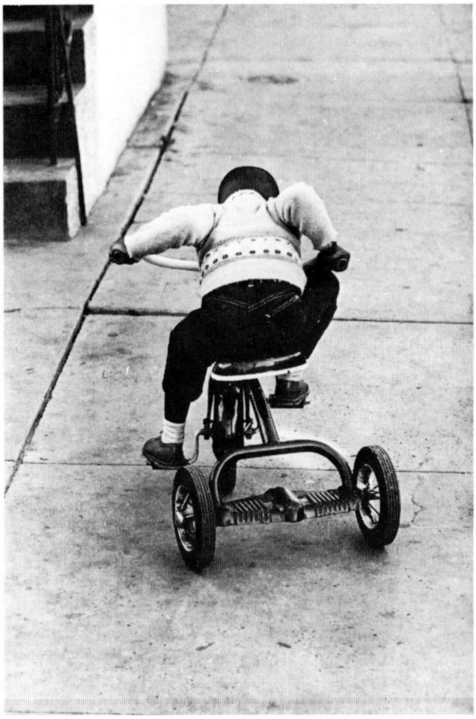

105 Every story needs a good ending; this also happens to be one of my favourite photographs.

GLOSSARY

Accelerator The chemical constituent of a developer which accelerates development; the most common examples are sodium carbonate and borax.

Acetic acid Acid which, in diluted form (about two per cent solution) is used as a stop bath in film and paper processing, and also as a constituent of acid fixing baths.

Acid hardening fixer Acidic fixing bath which contains a hardening agent to toughen the paper or film emulsion and therefore protect it from minor abrasions.

Acutance Micro contrast of edge detail which is measured by the rate of change of density across a sharp edge of the image. High acutance developers build up contrast at the boundaries of image detail and improve apparent sharpness.

Ammonium thiosulphate The main constituent of rapid fixers which are employed when fast processing is needed. Rapid fixers are not recommended when prints are likely to stand for some time in the fixer because of the risk of image bleaching.

Anti-halation backing Coated layer of a photographic film which prevents light reflecting back from the film base to create 'halos' around very bright objects (eg. street lights).

ASA American Standards Association. System used to measure the sensitivity of films. The ASA scale is arithmetic eg. ASA 200 film is twice as fast as ASA 100 film, and half the speed of ASA 400 material.

Available light General term usually referring to low levels of existing illumination, which require fast films, wide lens apertures, and/or slow shutter speeds.

Bellows Concertina-like device which is placed between the lens and camera body, so that very close subjects can be sharply focused. Bellows units are used for close-up photography within the magnification range of about X1 to X10.

Bellows extension Distance between the lens and the film when a bellows unit is fitted. This distance can be used to calculate the exposure increase required when magnifications are X¼ and greater.

Bleach Chemical solution which reacts with the silver formed by the developer, and either converts it back to silver halide (rehalogenating bleach) or dissolves it completely.

Borax Mild alkali used in some developer formulations.

Bracketing Range of different exposures which is on either side of a 'normal' exposure and thereby ensures that at least one exposure is correct. Bracketing is employed when exposure estimation is difficult eg. with back-lit subjects. For most black-and-white photography a one stop interval between each exposure is sufficient.

Bromide paper Cold-toned photographic paper using silver bromide emulsions.

Buffer Chemicals which help to maintain a constant pH (acidity/alkalinity) for a processing solution, thereby precisely controlling the activity of the solution. Common buffers for developers include borax/boric acid and sodium carbonate/sodium hydroxide.

Cadmium sulphide (CdS) cell Sensitive cell which alters its electrical resistance as the light incident on it changes, used in some lightmeters. CdS meters can be built into cameras or made as separate units. Their battery needs replacing about once a year.

Camera movements Refers to the ability of some cameras, mainly large format (5 x 4in etc), to alter the relative positions of lens and film planes. Camera movements are extremely useful for increasing image sharpness and changing image shape.

Catadioptric lens Lens which uses both mirrors and refractive elements to produce an image. Most camera 'mirror' lenses are in fact catadioptric and are used when lightweight long-focal-length lenses are needed.

Changing bag Light-tight bag used to handle film when no darkroom is available, for example, on location, to load sheet film into film holders.

Chloride paper Slow photographic paper used at one time for contact printing, and consisting of silver chloride emulsions.

Chlorobromide paper Warm-toned photographic paper consisting of a mixture of silver chloride and silver bromide emulsions.

Chromatic aberration Lens fault which causes light of different colour, but emitted from the same subject point, to come to focus at different image points. Lenses with poor correction for chromatic aberration produce colour fringes, resulting in a loss of sharpness in black-and-white photography.

Coating of lens Very thin layer(s) of chemicals, such as fluorides, coated on to lens elements to reduce the amount of non-image-forming light reaching the film and causing 'flare'.

Cold cathode Form of fluorescent tube used in some professional enlargers which sometimes has a blue colour. A cold cathode enlarger is not suitable for colour photography.

Colour head Illumination unit made to fit a specific enlarger which has built-in filters to control the colour of the light. Colour heads are primarily for colour printing but can also be used for black-and-white work.

Compensating developer Developer which reacts more vigorously on the less exposed parts of the film (ie. shadows) and less vigorously on the more fully exposed areas (highlights); overall, there is a slight reduction in negative contrast. The effect is most pronounced when using dilute developers with minimum agitation.

Condenser Simple lens which is used to converge light. Condenser enlargers employ one or more condensers to direct light towards the film. The position and focal length of the condenser(s) depends on the focal length of the enlarging lens.

Contact printing Technique of placing a negative (or positive) film image in close contact, usually emulsion to emulsion, with a piece of photographic film or paper. The unexposed material is exposed by shining light through the image on to the sensitive film or paper. No lens is required and image size remains constant.

Contrast Rate of change in tone when the viewer looks at differences between shadows, mid-tones, and highlights. Contrast is a subjective 'feeling' and depends on such factors as subject brightness range, film type and development, printing, and viewing conditions.

Contrast index System designed by Kodak to standardise the printing characteristics of black-and-white negatives.

Copper toning Chemical procedure which converts the 'neutral' tones of a processed black-and-white print to reddish-brown tones.

Cross front Movement available on most larger format or a few smaller cameras which allows the lens to be shifted sideways in relation to the film back. Cross front is used when 'head-on' photography is undesirable (eg. camera reflecting in the subject) or impossible due to obstructions.

Deep tank Processing tank which holds a relatively large volume of solution and is replenished after film is developed. The tank is only emptied when the solution starts to lose its effectiveness or becomes unclean; this normally occurs after about three months or more of constant use.

Definition General term describing the clarity of a photographic image. For more precise evaluation of image definition see *MTF* and *resolving power.*

Densitometer Instrument which measures the opacity (density) of processed film and paper, and is used to monitor the quality of film/paper and its processing. Density readings can be plotted to give graphs such as D/Log E and Gamma/Time.

Density Measure of the light-absorbing properties of a particular area of film or paper. The darker parts of black-and-white prints have a density usually greater than 1.4, and white areas have densities close to zero. Density is a log reading, with a 0.3 difference between readings signifying a doubling or halving of the light absorbed.

Density range The difference between the density of the darkest and lightest part of a film or paper ie. D max–D min. For example, the density ranges for black-and-white paper vary from 1.3 to 2.1.

Depth of field Distance between the nearest and farthest parts of the subject which appear as acceptably sharp in the final reproduction (ie. print or slide). To increase depth of field use a smaller aperture, a shorter focal-length lens, and/or move further from the subject.

Depth of focus Allowable error in lens focusing which still produces an acceptably sharp photographic image.

Developing by inspection Safelight viewing of film or paper to determine when the required amount of development has been reached. The technique is only suitable for blue-sensitive and ortho materials, and for very slow pan films which can be periodically examined under a very dim green light.

Dichroic fog Stain which can be formed on a film when it is transferred from the developer to the fixer without using an intermediate bath. Once formed, dichroic fog is impossible to remove. In practice, however, dichroic fog is rarely seen.

Diffraction Scattering of light when it passes close to opaque surfaces such as the lens diaphragm leaves. Consequently, lens definition is slightly reduced at very small apertures and diffraction losses are the reason why some lenses do not stop down to, say, less than *f*/16.

Diffuse light source Any light source producing subject shadows which are relatively light in tone and have soft, indistinct edges; specular highlights are also avoided.

Diffusion enlarger Any enlarger which uses a diffused light source rather than a condenser to direct illumination. Film should be developed to a relatively high contrast when a diffuser enlarger is used.

DIN Deutsche Industrie Norm. Film speed system instigated by Germany and adopted by some European countries. A change of 3 DIN signifies a doubling or halving of film speed. The scales are the same at 12, ie. ASA 12 = 12 DIN.

Electronic flash High-energy discharge between two electrodes sealed in a glass case containing an inert gas. The light emitted from the discharge is of very short duration (1/500 sec. or shorter) and extremely bright.

Elon Kodak trade name given to the developing agent metol.

Emulsion In photography, an emulsion is a suspension of silver halide grains in gelatin. Each type of emulsion has its own ingredients mixed in its own way.

Expiry date Date printed on the package of a photographic material which indicates when the material is likely to be below acceptable standards. Expiry dates assume average keeping conditions. If kept in cold, dry conditions, the photographic material can be safely used past the expiry date.

Exposure factor Increase in exposure necessary when using camera accessories such as filters, extension tubes, and bellows. The exposure factor is expressed as a multiplication factor; for example, a X2 yellow filter changes an exposure of 1/125 sec. at *f*/8 to 1/60 sec. *f*/8 or 1/125 sec. *f*/5.6.

Exposure latitude Range of exposures over which a particular photographic material still gives acceptable results. Exposure latitude depends on many factors including subject, lighting, processing, and what is considered acceptable.

Extension ring (tube) Spacer ring which fits between the camera lens and body and allows focusing on objects closer than the normal minimum lens focusing distance. They are available as sets of three or more different sized rings to give a wide choice of close focusing ranges.

Farmer's reducer Solution used to reduce the density of negatives and prints.

Fill light Any light which adds illumination to subject areas in shadow, so that these areas are recorded more pleasingly on the film. Fill lights do not change the overall character of the lighting, but lower overall brightness range.

Film holder Device for holding (normally) two pieces of sheet film, one on either side. The film is protected from light by a dark slide which is removed after the holder is placed in the camera and just prior to exposure; the slide is replaced before the holder is removed from the camera.

Filter factor See *exposure factor.*

Flare Non-image light which reaches the film and causes a loss of image contrast; its effect is most noticeable in the shadow areas of the subject. Flare is considerably reduced by lens coating and the use of a lens hood.

***f*-number** Series of internationally agreed numbers which indicate the brightness of the image produced by a lens. Irrespective of focal length and the film format for which a lens is designed, the same *f*-number on all lenses gives the same image brightness of the same subject. The series is 1.0, 1.4, 2, 2.8, 4, 5.6, 8, 11, 16, 22, 32, 45, etc. Changing from one number to the next in the series causes the image brightness to be halved (eg. *f*/8 to *f*/11) or doubled (eg. *f*/8 to *f*/5.6).

Focal length Distance between the lens optical centre and the focused image when the subject is at infinity. For a particular film format, the lens focal length indicates the angle of view of that lens.

Focal plane Plane behind the lens on which the sharpest image of the subject is produced; the film must be positioned in the focal plane.

Focal plane shutter Shutter which is positioned as close to the focal plane (ie. the film plane) as possible, and causes a slit of image light to move across the film. The exposure time is varied by changing the width of the slit.

Fog level Density of an unexposed area of a processed film or paper, due to the 'noise' in the photographic system. The fog level is influenced by the degree and type of development and the type and condition (age, storage, etc) of the photographic material.

Gelatin Water-permeable material which is used as a binder for photographic emulsions; it is obtained from animal hides and bones.

GPD cells Gallium arsenic phosphorus photo diodes (GPD) cells are incorporated in some light meters. They react extremely rapidly to light changes and do not have a 'memory' of previous light readings; they are therefore ideal for in-camera metering systems.

Grain Random pattern of silver halide particles within a photographic emulsion which, after exposure and development, gives an image consisting of random black metallic silver particles.

Graininess Subjective evaluation of the processed grain pattern. 'Grainy' photographs are produced when fast films are enlarged to a high magnification.

Granularity Objective evaluation of the processed grain pattern. Granularity numbers are obtained from microdensitometer (measures density of very small areas) readings, and it is then possible to compare the granularity of one film with another, or one developer against another.

Halation Ring of exposure on a film around very bright objects (eg. lights) caused by image light passing through the emulsion and then reflected back off the film base. Halation is greatly minimised by the coating of an antihalation layer within the film structure.

Halide Collective term for the chemical salts derived from the halogens. The halides are fluorides, chlorides, bromides and iodides.

H & D curve Alternative name for D/Log E curve, derived from Hurter and Driffield, two pioneer photographic scientists.

Highlight Light part of a subject which is not white. A highlight is a very crucial part of an image and needs to be printed carefully to show subtle detail.

Highlight mask Intermediate positive or negative which is used to retain highlight contrast in a duplicate negative or slide.

Hydroquinone Developing agent used in many developer formulations.

Hypo Common name given to sodium thiosulphate, the usual fixing agent in non-rapid fixers.

Infectious development Type of development which occurs with lith films and developers. The development is initially very slow, but as areas become developed the by-products of the reaction act as catalysts to promote more development.

Infra-red Electromagnetic energy next to red light in the spectrum and of longer wavelength which is not visible but can be detected by instruments and IR sensitive photographic film.

Infra-red setting Mark (usually red) on the lens focusing scale which enables the lens to be correctly focused when IR film is used. The lens is focused visually and the noted subject distance is moved until it is opposite the IR mark.

Intensification Method of rescuing a very light and otherwise unprintable negative by chemically adding density to the visible detail.

Leaf shutter Shutter consisting of five or more blades which uncover and then cover the aperture in a fan-like movement to cause exposure.

LED Light emitting diode, which is an electronic device now used extensively to replace pointers etc used in earlier cameras and photographic equipment.

Line image Image which consists of black and white without intermediate mid-tones, for example, pen and ink sketches.

Lith developer Developer which is formulated to give maximum contrast with lith films. Once made up, a lith developer is only active for a couple of hours, and is therefore mixed from two stock solutions just prior to use.

Macro lens Considered to be any lens which focuses very close subjects without the aid of extension tubes and other close-up attachments. Traditionally 'macro' refers to negatives of life size (magnification = 1) and larger magnifications.

Mask A photographic mask is an image on a piece of film which is bound up with the main negative or positive image to modify either contrast, colour or content of the image.

Metol Developing agent used in many black-and-white developer formulations.

Mirror lens Lens which uses reflective elements (mirrors) instead of refractive material (conventional lens) to produce an image. Also known as a *catoptric* lens. See *catadioptric lens*.

Monobath Single solution which develops and fixes an exposed film; and provided solution temperature is between 18–24°C the processing time is not critical. Although useful in an emergency, the results are inferior to separate developer and fixer solutions.

MTF Modulation transfer function. Complex mathematical analysis of lens quality which produces a graph of per cent response/spatial frequency (lines/mm). MTF curves are the most reliable method of forecasting lens performance but need to be interpreted by experts.

Neutral density filter Series of filters which absorb light but do not alter the colour of the light. Neutral density (ND) filters are normally available in values of 0.15, 0.3, 0.6, 0.9, etc, where 0.3 is equivalent to one stop (50 per cent of light absorbed).

Newton's rings Series of irregular patterns which are sometimes formed when two surfaces do not quite meet. Newton's rings may be produced when a negative is placed in a glass film carrier; the pattern will then be reproduced on the print. To avoid Newton's rings use either specially etched glass or preferably a glassless film carrier.

Notching code Notch on a piece of film which indicates the type of film and the side on which the light-sensitive emulsion is coated. The emulsion is facing towards you when the notch is on the right side of the top edge.

Ordinary emulsion Emulsion which is sensitive only to UV and blue light. Most black-and-white printing papers are coated with ordinary emulsions, and can therefore be handled in yellow-orange safelights.

Orthochromatic emulsion Emulsion which is sensitive to UV, blue and green light, and can be used in red safelights.

Oxidation In photography, oxidation causes the reduction of developer activity and therefore produces underdeveloped films and prints. To avoid oxidation store all developers in full, stoppered glass (or impermeable plastic) bottles.

Panchromatic emulsion Emulsion which is sensitive to UV and white light (ie. blue, green and red) and must be handled in complete darkness. Most camera films are pan emulsions.

Perspective Size and spatial relationships of the various parts of a subject. Perspective is changed only by moving to a different viewpoint.

pH Scale from 0–14 which measures the acidity or alkalinity of a solution; where 7 is neutral, lower numbers indicate acidity, and high numbers signify alkaline solutions.

Pincushion distortion Optical aberration which causes square objects to photograph as a pincushion shape, and straight lines near the frame edges to bow inwards at their centres.

Pola (polarising) screen Screen or filter which absorbs varying amounts of polarised light according to the filter's rotational position. A pola filter can be used to darken a sky, remove unwanted 'polarised light' reflections eg. road surfaces, water and glass.

Process lens Apochromatic lens of high quality used by the printing industry when copying artwork and photographs for reproduction.

Reducer In photography, a reducer is a chemical formulation which reduces the density (overall, or in selected areas) of the print or film.

Replenisher Top-up solution which keeps a processing bath at a consistent level of activity. Replenishers are used for deep tank processing.

Resolving power One measure of lens or film definition. Resolving power is quoted in lines/mm and is based on the ability of a lens (or lens/film) to resolve detail on a test chart. See *MTF*.

Reticulation Cracked 'mosaic' appearance of film caused by sudden change in processing temperature when being passed from one solution to the next. Deliberate reticulation is difficult to achieve, but can be produced by transferring the film from a developer at normal temperature to an ice-cold stop bath.

Sensitometry Scientific study of the sensitivity of photographic materials used by manufacturers and processors to monitor quality.

Solarisation Gross overexposure of a film or paper which produces a slight reversal (negative to positive, or vice versa) of the image. Solarisation should not be confused with the sabattier effect (pseudo-solarisation).

SPD Silicon photo diode. Very sensitive photocell used in some lightmeters which is sometimes 'blue' to compensate for excessive red response.

Spot meter Lightmeter which reads over a very narrow angle of about 1°, and is used for critical metering of a subject such as is required by the Zone System of exposure determination.

Spotting Elementary retouching of the white spots caused by fine particles of dust on the negative.

Stop bath Processing solution which halts the action of a developer, and usually consists of a dilute solution of acetic acid.

Synchro-sunlight Technique of using flash lighting in daylight scenes in order to 'fill-in' dense shadows and reduce overall contrast. Synchro-sunlight is most useful on bright sunny days when the lighting is very harsh.

Tacking iron Small electrical iron used to 'tack' (stick) dry mounting tissue to the print and then to the card. The print/tissue/card sandwich is welded together in a heated press.

Ultra-violet (UV) radiation Invisible electro-magnetic energy which is present in many light sources, including daylight and, if not filtered out, causes a slight bluish cast in colour films.

Universal developer Developer which can be used to process film and paper, but is normally mixed at different dilutions for the two types of material.

Wetting agent Chemical which is added to the final film rinse to lower surface tension and thereby promote even drying, so avoiding the formation of drying marks.

BIBLIOGRAPHY

Many general photographic books concentrate on camera work and the use of colour materials. However, a few give a useful basic introduction to black-and-white work. Books aimed at the 'art photographer' usually focus on black-and-white and fall into two distinct categories: picture books, and those which cover technical matters.

The picture books are either devoted to the work of one photographer or contain a selection from many sources (eg. year books). The majority of one-man books show the work of well established photographers or those of the 19th and early 20th Centuries. To view contemporary photographs you should read the photographic magazines and visit galleries specialising in photography.

Technical photographic books range from the more scientific, giving precise details of equipment, materials, and processes that should appeal to those interested in theoretical matters, to the more practical variety which give only information essential to the picture maker. Many books in both categories originate from the USA, but are usually available in larger bookshops, or can be obtained from libraries.

The list below consists of some books the author has found useful in dealing with black-and-white photography:

A Day Off / Tony Ray-Jones / Thames & Hudson

America in Crisis / Magnum / Holt, Rinehart & Winston

Basic Photography / Michael Langford / Focal Press

Design by Photography / Otto Croy / Focal Press

Interviews with Master Photographers / James Danziger & Barnaby Conrad / Paddington Press

Lighting for Photography / Walter Nurnberg / Focal Press

One Mind's Eye / Arnold Newman / Secker & Warburg

Son of Bitch / Elliot Erwitt / Thames & Hudson

The English / Ian Berry / Penguin

The Photographic Illusion / Duane Michals / Morgan & Morgan

The Photographic Lens / Sidney Ray / Focal Press

The World of Henri Cartier-Bresson / Thames & Hudson

ACKNOWLEDGEMENTS

The author would like to thank the following:

Agfa-Gevaert Limited
Eastman Kodak Company
E. Leitz (Instruments) Limited
Eumig (UK) Limited
Ilford Limited
Kodak Limited
May & Baker Limited
Paterson Products Limited
Philips Electronic and Associated Industries Limited
Vivitar (UK) Limited

and the Editorial and Design staff of Element, and to Lynne for reading the manuscript.

Photographs by the author except as follows:
Bob Irons 3, 4, 9, 20, 21, 22, 27, 35, 36, 38, 55, 59, 61, 75, 79, 87, 89, 100, 104

Paul Petzold 2·1, 46, 48, 53, 60, 62, 77, 82, 85

INDEX

R

S

T

V

W

Z